Odyssey to Ushuaia

Odyssey to Ushuaia

A MOTORCYCLING ADVENTURE
FROM NEW YORK TO TIERRA DEL FUEGO

ANDRÉS CARLSTEIN

Library of Congress Cataloging-in-Publication Data

Carlstein, Andrés, 1974–
Odyssey to Ushuaia : a motorcycling adventure from New York to Tierra del
    Fuego / Andrés Carlstein.— 1st ed.
    p. cm.
ISBN 1-55652-440-4
1. Carlstein, Andrés, 1974—Journeys–North America. 2. Carlstein, Andrés,
    1974—Journeys–South America. 3. Motorcycling. 4. North
    America–Description and travel. 5. South America–Description and
    travel. I. Title.
G465 .C296 2002
918.04'39–dc21

2002000573

Cover and interior design: Monica Baziuk
Cover photograph: Peter Santa-Maria

Published by Chicago Review Press, Incorporated
814 North Franklin Street
Chicago, Illinois 60610
ISBN 1-55652-440-4
Printed in the United States of America
5 4 3 2 1

➤ This book is dedicated to fathers and sons. I offer it in memory of my father, Dr. Rudolf G. Carlstein-Reyes, and to Charlie Stewart, formerly of Bethel, Alaska. Wherever you are now, Charlie, I hope you've reunited with your son.

Contents

Acknowledgments

➤ I SIMPLY COULDN'T HAVE done this trip alone. There were far too many people that helped me along the way to list them all, but there are several who merit specific thanks. I would like to thank first my family, particularly my mother, Ann Furlong, and my sister, Astrid Baker, who handled my stateside business while I was away. I'd like to thank Carl Williamson, Paul Morroni, Mark Van Horn, and all the friends who helped prepare me for, and shared in, the journey.

I extend a very special thanks to my writing mentor and friend, Robert Gannon, without whom this book wouldn't have been written.

My warmest appreciation also goes to Robert and Peter, my fellow rum riders, for their time, effort, dedication, energy, patience, and for being who they are. Luckily for me we didn't always get along, otherwise the trip would've been infinitely less entertaining. Thanks, guys.

I'd like to also thank the following trip sponsors and their representatives: Sheryl Bussard and Kawasaki USA; Larry Langley and Progressive Suspension; Paul Collins and Givi, USA; Carl Williamson and Williamson Sports Motors; Pat Widder and Widder Enterprises; Craig

Stenger and Clearview Windscreens; Andy Goldfine and Aerostich, Inc.; Sandra Blackmer and Russell Performance, Inc.; Mike, Doug, and Juan at Corbin Saddles; Doug Flagg and Kershaw Knives; Max Martin and Avon Tyres; and Rob Hart and Walter Goldstein at Crazy Creek Products.

Odyssey to Ushuaia

To Boldly Go Where
Other People Already Live

➤ MY SUNGLASSES HAD BEEN STOLEN from my pocket in a Peruvian coat-check, so I had to keep the tinted visor on my helmet down to curb the tremendous glare. Salt, pure and blazingly white, lay in all directions. There was enough salt to kill every last slug on the planet. Aside from the mountains visible to the southwest, there was no earth nearby. All around me lay a flat white desert of salt where not a creature could live. I wasn't taking any chances—the crusty white lake bed we rode on reflected the bold midday sun, sending rays into my eyes from all directions and threatening to cause a kind of snow blindness, even though there wasn't any snow in sight. Temporary blindness, no matter what the cause, was a condition that would make riding my motorcycle off the salt impossible. This was the Salar de Uyuni, a 7,500-square-mile dried lake at 12,000 feet, formed when a huge bowl of ocean water was driven skyward with the rising continent millennia ago. And we were stuck on it.

My two companions and I were unsure how to proceed. "I think we need to go southeast," I finally said. "That travel agent said there was a road down there, and we haven't crossed it yet. I'm sure that's the way."

Robert, a big, graying man in his fifties who looked like a retired lumberjack or burly ship captain, sat on his massive black BMW bike to my right. He flipped up his helmet and a bushy beard popped out. Reminiscent of something from a cartoon, his beard looked like an expanded white sponge that couldn't possibly return to its original size and fit back in his helmet. He slowly took off his gloves and examined the global positioning satellite receiver (GPS) mounted on his handlebars for what must've been the tenth time.

The third man in our group, Peter, sat on his large, red-and-white BMW bike with his legs spread wide for balance, arms across his chest in frustration. His piercing Colombian eyes were set with a gravity they rarely displayed. "Yeah, but the other guy said there's also a road straight south from the Isla de los Pescadores," Peter said. "We came straight south, and still there's no road. I think we need to go west. We don't have enough gas to run around looking for a road. It has to be one or the other."

We were at an impasse. Normally during a disagreement between two members of the group, the third person settled the tie. But Robert just looked at us in silence. Between the GPS, maps, and local information we had figured we couldn't get lost. And technically we were right. We knew exactly where we were, but we couldn't find a way off the salt. The solid land lay just a couple hundred meters to the south, but between firm ground and us was a wide moat of sandy-salty mush that would surely swallow up at least one of our bikes if we tried to cross. Normally foolproof, the GPS wasn't helping us because there were no good reference points in the software to tell us where the road was in relation to our position. The sacred GPS, as Peter dubbed it, could only tell us what we already knew: that we were somewhere along the edge of the salt lake, but not on hard land.

We didn't want to end up like that French couple last year—their truck sank into the muck and they were stranded, suffering in the burning days and freezing nights under the endless, cloudless sky for

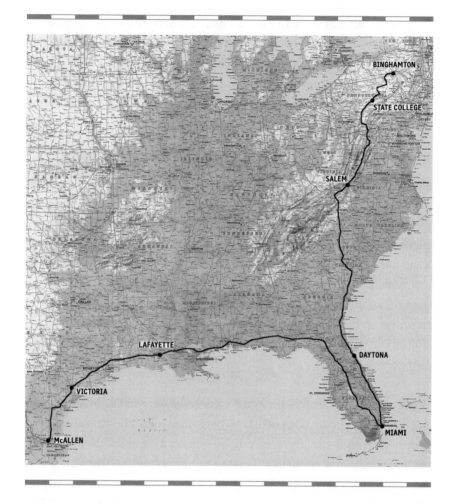

nearly a week before being rescued. They were consular representatives from France, and Bolivian Air Force planes began looking for them when they didn't arrive at their destination as expected. Nobody knew where we were, let alone gave a damn, so if we got stuck we'd have to be our own rescue party. Worse still, we were running out of water and gas, and we had nowhere to turn for more information. I was sick of the constant committee frustrations that come when making group decisions, and decided it was time to act.

"Look, we know there's a road over there to the east. Supposedly it also heads south, right?" They both looked at me noncommittally. "We haven't seen anything resembling a road yet, so if we go in that direction long enough we will cross it. We have to cross it. I'm going that way." I lowered my visor and started off. I looked back a few moments later to see them grudgingly begin to follow.

Fortunately I was right. We made it to the bridge and to hard, salt-free land. Robert, the big Canadian, stopped his bike next to mine and smiled. "That was a close one," he said. "We had to make a decision and it had to be right." I realized this must've been his way of complimenting me. I'm sure it was hard for him, considering how many times I'd done the completely wrong thing since we had been together. Who am I kidding? Half the time I'd been a two-wheeled pain in the ass, and saying these kind words was probably not unlike verbally passing a kidney stone. I nodded in appreciative silence, not wanting to screw up this unusual moment.

*

BACK WHEN MY BROTHER and I were kids, we used to dream of riding motorcycles to Argentina. We would joke about pulling triumphantly into the drive of one of our many uncles' houses—our loving family and beautiful female strangers (they'd heard about us and came from across the land in bikinis to meet the heroes) would embrace us at the door with the sun shining and our engines revving loudly. Since childhood we'd been infected with our father's love of motorcycle travel, but while we were encouraged to travel, we were discouraged from having bikes of our own. After our father's death, all his old treasures were sold, including a two-stroke NSU, a DKW, and a BMW touring bike. The motorcycle had left my presence, but it hadn't left my consciousness.

One hot summer evening just before my last semester of college at Penn State, the motorcycle dream came back to my mind. It came from deep in my memory, but for some reason, suddenly the message was loud and irresistible. I was having drinks with some friends in a pub when the idea crystallized—and I decided right there that, no matter what happened, I would ride a motorcycle south until I ran out of road in Argentina.

You know you've said something remarkable when people grow silent for a few moments, processing your words, eyeing you with quizzical concern, as if to say, "Should this person be on medication?" So after that evening at the bar where my friends replied, "Don't you know there are planes for that?" or "Hope you have a tough ass," I stopped telling others I planned to ride a motorcycle to the tip of South America.

How do you justify selling everything you own and riding a bike through the Americas? Thousands of people have done it, and thousands more will do it, probably all for similar reasons, but I'd be surprised if any of us could readily explain those reasons. Besides, people don't want to know the real reason—the truth is too simple, too boring. The general expectation is that such a grand plan must have a grand motivation behind it. I felt obliged to come up with elaborate rationalizations to hide what, to me, was acutely obvious: I simply felt like it. The trip seemed like the thing to do.

I suppose there was also the issue of roots. As a first-generation American, distance kept me apart from my large extended family—I had over thirty blood relatives in Latin America who barely knew me. I felt a need to connect with the Argentine part of my past, to know my inner workings by getting to know those most like me and ensconce myself in the enveloping warmth and camaraderie of my corner of the gene pool. Another benefit would be the perfect chance to improve my Spanish.

And there was the impending future. After Penn State, I'd planned to go on to medical school. I was in the world of exams and competition and applications and interviews. I had taken all the tests and been accepted to several schools, but despite the fact that I was successfully selling myself to people I'd never met, I didn't feel good about it. The dream of going to med school and becoming a doctor was one I'd struggled for years to realize, using all my motivation and discipline, but lately it didn't inspire me anymore. My father had been a doctor, and although he died when I was just eleven years old, I could still feel an unconscious desire to follow in his footsteps. Whether he planted that idea in my psyche or not, I was realizing more each day that the vision of my future in medicine was really more his than mine. As that insight sank in I started losing wind for academics. I felt directionless. Hollow. When the trip idea came along, suddenly life was inspiring again. Taking the motorcycle south was a dream all my own, and one that seemed undeniably worth following.

Planning the trip was tough. It took nearly nine months of careful research and effort, during which I realized that this was, by far, the most difficult undertaking I'd ever attempted. In the end, there was only one really critical ingredient. If you have it, all the less important things become attainable, or a way to succeed without them can be found. That key ingredient is motivation.

"You don't own a motorcycle." "Do you even have a motorcycle license?" "You're fucking crazy." Statements like these can be daunting for someone with insufficient motivation. For a properly motivated individual, the only appropriate response to these negative comments ("Bite me.") becomes immediately clear, thereby freeing the mind and social schedule for the more pressing tasks at hand, such as buying a motorcycle, obtaining a motorcycle license, and getting professional psychiatric treatment.

First I needed a motorcycle. After reading everything I could find on the subject of motorcycles and travel, and after talking to informed parties, a vision of the ideal bike for the journey became clearer. It had to be powerful, not too heavy, and suitable for highway and off-road use. The right motorcycle would be hard to break, and if broken, easy to fix. It had to stand up to some of the worst roads on the planet. I narrowed my focus down to a class of bikes collectively known as dual-sports, designed for the twofold purpose of riding both on and off paved roads. Dual-sports are tough and street legal. They're designed to go long distances on- or off-road and can take lots of abuse. They have big gas tanks, tough suspensions, semiknobby tires, and minimal frills. Imagine a motocross bike (the kind that flies through the air over tall jumps on dirt tracks), hop it up on steroids, weigh it down with a powerful engine and a big gas tank, and you'd end up with a good idea of what a dual-sport looks like. There are now many varieties of dual-sport on the market; the class has grown considerably since the advent of the annual Paris–Dakar rally, a torturous, high-speed, transdesert race where two-wheeled machines define the term "enduro."

Once I decided on dual-sports in general, I narrowed the search to a class with a single large cylinder, collectively known as "thumpers." Thumpers are so called because their single cylinder makes a loud, distinguishable exhaust note, not unlike the constant pounding of a drum. I preferred this kind of dual-sport because, as I had learned in my research, if anything goes wrong with that single cylinder, the bike is typically much simpler to fix than a multiple-cylinder ride. Since I had limited mechanical knowledge of bikes, simplicity was an important factor. Among the manufacturers I considered were Suzuki, KTM, BMW, Honda, and Kawasaki. I decided on Kawasaki, the model KLR 650.

About 60 percent of the riding I planned to do would be on pavement, and the rest would be in rocky, sandy, or muddy terrain, but nothing too technical. The need for long-distance comfort and power far outweighed the need for off-road superiority. The KLR matched my needs for several reasons. The bike excels at highway riding and has a range of almost three hundred miles with the stock six-gallon tank. Off-road the bike was above average, its greatest asset being a high-torque motor that pulls like a tractor. And it pulls, all right. I wouldn't be surprised if the thing could tear stumps from the ground. The KLR had been in production for thirteen years, and though some may consider that a liability (old technology), I considered it a strength because all the kinks had been worked out of the model long ago. Furthermore, many years of KLR production meant aftermarket parts were available to tailor the bike to my needs, and replacement parts were more likely to be available in Latin America. In terms of price no other bike even came close.

Having decided on the bike I wanted, I found a dealer who could supply one. I also began taking a Motorcycle Safety Foundation rider course and got my motorcycle license. I still needed riding gear for the trip, including a helmet, gloves, electric vest, boots, and a riding suit, to protect me from the elements and from unscheduled dismounts. The surroundings would vary from subtropical lowlands to glacier-covered mountains. Luckily, I found a single riding suit to accommodate these different climes. With a removable fleece liner, zippered ventilation, and wind- and waterproofing, the suit would serve as my own mini-environment for the next twelve months. The two-piece outfit also came equipped with armor pads in the shoulders, elbows, and knees and was made from ballistic nylon—superior even to leather for crashes at less than 80 MPH—to prevent the loss of highly valued flesh to any surfaces my skin might meet.

To protect my head, another item I value, I selected a full-face helmet. I chose to cover my hands with winter riding gauntlets for cold days and short elkskin ropers for the warm ones. For my feet, I settled on a pair of leather hiking boots I'd had for seven years. They were like a pair of old college drinking buddies that I didn't have the heart to toss out of my life—unpolished, comfortable, and with a slightly funky odor. I considered taking tall riding boots for the extra shin protection, but decided against them because of their bulk.

The Internet proved to be one of the most invaluable tools for researching all these decisions I was making. I spent a lot of time reading personal Web sites and connecting with others who had done, or were doing, similar trips. It was over the Internet that I hooked up with Robert and Peter, two experienced riders who eventually ended up riding with me for most of the way. Although I'd always imagined taking this trip alone, it made a lot of sense for safety and convenience to travel in a group for at least part of the journey.

While scanning the Net I learned of people who'd taken trips like mine and then some, like Ed Culberson, the first man to traverse the entire length of the Pan-American Highway by motorcycle. That's no small feat. The Pan Am, in theory, stretches from the top of Prudhoe Bay, Alaska, all the way to the tip of Argentina, ending outside of a little town called Ushuaia. It's supposed to be a road that connects the Americas, but in reality, the Pan Am is incomplete. There's a nasty stretch of jungle, about eighty miles in all, between Panama and Colombia, called the Darien Gap. There are no roads, so all travel must be made on meandering footpaths, or by hacking one's way with a machete. Imagine chopping a hundred yards of foliage in the swelter-ing, steamy heat, walking back to your bike and riding it forward, and then doing that over again—all day. As you can imagine, the going is slow. All rivers, of which jungles have many, must be crossed the old-fashioned way—by fording. To make matters even more interesting, the jungle also happens to be occupied by drug smugglers and terror-ist revolutionaries. People like that get very suspicious when tres-passers come out of the bush on motorcycles and ride across their cocaine fields. Then it becomes a matter of shoot first, mount your head on a stake as a warning to others later. Not to mention the various par-asites, bacteria, spiders, and giant snakes that also don't like to be dis-turbed.

I also read about Helge Peterson, the much-lauded Norwegian rider who circled the earth on a bike and documented his trip with photos. By the way, Helge has the distinction of also crossing the Darien Gap. Culberson was the first to do it from the north, and Peterson was the first to tackle it from the south.

Then there was my personal hero, Emilio Scotto, an Argentine man recorded in the *Guinness Book of World Records* for the longest motor-cycle ride around the earth. Scotto circled the globe seven times and covered over four hundred and fifty thousand miles on his Honda

Gold Wing, all while learning five languages, changing his religion to Islam, and marrying his girlfriend in India. When he started his trip, he left with little motorcycle experience and the equivalent of three hundred dollars in his pocket. Whenever he ran out of money, he'd park his bike, find temporary work, and save until he could afford to continue.

Money was an issue for me as well. As a relatively poor college student, finding funding for this trip was no simple task. My mother and stepfather were (at first) opposed to me taking this trip, so there was no financial help from my family. But I had some things going for me that made life easier, such as student loans and credit cards. For one, I could justify this trip as a kind of research. After all, weren't student loans intended for learning? Secondly, because I had taken a couple years off from school and worked, I had some small savings. I also had a small advance from my publisher, and several sponsors contributed parts, supplies, and assistance that helped me hang on to my cash. I sold almost everything I owned, which had the unplanned bonus of significantly reducing my storage expenses. Finally, my bank account received a needed boost when a family estate settled and I got some more funds midway through the trip. But I would have done this trip no matter what my financial situation. Perhaps it might not have been as comfortable, convenient, or glamorous, but I was going even if I had to ride a motor scooter and wear a trash bag for a rainsuit. As I said before, with proper motivation, anything is possible.

The more research I did for the trip, the more the tedious details surfaced, like worms on a rainy day. I was overwhelmed with wriggling minutia. I needed medical insurance in the event of an injury, medical evacuation insurance in case I had to be flown to an adequate hospital, immunizations, malaria pills, and an international driving permit. I needed copies of all my documents, including my passport, license, and credit cards. I even took a laminated paper copy of my aluminum motorcycle license plate, in case someone decided to decorate his or her den with the original.

I carried a dummy wallet (with outdated credit cards, an old ID, and a couple of dollars) for quick muggers, and a Multi-Tool with a folding, viciously serrated blade for the slow ones. I picked up an extra set of keys to hide on the motorcycle, along with wads of emergency cash and a credit card (you never can tell when a Latin American government might crumble, and dumping the bike and evacuating might be the only option). I also had a hidden pouch to stash documents and money under my clothes, some letters of endorsement from sponsors I'd hooked up with, and five hundred business cards to hand out to people I met.

My bike needed attention as well. I had to carry enough spare parts, but not so many as to weigh me down. The question of what to bring became more difficult when I asked for opinions; everybody had a different view of what was essential. Some insisted I take minimal tools on the premise that if I had any real problems I could just get the

bike towed to a decent mechanic. Others believed that leaving without everything, including a spare ignition box, was foolish, since you
never know what might be impossible to find down there. My packing plans lay somewhere between these two schools of thought. I took
the toolkit that came with the bike plus a few extra tools, and a variety of spare parts. The bike was brand-new, so odds of a major failure
were small. I was betting that most problems would be minor and
readily fixable with the available resources en route.

I had some aftermarket parts and equipment added to the bike to
increase comfort, functionality, and safety. These included luggage and
mounting racks, an entirely new suspension, braided steel brake lines
to improve the bike's stopping power, a custom motorcycle saddle,
cloth tank panniers, a higher windscreen, and new tires. Then I
packed a tent, clothes, riding gear, first aid kit, repair manuals and
guidebooks, a laptop, camera, and toiletries. With the bike ready and
my bags packed, I left Binghamton, New York on March 19, 1999, after
a warm, yet brief, send-off from my family.

I raced down the highway at 75 MPH on my overburdened bike.
The day was bitter, typical of the Northeast in March. With all my gear
on I was sealed up in my own mini-environment and couldn't hear the
road or sense the cold. The only way I knew it was freezing outside
was by the snowflakes that melted on my face shield and the stunned
faces of the people hurtling alongside me in their four-wheeled cages.
I had my electric vest cranked up to five, the heated bike grips on high,
and more attitude than a barnful of drunken bulls to keep me warm.
Nothing could stop me now. I was really doing it.

I sped to Pennsylvania to meet Mark Van Horn, a burly, bear-
pawed friend who had agreed to accompany me as far as Daytona,
Florida. I was headed to Miami to pick up parts from a sponsor and do
an interview about my trip with a reporter from the Miami *Herald*. I
was glad to have Mark along—not only was he a good friend, but he
was also a fantastic mechanic—a backyard MacGyver of sorts. He had
a bike like mine, and when I was studying at Penn State we'd often go

motorcycling together in the woods, or I'd watch him tinker with his bike in his garage while I poked at mine as though I knew what I was doing.

We reached Daytona in two days. We hoped to enjoy the weekend a bit, so after dinner we rode up and down the Daytona strip. Daytona's famous Bike Week had just passed, so a few motorcyclists were still around. Mark signaled he wanted to stop for a drink, so we pulled into a gas station. Some kids sat in a parked car, probably on spring break. We took off our helmets and walked inside, past a man so drunk he couldn't find the door—he was examining the windowpane to see why it wouldn't swing open. We came back out and leaned on our bikes as we sipped and soaked in the quiet evening breeze.

An approaching V-twin roared loudly in the distance. A single headlight bore down the road, attached to a customized cruiser, all chromed and chopped out. The rider revved the engine until it belched thunderously—probably for our benefit—as he pulled in and parked nearby. He was a small man dressed all in leather, with a greasy black beard and a tiny skullcap helmet. As he stepped off his ride and walked past I smiled and said, "Hey, how's it going?" The biker kept walking, but he glanced at me and my bike, Mark and his bike, and the kids in their car, in that order, and liberally passed scowls all around. The spring-breakers looked positively terrified. The lone rider continued inside without pausing or saying a word.

A moment later he reappeared and got on his chopper. We watched as the big machine misfired once, then burped to life. He revved his engine a few times, scowled one last time for the road, and then together man and machine rumbled off down the strip to feast upon whatever destiny had laid on their table. "That guy," Mark said reflectively, as the man disappeared in the distance, "is a horse's ass."

I noticed that the biker had an extra little helmet strapped to the passenger seat. Surely, somewhere out there, some lucky woman or man would just be tickled at the thought of joining our surly friend for a ride toward the horizon. And to think I hadn't even left my own country, and already I was learning what a rare and strangely wonderful world we live in. God bless that little horse's ass.

Two days later Mark wished me good-bye and I took off alone to Miami, where I took care of final details, spent a brief visit with family, and then curved around the Gulf to McAllen, Texas, to meet the two men I'd be traveling with for the next five months.

*

THE CLOCK ON THE MOTEL WALL read midnight. The windowpane I looked through reflected the street lamps and starlight. A chilly draft wafted across the parking lot, mingled with the heat from my bike's motor, and together they dissipated into the Texas night. In a couple of days I'd be leaving my country for the next year. I bent down to check the wear of my tires as the sound of heavy feet approached.

And there he was. After nine months of planning and six months of Internet conversations, I finally met the first of two mystery men who would join me on my journey across Latin America. Robert was much larger than he appeared in the motorcycle trip photos I'd seen of him posted on the Net. I'm not small, at 6′1″ and 185 lbs, but this guy had mass. He was at least as tall as me, with an additional thirty pounds of muscle. His limbs were long and thick, his beard bushy and white, his gray, wavy hair neatly combed. Round glasses settled over a pair of small, dark eyes, completing the portrait of a man who was every bit Kriss Kringle, the jolly old elf himself—except this Santa Claus could rip the roof off a car. "I'll help with your bags," Robert said. "Why don't you bring the bike around back to the room? You can leave it next to mine." I parked next to his massive black BMW and started removing my luggage. My bike looked dwarfed next to his. With no luggage and a full tank of gas, my KLR weighed in around 380 lbs. Robert's machine had a motor almost twice the size of mine and porked out at over 500 lbs, unladen. He had to be strong, because if that thing ever fell over with a full tank and another 80 lbs of luggage attached, it would take two average guys to pick it up. Robert hefted a bag in each burly paw, and I grabbed the rest as we climbed the stairs. I had a lot of luggage: two plastic saddlebags, a top case, a set of cloth panniers, a tank bag, and a pair of replacement tires I planned to ship ahead to Panama. "I was expecting you to be traveling heavy," Robert said with a laugh, "but not this heavy."

The motel was full and Robert graciously let me stay in his room. We'd been planning this trip together for some time, and he had our route mapped out to the day. I'd done so much thinking about this moment, and now it had suddenly arrived. I was overcome with excitement to be there, to be making the trip a reality. In my exhilaration I found myself gibbering like an idiot. After so much preparation and expectation, I was ecstatic to converse with someone who could really appreciate what we were about to do. Words dumped out of me like alphabet soup. As I unpacked, I withdrew the Miami *Herald* article and other clippings written about me and the trip we'd planned. There were also the letters of introduction from my sponsors. "May come in handy at border crossings or something," I said. I was spouting a rush of words, but Robert just looked at me in silence.

I was making him uncomfortable; unfortunately I was too wired from the ride and the excitement to notice. But I slowly picked up on it, like waking from a deep sleep, and all of a sudden it occurred to me that something weird had entered the room. I suspect Robert mistook my giddy speech and paper shuffling as the ramblings of a braggart. I'd merely wanted to show my worth, that I wasn't just some rookie punk he'd have to babysit. Faced with a man of such experience, I felt the need to show that I too brought something to the group. I don't think that's how he took it. That moment set a tone of awkwardness to our friendship that was at best an inauspicious way to begin a transcontinental road trip. At worst it might become a permanent detriment to our ability to function as a team. To be fair to myself, perhaps this mood wasn't really caused by my eager babble. Perhaps it was just our conflicting personalities or our difference in age, experience, or whatever. I don't know what the reason was, but somehow I pinned the corsage on wrong, and the rest of that prom night was fucked.

The following morning I realized our next biggest (and somewhat related) problem: Robert and I just couldn't communicate well. We were walking to the restaurant next door for breakfast. One of us forgot something and went back to the room, and then somehow in the confusion we were separated, and it took us several minutes to relocate each other. Already we illustrated our inability to effectively convey even the simplest ideas—not a good omen. When doing a bike trip, losing other riders in the wilds can be life threatening in the event of a serious injury, hostile natives, or inclement weather. Losing other riders when walking next door for chow is just pathetic.

I quickly learned a lot about Robert. He was married and lived in both Canada and the United States. He worked as a petroleum engineer, mostly on a consulting basis, and he'd declined the next few contracts to have time for the trip. Sandy, his wife, was apparently OK with the idea of him leaving. Robert had been traveling by motorcycle for longer than I'd been alive, and he was a well-versed mechanic. Trips like this were part of his blood. He was the grizzled authority of our group, the man to turn to for advice and expertise.

Peter Santa-Maria was to arrive later that day. The final member of our triumvirate, Peter was in many ways our salvation. He was a United States citizen raised in Colombia, and his savvy and experience with potential Latin problems like corruption, bureaucracy, and how to dance salsa was going to save us scads of frustration and generally make life more enjoyable. He also spoke perfect Spanish. My Spanish was passable, but it couldn't compare to Peter's native fluency. Robert knew little Spanish and would come to rely heavily on Peter and occasionally on me for translations.

Peter was about my height, slim, and in his mid-thirties, with a handsome, everyday-guy face and receding hairline. Like Robert, Peter was married, and he lived with his wife in New Mexico. He'd worked as safety manager for a waste management company, but quit his job in order to take this trip. There were many factors motivating him for the journey, such as a general malaise with his career and frustrations on the home front, but like me, I suppose he mostly just needed to dream. Robert and I were working on our bikes when Peter rolled into the parking lot that afternoon. Peter rode a big red-and-white 95 BMW GSPD he dubbed the Virgin Queen because of its immaculate condition. Peter's bike didn't feel as heavy as Robert's because of its lower center of gravity, but the Virgin Queen was still seriously portly. A huge, homemade aluminum box was mounted on the back, where he kept his sleeping bag, tools, and spare parts. Two black cases with the rest of his supplies were attached on the sides.

Our circle was complete. The plan was to ride through Mexico and Central America in about one month and reach Panama by May. From there we'd ship the bikes to Ecuador, then continue overland to Peru, Bolivia, Chile, and end up in Buenos Aires, Argentina. At that point Peter and Robert would continue north to Brazil, up through the Mato Grosso into Venezuela, and then either ship back to Miami or to Central America and ride home. I planned to visit family in Argentina for a few months and then continue on to Ushuaia, Argentina, the southernmost city in the world, for the millennium celebration. After Ushuaia I'd ride back through Uruguay, Paraguay, Brazil, the Guyanas, and Venezuela, then ship to Central America and return to the United States. In that way I'd have touched all the countries in Central and South America. Well, those were our plans, anyway.

The next day was full of last-minute preparations. We packed and repacked, bought batteries and film, and the guys helped me select items to discard from my overloaded saddlebags. "No, no, no, yes, no, no . . ." While they inspected and commented on my gear, I noticed the uniqueness of Peter's accent. He spoke English with an inflection that I can only describe as a Spanish lilt, which made him appear sophisticated and silly all at once, like a man holding a dainty cup with his pinky thrust out. This humorous effect was augmented by things that came out of his mouth, giving us a keen insight into Peter's world of the absurd.

"What would you guys have done if I rolled up on my bike today wearing only a pink T-shirt and skintight bicycle shorts?" Robert and I looked at each other dumbly. Peter burst out in a hyena-like laugh. "I was going to play a little joke on you guys to see what you'd have said, but I decided at the last minute not to do it. I should have done it—you guys would've freaked out!"

We were supposed to leave the next day, but due to the first of many problems I'd cause on the trip, we were delayed. And this first problem was a big one. I didn't have the title to my motorcycle. In order to take a vehicle out of the United States and into other countries, authorities generally need to see proof of ownership like a title or a notarized permission from the owner. In my case, the previous owner was the bank that financed my motorcycle loan. Although I'd paid off the loan and sent the paperwork to the Pennsylvania Department of Motor Vehicles a month before, there had been no word back from them. I waited as long as possible, and when the paperwork didn't arrive I started the trip, hoping it would arrive at home, to be forwarded to me in Miami. In Miami there was still no sign of the paperwork, so I kept riding and hoped to get it in McAllen, preferably without alarming or angering Robert and Peter with the news.

"What do you mean, you have no title?" Peter said alarmedly.

"This is a major problem," Robert said angrily.

I couldn't go anywhere without the paperwork. They weighed several options, including their leaving ahead (I would hurry up to meet them later), but Robert was against that idea. "Once you get separated it can be very difficult to get back together again," he said. But I was already aware of that; we learned that lesson on the way to breakfast.

What I hadn't learned was that the DMV office in Harrisburg had lost my title application. No amount of waiting would've made it appear. Fortunately a guy named Mike in the State College office came through for me. He called Harrisburg and got the assistance of a woman named Linda, who did a rush production of the title, and then shipped it overnight to McAllen. Their kindness and help probably saved me from riding into Mexico alone, a scenario I wasn't looking forward to. I was so uncomfortable with the idea that, according to Robert, I woke him, muttering in my sleep: "I can't believe it, those guys left me . . . they left me."

The title was to arrive the following morning. The rest of the day I changed the bike's oil, mailed my spare tires to Panama, and tried not to irritate my riding buddies. There was a little tension, but nothing out of the ordinary for the day before such a big trip. The next morning would go like clockwork: get up, eat, get ready, get the title, and cross the border to Latin destinations unknown. No problem. So the adventure had arrived. The mission? To explore new lands, to imbibe many drinks with little umbrellas, and to boldly go where other people already live. The trip of a lifetime was about to begin.

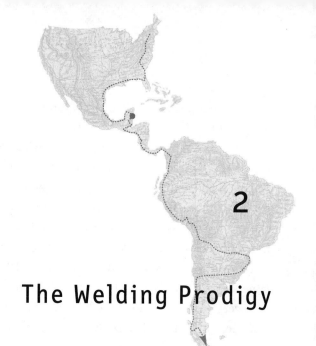

2

The Welding Prodigy

➤ YOU COULD SAY THAT THINGS went like clockwork that morning—if the clock you're referring to is broken or several hours slow. The title paperwork for my motorcycle arrived at 10:30 A.M. but we didn't actually leave McAllen for Latin destinations unknown until noon. It was all my fault. I was copying important documents and e-mailing a final update, and when I realized the time I rushed to the motel in such a hurry that I dropped my bike in the parking lot. Peter was not his normal, joking self. Robert glared at me so hard I got welts.

We hopped on our bikes and bolted out of McAllen, straight south. The sun was reassuring, penetrating down through my protective suit. When we stopped, the heat under the helmet and other gear became intense, but as long as we were moving I was fine. The customs and immigration checkpoint at the United States/Mexico border was a big parking lot with a few scattered concrete buildings and men in beige uniforms and orange vests walking around. There were also some travelers: truckers, old men in small Japanese compacts, families in pickups. The guards looked bored and universally annoyed. They shuffled people through quickly and with as little interaction as possible.

We were nervous. Peter triple-checked his documentation and repeated back everything the guards said to make sure he understood, and then he translated for us as we signed this and handed over that. "Hey, Andrés—they think your title is a fake," Peter laughed. "They want to see the real one." I managed a self-conscious smile but noticed that Robert wasn't amused. He was sweltering from the heat in his leather riding pants, obviously still stressed from the morning's delay. When under pressure, Robert became even quieter than normal, and did everything more slowly to be sure he did it right. Peter and Robert wandered ahead to the next line. Fast Spanish was spoken at me, and I struggled to understand and answer back politely. I kept worrying that someone might steal something off my bike, or that I might not get back all my documents or some other little important thing. My forehead was drenched in sweat. We must've looked like wrecks. The only entertainment those border guards must've gotten was from watching people like us.

We finally returned to the bikes (nothing had been stolen—in fact, nothing was ever stolen at a border), stuck holographic Mexican vehicle permits onto the windshields, and rode out onto the highway. Robert led, Peter was second, and I pulled up the rear. Fields of rusted-out trucks and impounded school buses bid us good-bye as we rode out of sight of the border.

The ride on Highway 97 South was long and straight pretty much all the way to Tampico. We tore along the tarmac to arrive before dark—Peter had heard there were muggers on the roads recently, and we weren't going to wait around to see if the reports were accurate. We stopped only once for gas, which further hassled Robert because Peter and I had to borrow pesos. We had forgotten to change dollars in the United States. The fresh blacktop in the parking lot was so hot from the sun that my motorcycle kickstand sank in and the KLR fell over. Hot, messy tar stuck to the handlebars and saddlebags after I

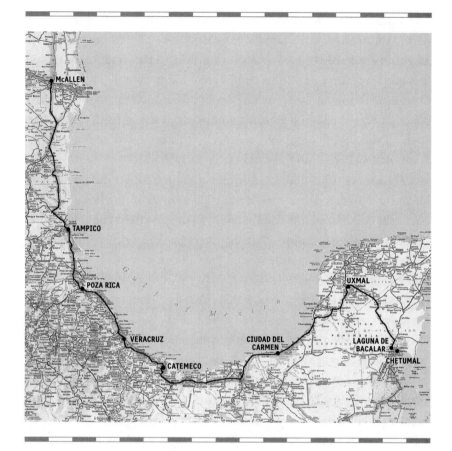

picked the bike up. I was having quite a day. We had a cool drink and didn't talk much. As we were leaving I said something forgettable like "Let's make some miles," just in case anyone had forgotten what a fool beginner I really was.

We passed several fires burning alongside the road; the smoke was visible for miles. I never learned why, but fires burned on roadsides in the north, the south, and all along the coast. Nobody around seemed to notice or care, and soon neither did we.

Just as the navy blue cool of the evening spread across the horizon we pulled into Tampico, a town on the Gulf Coast of Mexico about

280 miles south of McAllen. The city was well lit and filled with wandering tourists. It was *semana santa*—Holy Week—and people all over Latin America were traveling and celebrating. Peter had known about this and forgotten, but Robert and I were taken completely off guard. It seemed to me an ugly turn of events that our first night in Latin America was spent in a Howard Johnson's, but the reality was that, with all the vacationers, we were lucky to find any accommodations at all. At least we didn't have to eat at McDonald's.

The ornate third-floor balcony of the restaurant we did eat in overlooked the plaza in the center of town. The surrounding buildings had beautiful colonial architecture, preserved despite their conversion into offices, banks, and shops. The city was packed with people. Men, women, and even a couple of children drank alcohol openly in the plaza and on the street.

"We gotta stay together on these things," Robert said sternly, in between slowly taken forkfuls of *carne tampiqueño*. "We can't go on like this." I was gritting my teeth as he spoke, but he was right, of course. These first couple of days I hadn't exactly shone. Nobody likes to wear the dunce cap, whether it's self-donned or not. Children shrieked and chased each other around a vendor's cart in the plaza below. The first day of my Latin American adventure hadn't passed as I'd hoped, but I promised myself tomorrow would look better.

The next day we rode 170 miles to Poza Rica on the same kind of straight paved highway as before, the only difference being the temperature. Robert's full leather riding pants looked absolutely painful in 100°F heat. Peter and I both had zippered nylon suits that we could open and ventilate, but Robert got no such relief. Peter and I also had portable water systems with long tubes for drinking while riding. Generally even the scorching Mexican weather was tolerable provided we had lots of water and never stopped moving, but when traffic slowed or we stopped for gas, we'd bake on the black tarmac and every five seconds Peter shouted, "Hurry up, Slow Boy, I'm a-dying of heatstroke!"

El Tajín was the first in a long line of archeological sites we'd see. Being an avid fan of ancient cultures, Robert had plotted our map route like a game of connect-the-ruins. The highlights of El Tajín included detailed wall relief in good condition and an expansive set of buildings—overall, an excellent impression of the grandeur that once was. Crowds were given free reign to climb on virtually everything. I doubted that this policy was good for the site; in fact, the extra traffic was a likely a major contributor to its current rate of deterioration. If these ruins were under the auspices of the States, there'd be safety handrails, roped-off trails, and litigation-proof signage warning of the dangers of leaving the path (not to mention the obligatory animated mascot, like Maria the Montezuma Quail, or Smeller the Shorthaired Chihuahua).

According to Robert, this particular site had several good examples of the famous gaming courts where teams vied to force a small rubber ball through a ring set high on a wall, without using their hands. The games culminated with the decapitation of one or more of the players. Originally it was believed that the losers were decapitated, but new theories suggest that it may have been the captains of the winning teams that were sacrificed, since they would be a worthier offering to the gods.

The other attraction at the ruins, no less famous, were *Los Voladores,* or the Fliers. There are groups of Voladores performing in many places now, demonstrating this tradition for tourists, but the ceremony used to be deeply significant for several of the indigenous peoples in the Veracruz region. The intent was to give thanks for the harvests received during the year and to ask for rains to nourish the lands in the coming seasons, thus bringing prosperity and wealth. The Fliers are groups of five men that ascend a metal pole about three stories high, with a rotating apex and four ropes wound about the top. The men wear colorful traditional garb and four of them carry flutes. The fifth man is the leader, and he carries a small drum. The ceremony begins with some dancing, and then the four flautists ascend. Each of the four winds a rope about his legs, and then the leader climbs up. He perches atop the spinning peak and keeps the rhythm while the other four leap out headfirst at the ground, playing their instruments as they swing by their feet in an elegant, ever-widening, four-pointed spiral. The ropes they hang from slowly wind out as the men rotate to the earth. Just before they touch down, the fliers nimbly unwrap themselves from their cables and land on their feet. After the four have landed, the leader then descends one of the cables with his bare hands, demonstrating his valor and agility. Then the group tours the crowd and reminds everyone that the spectacle was not for free.

The next day we moved on. Oncoming traffic was a major concern. Cows and dogs wandered the streets freely, as did children, drunks, and the elderly. Hazards could (and did) spring up at any time. The highway often crossed in and out of towns, and in one of them we encountered eight-inch-tall, monster speed bumps right across our path. Peter wholly nailed one, his rear suspension rocking and bouncing in the air. Seeing his mistake saved me because I had enough time to slow down. These speed bumps became familiar and bore different names in different countries, but here in Mexico they were simply called *topes*.

In a moderately sized city, standing near a gas station, was a group of young women clad in racy white seventies-style basketball shorts and tank tops with red trim. They waved and smiled, bouncing and dancing on the roadside near a juice stand. They tried to flag everyone down, even us, but the truck drivers seemed to be their target market. What a country. Where else can you hire five gorgeous young women to frolic half-naked every morning to promote juice and still make a profit? Perhaps Mexico has exceptional juice. Perhaps Mexican truckers are exceptionally thirsty. Or perhaps there was more for sale at that juice stand than just beverages.

My motorcycle skills improved daily, but the differences between Peter and me were significant, and the differences between Robert and us were extreme. Each of them had a lot of practice riding, years in fact, but Robert was so far out of our league it was laughable. I first noticed his style in McAllen. He always sat bolt upright in the saddle, even during the ten-hour days we occasionally did. No matter how long he'd ridden, he always looked the same. What really made me take note was how he flowed in traffic: pulling up behind a car, passing, and resuming with a steady rhythm, he never needed to accelerate or brake aggressively. For a long time I never saw his brake light come on at all. At first I thought it was broken, but then I realized that he purposefully rode that way, controlling the timing and distances so that he seldom braked. Up to this point I never felt I was endangering myself to keep up, but I was definitely pushing the limits of my ability.

On a particular road in Mexico I was stuck behind a big eighteen-wheeler. Robert and Peter sneaked past the driver while going uphill, where he was at a disadvantage for lack of acceleration, and by now they'd gotten pretty far ahead. By the time the truck driver got his rig up to the plateau and I had an opportunity to get by, he'd decided enough motorcyclists had passed him that day.

Unaware of his decision, I casually began to overtake him and he sped up next to me. I didn't know what was going on so I tried again and he scared the hell out of me when he swerved a bit into the other lane, cutting me off. I was outraged. This guy could kill someone with his massive machine and he was fooling around? My heart pounded in anger. Deciding I was finished with this game, I pulled up tight behind his rig and downshifted, waiting for oncoming traffic to disappear. When the other lane opened I blasted out from behind him— full throttle and pushing the red line—by the time he saw me I was even with his cab. I shifted up and kept going, thumping along righteously.

He looked at me in surprise and then with disappointment as he realized his fun was over. There was nothing he could safely do to stop me, so he let me by. "Bite me, asshole," I thought, and flashed him my middle finger over my shoulder with my left hand while still twisting the throttle with my right.

I was satisfied and continued ahead until I noticed the trucker was now bearing down behind me. At that point, upon reconsideration, flipping him the bird seemed a little rash. I accelerated up from 70 to 80 MPH, then from 80 to 90 MPH, and even up to 95 MPH to keep a safe distance, but he was still coming. I could feel his grille coming up behind me. My needle was running out of speedometer, and the downgrade in the road helped him to keep up the pressure.

What an unexpected turn of events—was my trip going to end so soon? Thankfully some curves appeared ahead. I knew I'd smoke the bastard now. If he tried to enter those curves at anything over 45 MPH he'd have flipped, whereas I could take them safely at up to 70 MPH. I swooped into the turns with my face suspended just a few feet from the blacktop. I listened to the hum of my tires and the roar of the wind as I sliced the curves at speed, and over my shoulder the truck faded into the trees.

A few moments later I came upon Robert and Peter by the side of the road, waiting for me to catch up. "Get moving, a psycho truck driver's coming over that hill any second!" I neglected to tell them I'd also enraged him by giving him the finger—why waste more time with needless details? As we pulled away from the berm Robert dropped his water bottle. I frantically signaled for him to forget it. He looked at me quizzically but did as I asked. Luckily we never saw that trucker again.

Ciudad del Carmen is a quiet ocean town with sanded streets and salty tangerine sunsets. We rolled in during the late afternoon calm, attracting gaping stares from old women bent with groceries and young boys kicking a tattered leather ball. Scouring the guidebooks, we selected some decent-sounding hotels, then went to all of them inquiring for the best deal. Just down the street we found a little scenic nook in the typical mud brick style, with whitewashed balconies overlooking the ocean. This refuge was ours for a mere ten dollars each. We looked for triples when available, because they were always the cheapest. Enclosed, and preferably monitored, parking was also desirable. If a hotel had no parking, they'd usually help arrange something around the corner at a private lot, and on rare occasions we were even allowed to roll our bikes into the hotel hallway or lobby. In this case, a ten-foot stucco wall with a padlocked door surrounded the courtyard, and we parked the bikes right in front of our window. Finding shelter for the bikes was never hard.

The next morning was a wakeup to the bizarre. We stopped for gas at a station along the highway. The girl attending the car in front of me was dark-haired and attractive and wore a gray mechanic's coverall mottled with grease. Two other similarly dressed women worked alongside her while a portly man in his mid-fifties, short on height and even shorter on hair, wandered around, apparently supervising. Out of pesos, I asked the girl about changing dollars. She offered to charge me a full percentage point extra on the exchange rate. Although it was common to charge a modest fee for exchanging dollars, the rate she offered was ludicrous. Peter also needed pesos and tried to talk her down, but she wouldn't budge. Out of spite we finally borrowed some pesos from Robert to avoid getting shafted by the unfair rate.

Pesos in hand, I opened up my gas cap for her to fill the tank. She smiled briskly, put the gas nozzle inside, and we both watched the pump as the meter started to count off. Glancing down, I noticed she wasn't squeezing the nozzle's trigger. No gas was pouring into my tank. Her other hand rested casually on the side of the pump and apparently she'd flipped some hidden switch to make the meter count without pouring. "What are you, some kind of thief?" I said. She looked at me with feigned shock and innocence and I shouted at her to stop what she was doing. Several of the patrons were staring our way and she just glared at me angrily. Busted. The manager quickly waddled over. He apologized profusely and tried to pump the gas personally, but I'd have none of it. I took the nozzle from his hands and forced them both to stand back while I pumped it myself. Under any other circumstances I would've just left, but I felt trapped. Who could tell when the next station would appear?

Peter laughed at the girl scornfully. "First you want to hit us with a ridiculous exchange rate and now you steal from us outright." Looking at the manager, he added, "Some business you have here, Boss."

The man started to speak and the girl blurted out: "Yeah, but when we go to your country you murder us." Her eyes burned furiously.

I looked at Peter in disbelief. "Did she just say what I thought she said?"

"Excuse me?" Peter said to her. I didn't perfectly understand what she said next, but she seemed to believe it was United States policy to shoot Mexicans on sight, simply for crossing the border. Peter and I looked at each other in openmouthed silence. He abruptly turned and walked back to his bike, shaking his head. She again focused her attention on me, arguing the point. I put on my helmet and gloves while she foamed and seethed, and I said, "That's not true, this is madness, you're mistaken." I started the motor, slipped on my sunglasses, and pulled out of there.

"*Cabrón!*" she shouted after me. "*Hijo de puta!*"

The day was gorgeous and incredibly hot. Three men on bikes snaked along a scenic coastal highway. Ambient heat trickled skyward from the asphalt, blurring the view of creamy beaches like crumbled bone dust before an ocean of piled emeralds. This was the kind of beauty that poets write of and politicians war over. Robert was far in the lead when Peter pulled up next to me, waving for my attention. While he rode alongside he formed his hand into a C-shape in front of his face and wiggled his index finger. He was signaling to stop for a photo. I pointed in Robert's direction, thinking to stop him too. Peter just waved off my suggestion as if to say, "We'll only be a minute."

"Quick, we'll drive over this hill and get a shot of the bikes on the beach, in front of that incredible water." Peter smiled excitedly. We'd only just pulled over and removed our helmets, but already the sweat rivulets ran down his forehead. "What a day." We turned the bikes up a sandy track through some underbrush, over a small series of dunes, and onto the beach. We worked the bikes carefully through the sand,

and they handled terribly since they were fully loaded and the tires were fully inflated. In fact, both our bikes sank in axle deep, standing upright on their own, so we hopped off and snapped photos of each other without even dropping the kickstands. Laughing and sweating, we struggled to keep the motorcycles vertical while we unburied them, turned them around, and wobbled our way off the beach.

Robert had vanished. We rode on, expecting to see him waiting for us by the roadside, but there was no trace. We pulled into a gas station, our suits dripping from our excursion. My helmet felt like a warm, soggy pear on my head. A brown young girl giggled at us in all our gear and said, "You two cold?"

When Robert didn't show for about a half hour, we continued to Edzna, an archaeological site en route, thinking he'd meet us there. When he finally motored into the parking lot of the ruins he found us talking with two world travelers, a German woman named Birgit and a South African man named Sam. They'd been circling the earth on their BMWs, and already they'd covered Africa, eastern Europe, and South America. Their plan was to ride north to the United States and Canada and round out their trip with Australia, Asia, and western Europe. We were all chatting as Robert pulled up. He was visibly annoyed. Although he put up a good front and was polite for the newcomers, his smoldering curtness revealed how angry he was with Peter and me.

As we toured the ruins of Edzna, Robert lightened up and told us some of the history of the Maya. He said the local pre-Colombian cultures had a fundamentally religious basis, and human sacrifices were common. Sacrifices usually involved removing the live beating heart before tossing the poor bastard down the temple steps like a half-eaten drumstick. Robert described these grisly acts with a faraway, almost wistful look in his eye, and I sensed that perhaps he was imagining Peter and me as his victims, our moist violet hearts pulsing and coughing in his hands. Apparently all these involuntary organ donations were performed with flint knives, which are quite dull compared to a modern blade. A lucky victim probably would've been in shock and unable to feel the intense pain as his heartless body was pitched down the steep stone walls. According to Robert, the victim's blood was then collected to be drunk by all the priests in attendance and smeared into their hair, which they supposedly never washed.

As we pulled out of the site, I dropped my portable water system. Far down the road we came to a fork, and realizing it was missing, I turned around to quickly look for it. I didn't mention anything to Robert or Peter because I thought I'd just dropped it, and it was therefore probably somewhere nearby. I was just going to do a quick scan, grab it, and then turn around and catch up with them before they knew I was gone. I backtracked, looking by the sides of the road and in ditches, and as I searched I lost track of time and ended up riding all the way back to the ruins. No one there had seen it, so I gave up and went back to meet the others. Soon their two headlights approached, and Peter asked me what had happened. When I explained that I was looking for my water bottle, they were furious. Well, I think at this point Peter had given up on me entirely and could no longer get mad. He just shook his head. But Robert still held a smidgen of hope that I'd improve, and once again that hope was dashed like a kid's favorite action figure under the bully's baseball bat.

They'd noticed I wasn't behind them, and when they turned around to find me, a man in a pickup was waving at them and pointing to the side of the road. In their minds, this guy was telling them I was lying in a ditch somewhere. They came back looking in all the ditches along the roadside, and in that time I'd wasted two hours and nearly run us all out of gas. I think Robert's fantasies of ritualistically flaying me and using my blood for hair gel were becoming more vivid in his mind.

We finally made it to the ruins at Uxmal, where we stayed at a Club Med built on-site. I bought a peace offering, a six-pack of Coronas. Peter had screwed up in a big way by getting us separated from Robert on that morning's photo op, but since I messed up later on, alone, and in a bigger way, I absorbed all Robert's anger for that day's fiascoes.

"We can't help it that we are the two dingbats of the group," Peter said, apparently trying to console me.

"You should be glad I'm around, I make you look like an angel."

"I think I agree. Just try not to screw up anymore, Devil Boy."

As if it wasn't enough that I was the rookie fuckup, I was also feeling a bit of stress because of our pace. We were absolutely sailing through Mexico. We'd spent so much time in the saddle (over three thousand five hundred miles a week) that Peter was literally getting blisters on his ass. There was so much to see and do and we were moving too damn fast. I couldn't get past this idea. I felt my dream trip was passing me by.

Robert's reasons for rushing us through Central America were twofold. On a personal level, he wanted to spend as much time as possible in Peru. Peru had always fascinated and eluded him on his previous trips, so he scheduled forty days for Peru alone—one-third of our total time together as a group and more than one-fifth of his entire scheduled trip time. Therefore something had to be sacrificed, and that ended up being Central America. Robert was also well aware that the Central American rainy season was coming, and he knew exactly what that meant to a motorcycle traveler. Since we began in April, we only had about a month before the rains would arrive. That would be just enough time to make it out, as long as we didn't dawdle. We'd have been very foolish to allow ourselves to get caught in the monsoonlike deluges somewhere in El Salvador, and then watch our trip plans end in knee-deep mud and washed-out bridges. That was the other reason Robert was keeping the pace up. We really had no choice and he understood that better than anyone.

Peter and I, on the other hand, needed to see and do as much new stuff as possible. And for us, everything was new. We felt it was a crime to zip through countries in two to three days. Robert had planned the trip well, but not according to our interests.

Despite the pressure to keep moving, Robert told us there was some small amount of flexibility in the schedule. If we found a really great place we could pass an extra day there if we wanted. In the Club

Med near the ruins of Uxmal, we needed very little coaxing to stop. Our room was about three hundred feet from the ancient stone wonders and ten feet from the pool. Besides, Peter's swollen ass needed the break, and we all needed to enjoy the sun without our helmets and jackets for a change.

Already our equipment was showing signs of wear. My saddlebag mounting racks needed work and I went looking the next day for a welder nearby that could help. My saddlebags were hard, waterproof, plastic luggage that locked onto tubular steel racks on either side of the bike. They're one of many aftermarket bags available for the KLR, and in my (and Robert's) opinion were the best choice to bring along. Robert used a pair of plastic cases identical to mine. On a previous trip, he'd seen several sets of very expensive custom aluminum panniers burst open at the seams from the constant vibration. He also saw a set of those panniers after a wreck. His opinion was that once a set of the metal panniers had been crashed, they usually stayed crashed—and finding an aluminum welder in South America can be like questing for the Holy Grail.

The plastic bags, I discovered, were indeed durable and could withstand multiple crashes. But the mounting system proved less than adequate. "Hey, Devil Boy," Peter said. "Your bags are flopping around on the bumps. That doesn't look too good." I took a look and saw that the bag on the right side of the bike had begun to sag dejectedly, warning of an imminent structural failure.

The repair shop I found was just a garage with no door and an unobtrusive, hand-painted sign that read "welder." Outside was a short, gray-haired trucker with muscular forearms and wrinkled cheeks banging a pipe on the rear axle of his rig. BANG! BANG! BANG! He hammered away loudly like a hammering fool. Men and boys worked and wandered around inside. Some were actual apprentices, and some just kept their friends company while they worked. A couple of kids were barefoot, and everyone was filthy.

A group of men gathered around me, asked me some questions, and listened gravely as I described the work I wanted to have done.

They conferred for several minutes, pointing and gesturing animatedly at the bike. One of them questioned me again for clarification, and then finally they sent an eight-year-old with plastic flip-flops and scarred knees running into the back of the garage. The child, whose face reflected the gravity of the charge he was given, came running back with another boy, a fourteen-year-old they called Surgeon. The men all nodded at Surgeon approvingly, arms folded on their chests as they smiled proudly. I gathered I was in the presence of some kind of metalworking boy genius, a welding prodigy.

Surgeon had black hair, coal eyes, and a pudgy face. I began to ask him if he could do the work and he nodded yes without even letting me finish my sentence. Asking a Latin male if he can accomplish anything mechanical is a waste of breath. Every single mechanic, carpenter, craftsman, or kid with a wrench in his hand won't admit something can't be done until he has tried everything, including calling in every other kid with a wrench that he knows.

It's part of the Latin culture to be as helpful as possible. A great example of this is in the giving of directions. When getting directions, it's best to verify them with at least five different people to get a solid feel for which way to go. In Central and South America people will tell you how to get somewhere even if they haven't a clue. They offer up their best guess as fact, and smile contentedly as you wander off with a relieved look on your face. It's not a malicious thing; they just really want, at the very least, to appear to have helped.

I followed Surgeon across the shop, stepping over shards of scrap metal, ancient 2x4s, soda cans, rusted bolts, and twisted nails. I selected from the materials he offered, and watched as he bent and worked the long metal wire over an anvil and occasionally over his knee. The eight-year-old sandaled runner stared at me while I waited, a little potbelly poking out from under his navy blue T-shirt. I stared back at him while he drank tap water from a greasy jug he found on the floor.

Surgeon was patient and persistent. He cut each piece with a hacksaw fashioned from rebar and double-checked the sizes. He stuffed a wet rag around the battery of the bike to prevent a possible explosion, and then attached a welding lead to the frame. As he welded, he held a piece of darkened glass in front of his eyes, shielding them from the intense light. I was glad to see he had the training and brains to avoid damaging his vision. Just a few minutes before, I had watched that stumpy, hammering maniac outside weld an axle piece onto his rig with no eye protection whatsoever. Just one more scary thing to think about when facing a big rig bearing down the road at you—it just might be an old trucker blinded by arc welding who was driving that ten-ton load on a bum axle.

When the work was done, Surgeon sheepishly charged me two dollars. He apologized, saying it was a rush job and he'd used his best materials. I practically blushed from shame; he felt bad for charging me two lousy dollars! I paid him and then slipped him an extra three

dollars and told him not to tell his boss about it, and waved thanks as I drove off.

The Club Med was like heaven, sort of. It was both a paradise and a rip-off all at once. There was excellent fresh-cut papaya, pineapple, and watermelon every day at breakfast; the pool area was beautifully appointed with palms, bougainvillea, cotton plants, and a stunningly clear sky each night. As is typical of resorts, the prices were disproportional to those of the surrounding towns. The laundry service wanted to charge me two dollars to wash a single pair of jeans. I'd just watched a fourteen-year-old maestro of welding work for three hours and then balk at charging me two bucks. Of that amount he was probably paid fifty cents. I'd rather have paid Surgeon to weld me a new pair of pants than to let these hotel owners profit so grossly, by comparison, from washing my old ones. I scrubbed them as best I could in the sink and hung them out the window.

The last day at Club Med was screaming hot, and we carefully rationed our time between lounging by the pool and ordering refreshments. Robert wandered off to read in the shade.

Two pasty-white girls in bikinis lay on the chairs next to mine. They were blond and tall, and speaking in a language I couldn't place. The Club Med was filled with Europeans, lots of French and Dutch, but these girls were speaking something very unfamiliar to me. They also spoke in English a few times, and Peter suggested it was for our benefit since we spoke predominantly (and after a few brews, rather loudly) in English. As it turned out, the women were speaking Swiss German. I could've guessed they were from Switzerland. They were definitely chocolate girls, pale skinned and plump, raised on milky Swiss goodness and European morals. They had enormously soft, pillowlike breasts under their bikini tops, an air of general benevolence for humanity, and a "why exercise" languor. I loved them simply for existing. They looked to be in their mid-twenties, and I was certain they wanted some conversation. The more we drank, the more certain I became. I started a conversation with them, and they smiled and introduced themselves. We shared the typically stale travelers' chatter, but it led to the four of us having drinks after dinner that night.

Actually I invited myself to sit with them after they ate and Peter joined us a bit later. Robert noticed what we were up to and was either still too irritable to be social, or he decided he didn't want to mess with what we were getting into. So the four of us sipped our drinks and reveled in the soothing cool of the Mexican evening. Their names were Simone and Ann Marie. They looked at each other and laughed, not shyly, while we talked, seeming to tolerate us for no other reason than they had nothing better to do. The conversation turned to how everyone hates Americans. "No, the French like them," Ann Marie said.

"No, they do not. The French hate them more than anyone," Simone said.

"Some of the French do seem to like them," Peter said, "but only because they hate the English more."

"Yes, but the French hate everyone," said Simone.

"They love themselves," Ann Marie replied. We all reflected on this insight while we sipped our drinks. The talk then turned to stupid American laws, how Americans are all drunks, and that we don't really care about what's going on in Kosovo, even though our soldiers are fighting there. The general feel was that Americans were pretty much bad news all around, but we were particularly bad in light of our alcohol consumption and our foreign military policy.

"Oh, who cares about foreign military policy," I said. "Let's have another drink."

"My point exactly," Ann Marie said. I swear nobody gets my humor.

Peter and I were on fire; we were an unstoppable team. I hardly did any work, though, except for the initial introductions that afternoon. I didn't have to, because an expert had taken over. Most people are so easily snagged by Peter's subtle, friendly way that they don't realize they like him until it's too late. This was no exception. I sat back and watched from a safe distance, like Marlin Perkins on *Mutual of Omaha's Wild Kingdom*, while he, like Marlin's assistant Jim, fearlessly wrestled the giant, surly anaconda. And because Peter happened to be completely devoted to his wife, all the benefits of all his hard work were laid squarely on my shoulders. It's as if Jim single-handedly killed two feral beasts, then handed them over to Marlin, saying, "You keep them, I don't wear animal skin."

"Come on ladies, let's do another round of tequila." Peter was working his magic. "Well," he said diplomatically, "I can see you are a bit hesitant. I'm going to order four shots. They'll just be there in front of you, innocently waiting. If they should happen to get drunk, fine; if not, that is also fine. Don't feel bad if you don't want them, me and Devil Boy over there will take care of them."

Before any of us knew what was happening, Peter led us through four rounds of shots on top what we'd already drunk. Fortunately the bar closed at ten—even though I'm a drunken, uncaring, stupid-law-abiding American, those damned Swiss girls were going to put me under the table. I could hear Marlin's narration in my head as *Wild Kingdom* continued: "After wrestling the giant anaconda and administering the oral tranquilizers, Jim begins part two of his brilliant plan for further studying the magnificent creatures—the romantic walk."

We meandered down to the ruins, and Peter mischievously convinced the guards to turn a blind eye so we could walk the decaying structures at night. There was excitement in the air. After so many days on the road with two strange men, I was thrilled to have some female company. The Uxmal guards were quite willing to be Peter's co-conspirators. The only condition was that we "be mindful of the fierce guard dogs and sleeping archaeologists." The only guard dogs we saw were pathetic mutts with xylophone rib cages, and they were hardly fierce—they'd have lovingly followed us anywhere if we tossed them a piece of shoe leather. The archeologists were nonexistent.

The ruins at night were vastly more impressive than the farcical Uxmal laser light show we saw earlier would've had us believe. Peter, Robert, and I all attended the show that evening, and it was all I could do not to ask for my money back. The ancient constructions were black as we walked between the courtyards and the ball game arenas. We joked and stumbled on boulders and loose stones and climbed up to the top of a ruin we dubbed the Sacrificial Temple. It had gotten so dark because the clouds had set in, and I had a problem.

I liked both girls physically, but was more attracted to Ann Marie's spunky personality. However, Simone seemed more interested. Had Peter been available I'd have let him choose, because, after all, he did all the work. On top of the temple and unable to make up my mind, Simone stood next to me, leaning her body close to me in the dark, so I took her by the arm and kissed her. The warm skin of her chest pressed against me. I had come a lot of miles to be here, and I couldn't have asked for anything more than to be in the arms of a gorgeous young Swiss girl. Next thing I knew we were removing clothes. We stumbled into an alcove and I swear this is true, and you won't believe me, but the clouds gave way and a faded magenta crescent moon poured red rays down over us as we had sex on our feet on the top of the temple. (The part you're not supposed to believe is about the moon.) Peter and Ann Marie were just around the corner, which was weird since we could overhear their conversation.

When it was time to go, we walked the girls back to the hotel. Peter's watch read 3 A.M. by the time we wandered up to our room. "Damn, Devil Boy, you are bad," Peter said, laughing in his exhaustion.

"What about you? It was your idea to do the shots and trespass on private property. What happened, anyway?"

"Nothing happened. But it was bad there for a minute." His face looked worried. "When you two were preoccupied, she became very friendly, and she was sitting next to me, leaning on my shoulder, and her breast brushed against my arm. I just sat there thinking 'God give me strength,' and kept talking until you came back."

I felt bad for him. Obviously he missed his wife. Both he and Robert seemed to really love their spouses, and as far as I could tell, wouldn't have broken faith with them. Both wanted their wives to come, but for their own reasons their partners chose not to. I can't imagine what it's like to leave a significant other at home for six months, but I bet that's much easier than being the one who waits at home. Since I was the only member of the group that was unattached, Peter and Robert were relegated to living vicariously through my experiences with women—a role that I don't think either of them liked too much.

We were on our way to Chetumal and then Belize. All told, three days and two nights at the Club Med cost us about $150 each. We were sorry to see it go. Especially since we were leaving at 8:30 A.M., and Peter and I felt like our hungover heads were tightly wrapped in steel wire. The roads to Chetumal were relatively straight, the climate, beautifully hot. I was acclimatizing to these temperatures in full riding gear, and more than once it occurred to me that we might've been in more danger of dehydration without the jackets and helmets, which helped maintain moisture. Robert postulated that we also might've gotten heatstroke without the gear to shade us from the intense sunlight.

About midday we came upon a military checkpoint. We slowed to 10 MPH and approached the line of stopped vehicles. There were machine gun nests with helmets poking out. A soldier was propped against a wall of sandbags ahead of us, smoking and cradling his rifle, the muzzle pointed at the ground. He seemed to admire our bikes as we passed. About thirty yards further down, three men in fatigues pulled us over and asked for ID. They asked us where we were headed and inspected our passports. They quickly handed back our documents, nodding for us to be on our way. We were stopped by the military police five times in Mexico, and twice we had to open up our saddlebags to show the contents. Fortunately we didn't encounter any of those horrible situations I'd heard about where guards make you unpack everything and repack it all, just because they can. The Mexican military police I met were courteous and professional. After a brief document check and visual inspection of our bikes, we were again on our way.

Later that day, in the middle of some wild, twisting back roads, I noticed a bright red splotch on the side of the pavement as we roared past. I slowed and turned around, pulling up next to a small group of women, children, and one pleasant-faced old man with a wide-brimmed hat and a hopelessly dilapidated bicycle. They stood in and around a pile of tomatoes—as much as one ton of tomatoes—with shattered wooden boxes and crate pieces poking out everywhere. Drying rivers of red ooze drizzled all around, and scattered squashed tomatoes dotted the roadway. It was a fruit cataclysm. Apparently there'd been an accident involving a tomato truck, but the truck had since been righted and removed. The tomatoes, which had broken free of their crates in the fall, were obviously written off as a loss. The truck's loss was the peoples' gain, and the opportunistic tomato scavengers happily picked over the remains.

We also discovered a surprise ruin. Robert and Peter pulled over to check out some interesting structures we'd passed along a road I promised not to name. Unlike the other archaeological sites we'd seen, these ruins were completely unmarked. No signs on the roadway explained their presence, they weren't listed on our maps, and there was no tourist infrastructure built nearby. Curious. We found what looked like a road in, but the entrance was gated and locked, and a sign read: "Please spare me the embarrassment of denying you access to these ruins if you are not a member of the family or of the archeological team. —Signed, the owner."

We were still reading the curt warning when a short young man with a blue baseball cap approached from a house inside the fence. We exchanged greetings and asked about the buildings we'd seen. "The owner," the young man said, "is a private person who wants to develop these ruins and then charge admission to the public. He discovered them by accident one day on this farm, and since then archeologists and government people come here all the time." The ruins had a Mayan name that I promised not to reveal, and the young man, whom I'll call Francisco, said he worked for the owner as a farmhand.

"Where is the owner now?" Peter asked. Robert and I sat back and watched the master begin his work.

"Oh, should be gone all day," Francisco said, removing his cap to drag his forearm across his brow.

"I see," Peter said. Peter had a spare tire strapped to the back of his bike, and he kept all kinds of goodies stored in the hollow inside it. He pulled out a fat green mango, some salt, and a liter of water, and then began peeling and cleaning the fruit as they talked. Francisco watched as Peter cut and salted the underripe mango, which is, in some parts of Latin America, the only way to eat one. Peter held out a piece for him at arm's length. Guessing at what Peter was up to, I pulled some small sweet plantains out of my top case and offered our new friend a couple.

"All day, huh?" Peter smiled as he crunched the sour mango. "Any chance we could take a quick peek? We would, of course, compensate you for your time." Francisco was game, and he happily accepted our fruit. We later gave him three dollars as well, which didn't make him very happy. I think he had higher hopes for Peter's "compensation," but he still gave us a tour.

Francisco led us over to one side of the property, across a cow pasture and through a small semijungle with tall tropical fronds and huge trees hung with vines and dropping hard, round nuts. The mystery of the silent stone structures was only heightened by the rampant undergrowth. Most of the ruins we saw were well maintained, or at least free of any nearby foliage and large trees to obstruct the view. But this place was pristine, with no graffiti, no tourists, and the threatening tropical forest all around. This couldn't have been found in any guidebook. Robert was practically orgasmic; to have solitary access to a place that so few had seen, in this condition, was truly a once-in-a-lifetime event. We felt like explorers of old. When it was time to leave, we thanked Francisco for his disobedience, fired up our bikes, and continued down the road.

On the way toward Chetumal the stunning crystal waters of Laguna Bacalar beckoned to us, so we stopped and found a hotel on its shores. The hotel sprawled across the waterfront, with white plaster walls and rhubarb-colored roof tiles. Turquoise paint accented the borders of the walls and fences. Our room was clean and modeled in a sea motif; lamps made from giant conch shells hung over the beds, and seashells decorated the walls. Even the bathroom was affected—there was a clear polyester countertop, yellowed by time, with starfish, shells, sea horses, and fishes mummified inside.

Staring at the sea decorations on the ceiling, exhausted from the ten-hour ride, my mind gave way to fantasy. Lying on the bed in the Hotel Laguna de Bacalar, I felt a sense of discovery and a strange kinship with the earlier conquerors. To me, it always seemed laughable when historians spoke of the Vikings or Columbus "discovering" America, or any other place for that matter, where native people had lived for centuries. But now in my own way I could relate to the explorers. In only a few days, I'd participated in blasphemous sexual acts on a ruined temple, seen a prohibited archeological wonder, and now had the world's most beautiful lagoon all to myself for ten dollars a night. That tacky conch lamp above my bed was mine—all mine. These places were so far out of the perspective of my usual world that by writing about them and bringing them home, I had indeed conquered them.

Peter came back with three Dos Equis beers, stirring me from my daydreams. We changed into our trunks and raced to the lagoon. Rejuvenated, we dove like children off the old wooden pier with rusty nails sticking out of it. We splashed in the warm blue water, shoving our thumbs in the bottles and leaping in with our beers so we could sip them as we swam, maximizing the refreshment inside and out. The sun, less wrathful by now, hung softly in the fading summer sky as we relaxed on our last night in Mexico.

3

Attack of the Flesh-Eating Minnows

➤ THE BELIZEAN BORDER WAS HOT. We stripped off most of our gear while crossing from the Mexico side, and we now waited in the Belizean immigration lines to get our papers stamped. Before we could even bring the bikes into the country we had to shell out fifteen dollars for two weeks' vehicle insurance. But in just a brief moment we were stamped, authorized, and on our way. None of us realized or appreciated how easy those first border crossings were, in comparison to those waiting farther down the line.

That morning we'd satisfied Robert's schedule—we were washed, fed, packed, and ready to go by 8:30 A.M. We were getting better at this, but it wasn't always easy, especially when it meant leaving a place like the gorgeous Laguna de Bacalar behind.

The main road through Belize, like many in Mexico, had *topes*, or giant speed bumps, in every city. As we slowed down and bounced our way through the towns, we got a chance to look around. A parade, really just a lot of drum beating and schoolchildren marching, had taken over one village and blocked the main road. An observer on the street told me it was known as a "jamboree," and its purpose was to "celebrate the many cultures in Belize, and the pride we take in them."

There was indeed a lot of cultural diversity in Belize. Aside from the obviously African, European, and Hispanic influences, there were also many Asian-run businesses—the vestiges of the immigration boom when Belize had work. There was also a large Mennonite population. They'd been the victims of recent kidnappings because of the tremendous wealth they could access. A few years before, a Mennonite had been taken hostage, and the family approached the community for help. Each of the other families gave a thousand dollars. In two days they had enough to cover the exorbitant ransom, and the hostage was released. Later on, another kidnapping was botched and the captive escaped. Now the Mennonite policy is no more negotiations with terrorists. "Pray, don't pay."

That morning I felt overwhelmingly happy to be in Belize. There was something in the air—I felt an intoxicating sensation from my surroundings, a mix of the intrigue from the country's pirate history, awe at its tropical beauty, and joy from the cheerfulness of the people. There was also a dash of innocence thrown into the equation somewhere. Despite learning of the Mennonites taken for ransom, I had the sense that many of the bad things that happen in other places happened here much less frequently, if ever. Even the name sounded wonderful when spoken aloud—like something a gorgeous, exotic actress might call herself—just the one name, not Ms. or Miss Belize—just Belize. The only thing I disliked was the roads; they were about as straight and fun as a vaccination needle. Plus, stray animals were a hazard. I almost hit a small pig, a dog, and two wandering horses. Robert nailed a fat iguana earlier that day, cleanly decapitating the critter, spitting out its severed body behind his rear tire in a flopping, bloody arc. Robert: 1, Indigenous Wildlife: 0.

We stopped for a mango break just before San Ignacio. Robert was becoming a fanatic of the underripe mango, and Peter practically lived off them. In town we found a room for the night at Caesar's Place Guest

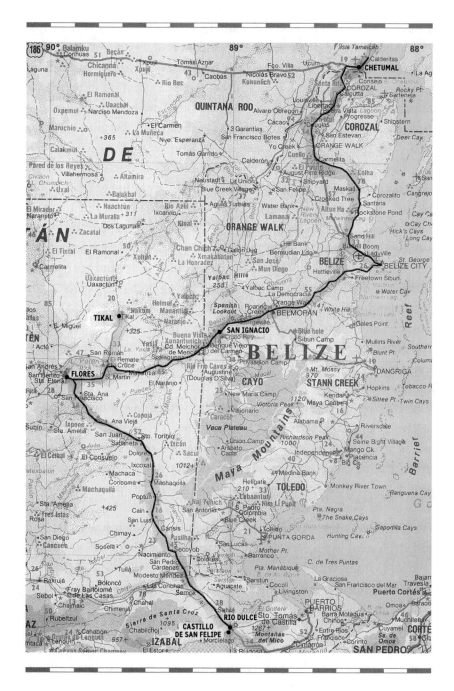

House, a hostel run by a world-roaming South African man. The triple was about thirty dollars, and we Roe Sham Bo'd for the best bed. The Roe Sham Bo game, also known as Paper, Rock, Scissors, was the simplest way for us to settle who got the best of a situation in which we all contributed equal amounts. The only problem was Robert. He continually confused Peter's and my strategies to win, because he never really got the feel for Roe Sham Bo. Or so it seemed. At first he had beginner's luck, winning with a string of rock victories. But we gathered he always just threw out a fist because he couldn't get the timing of the "one, two, three, shoot" part. After that, Peter and I always eliminated Robert first. We'd simply both choose paper, and when Robert threw that big ol' fist out, he'd be eliminated and we'd settle the victory between us. This worked fine until one day the burly Canadian came out with scissors, thereby defeating both our papers in the first round. What happened? Beating Robert had been child's play. Stunned and confused, we floundered in a paper, rock, scissors delirium, unable to put together coherent attacks. We soon recovered, however, but by that time Robert had gotten the hang of the game and it became a fairly even contest.

After we determined who would sleep where, we found the creek in the back of Caesar's hostel. "Hey Devil Boy," Peter called out. "Come on in, it's great." Peter was up to his chest in the water, and Robert stood dripping wet on a concrete platform nearby. A warning alarm was going off in my head—something in Peter's tone was odd. "Don't be a candy ass," he said. "Just jump in."

Why were they both watching me? I put down my towel and slowly untied my sneakers, buying time to analyze the situation. "What's wrong with the water?" I said to Robert.

"Nothing." He wore a big smile, and water drops casually fell from his woolly beard.

"It's freezing, right?"

"Not at all," Robert said, still smiling foolishly. He's not a subtle man, so I knew something was wrong. But then again, I'd never known

Robert to lie. His beefy arms hung limply at his sides. He just stood there, watching and anticipating my next move. Creepy. He looked like a big flesh golem, waiting to perform whatever evil function he was created for. I decided that if Peter was in there it must be OK, so I jumped in. The water was refreshing, not overly warm or cold, and there was nice current. I resurfaced and Peter and Robert were still watching me.

"What the hell are you freaks staring at?" Then I sensed it. I felt as though I was being touched with a fine paintbrush at first, then there was a sharp prick on my skin, followed by several more. I looked down as I felt five or six such pinches—and some of them really stung. There were dozens of tiny minnows swimming around my legs and torso biting me! I was startled at first, but then I realized that they were just nibbling and not actually capable of tearing anything off, so I relaxed. "What are these things?" I said, shooing them away with my hands. Peter and Robert were laughing at their prank enough to convince me that they were, in fact, ten-year-olds in disguise.

A decrepit old rope dangled above the deep water. The rope was about twenty feet long and reached as far as the dangerously shallow areas on the other side of the creek. Robert walked around to the edge of the concrete and pulled the rope toward him with a stick. Grabbing on with both hands, he swung out and back, crashing into the water with a healthy splash. The trick was to swing wide out, wait for the rope to make a pendulum motion carrying you away from the shallow water and sharp rocks, and then let go over the deep part. Letting go too early meant tasting the pointy stones in the shallows—too late meant slamming back into the concrete platform where you started.

"Ow! The little bastards are biting my nipples!" Peter shouted, splashing vigorously. He moved out of the deeper water to avoid the licentious minnows. I climbed out to sample the rope swing and Peter followed right behind, rubbing his pectorals. As I reached out for the rope with my hands, Peter said, "Wait, Andrés, let me get the stick of happiness. Santa Claus—where did you leave the stick of happiness?"

Everything Peter spoke of was embellished to fit his worldview. A stick wasn't an ordinary stick, it was a stick of happiness. His multifunction watch with built-in altimeter and thermometer was the super watch. Robert's global positioning satellite receiver wasn't just a GPS; according to Peter it was the sacred GPS. I was Devil Boy, Devil-o, and Danger Boy. And Peter called Robert Santa Claus, unless he was trying to maintain a veneer of respect, as when asking for directions or the history of particular ancient peoples. Otherwise it was: "Hey, Santa, grab me a beer, will you?"

We played a while longer in the water, careful not to crash into anything hard. I took one final swing, and the abused rope gave in to entropy and snapped, sending me crashing on my back into the water. Fortunately I was near the midpoint of the pool so that my head wasn't split upon the sharp rocks or the deadly concrete. If I'd hit anything solid, the blow could've easily ended my trip. I envisioned the headlines: "Adventurer Dies in Belizean Rope Swing Fiasco While Braving Flesh-Eating Minnows."

San Ignacio was incredibly hilly, built in a style reminiscent of a colonial shantytown. Beautiful old houses in various states of disrepair stood next to shacks with corrugated tin roofs. We rode, unburdened by our luggage, across a rickety bridge to the main street and found Eva's Café, which advertised Internet access and seemed quiet and clean.

The greatest thing about the Internet on a trip like ours was that no matter where we went, whatever town we stopped in, as long as there was a computer with Web service, I had mail from home. I hadn't felt homesick even once. How can you feel far away from people you care about when you can communicate with them daily and receive correspondence in seconds? Soon there'd be no more remote areas—the Internet was changing the whole face of travel. But after waiting my turn for the computer, I discovered that the machine refused to connect to the server. I was annoyed, to say the least. I wanted my instant gratification, and I wanted it now! How dare this crappy little joint boast of Internet to sucker me in here and get my beer money, only to pull the Web out from under me?

A complaint to the barman seemed in order. He was behind the counter, about 5'8" and balding, with tattoos on both arms. I walked right up to where he stood stacking bottles on a shelf. He had, I noticed, a Smith & Wesson automatic tucked into the back of his shorts. This was definitely no longer Mexico; the only guns I saw there were held by professional soldiers. But this guy had a very real, and very deadly, gun. "Need something?" the bartender said impatiently over his shoulder.

"Just another beer, please."

In the cool of the evening Robert and I read and wrote letters home in the hostel dining area. He lettered in a smooth hand, even, neat, and methodical. He wrote like he rode motorcycles. "So why do you write a journal, Robert?" I asked. He looked up at me from his notebook and paused to consider the question. Robert never responded immediately; he always seemed to weigh his words carefully—a quality I admired in him.

"It's a neat way to look back on the trip." He put down his pen and adjusted his hat, a leather Harley-Davidson cap with a chain across the narrow visor. "Plus Sandy really enjoys reading them." Satisfied, he picked up his pen and continued writing.

We made our way into Guatemala the next day, past dozens and dozens of trucks, old diesel flatbeds, loaded heavy with green sugar-cane on top, driving in the same direction like enormous leaf-cutter ants in a column. As we left the undulating terrain of San Ignacio behind, we crossed roads covered in white dust that spewed clouds from our tires like powdered sugar. At the border we were practically assaulted by the money changers, who hoped to pay for their kids' orthodontics or their next drink with our ignorance of the exchange rates. I found it disconcerting to trade in my trusty dollars at a foreign border to end up with a stack of high-denomination, pastel-colored paper depicting generals or crumbling ruins, never quite knowing if the filthy wad of bills we clutched was indeed legal tender.

By far, the most affable border officials we met were at this Guatemala crossing. I was especially impressed considering that they hand-typed all of our paperwork, a mound of it between the three of us, on a machine that predated the Maya, all the while joking and chatting. After changing our money and finishing the paperwork, we turned our sights toward Tikal, our first stop.

Tikal is an impressive collection of ruins set deep in a national forest, and its pristine location is rigorously protected by the government. Admission is charged just to enter the national park, and another admission is charged to tour the site. Development is regulated—all the hostels nearby are powered by portable generators that shut down at 10 P.M. Animals rule the temples, and even the archaeological workers repairing the decaying structures must use silent, hand-powered machinery to avoid disturbing the resident wildlife. Peter and I had no idea what to expect, but Robert knew what we were getting into; the ruins at Tikal made other places we had seen, such as Uxmal, look like glorified children's sand castles.

A few tour buses chugged up the road, and widened eyes and astonished expressions greeted us in the windows as we motored past them. I'll admit, I loved the envious looks and the near celebrity treatment we occasionally got from people when they saw how we traveled. I think we all enjoyed it. Things might've looked different had I been alone and felt all those eyes on me—you probably could've bottled the paranoia as it oozed from my pores.

Earlier that day we got a chance to stare at other people on bikes for a change. While enjoying the morning sunlight on a gently curved road, a pair of big dual-sports with bright headlights flashed past. You can hardly mistake world travelers. They usually rode big, fully loaded bikes like ours, and often wore expensive riding gear. Even if their motorcycles were far off in the distance, world riders stood out because their main headlights ran during the day. The United States, Canada, and most countries in Europe have laws requiring riders to keep the headlights on at all times when a motorcycle is in operation, as a safety precaution, and bikes sold in those countries leave the factory with daytime-running headlights. Most experienced riders whose headlights do have an off switch still prefer to ride with the lights on. It's just common sense. The headlight increases the odds of drivers seeing you, thereby minimizing the odds of becoming a grille stain. Daytime headlights aren't mandatory in Latin America, and many Latinos intentionally ride without them—surprising as it may sound—even at night. The belief is that constantly running lights ruin a battery by overuse, so it was common (and frightening) to see cars and trucks driving at night with no lights. Just one more good reason to follow the world-rider mantra: Never Ride After Dark.

I pulled over, and the passing bikers slowed down and came back around. Robert and Peter turned around and came back as well. As I suspected, they were indeed riding the earth, and wearing a lot of it as well. Their big Africa Twins were battered and covered with dirt, and grime caked their sheepskin seat covers and riding gear. Both bikers and their machines looked like they'd stepped off the set of a Mad Max flick, right after the scene where Max makes the motorcyclists chasing him crash violently. They were an Austrian couple in their late twenties, and they'd shipped their bikes to Buenos Aires from Europe. They'd ridden south to Ushuaia and now were on their way north to Canada, where they planned to pack up and send their bikes back home.

In broken English they related their troubles. The man's rear suspension had failed and he'd ridden for the last eleven miles with a stick wedged in it. But he was lucky—the woman had crashed, partly flipped the bike, smashed the windshield and front end, and landed painfully on her face. Her helmet was damaged and she'd injured her nose in the process. She was a small woman on a bike bigger than mine, and I was impressed she could even climb on that thing, let

alone control it. They gave a poor account of the Argentine roads we planned on taking. "A nightmare," she said, "the worst roads I've seen. We had to change all our wheel bearings." We wished them well and parted.

In addition to interesting characters and danger, one thing that's easy to find on the road is time to think. These days I'd been alternately lamenting the speed of our travel and considering my place in this group. I didn't let on to the others, but I was starting to wonder if I belonged with these guys. Nobody was forcing us to stay together. Peter later confessed to me that "if you and Robert turned out to be dorks, I was going to bail and go it alone." My problem wasn't quite like that, I liked Robert and Peter, for the most part, but I was seriously starting to wonder what purpose I served in the group. Peter spoke far better Spanish than I did. Robert had more mechanical aptitude than an entire pit crew. They both had more experience and could outride me. My first ten days of fumbling had shown what a pain I could be, but I hadn't done anything to show what, if anything, I brought to the party.

The Tikal ruins had a couple of hotels nearby, and we pulled up to the first one we saw, the Hotel Jaguar Inn. Peter and I talked prices with the kid behind the bar while Robert looked on. The barman looked like a young, bronzed version of Moe from the *Three Stooges*. Peter's charm wasn't working on Moe and his frustration began to show. This place was just as expensive as the Club Med in Mexico, but with none of the perks. Suddenly I got an idea and walked out to my bike. I pulled out all those letters of introduction and articles that had made Robert uncomfortable back in McAllen and returned to the hotel. Things were going to change today. I'd finally figured out a way to carry my weight.

By now our swarthy stooge had Peter vexed—Moe refused to give on the price. The kid was a hard nut. "Excuse me," I said, putting my papers on the counter. I tried to sound as self-important and authoritative as possible. "Can you please bring your manager here?" Bureaucracy is a time-honored tradition in Latin America, and impressive-sounding titles and official-looking documents can carry a lot of weight. The kid took one glance at my notarized letters, turned, and walked out, happy for a reprieve from Peter's dogged negotiating.

"What are you doing, Devil Boy?" Peter seemed annoyed by my interruption. A different young man came out, arms folded across his chest, obviously practiced at dealing with whining gringos. I don't remember my exact words, but I managed to convince him to give us a discount on the room. I told him we'd come from the United States by motorcycle, and that we planned to ride all over Latin America for the next year. I said that we had a lot of expenses over the course of the year, and if he could help us out with the price, I'd include his hotel in a book I planned to write about the trip. I held out my documents and the young man reluctantly looked them over. "Any discount you can offer is appreciated," I said. He wore a red T-shirt with the hotel's name and logo on it. The feline pawprints of the iron-on logo were cracked and peeling and he absentmindedly picked at the pieces while mulling it over.

"Well," he said, "all I can offer you is this." He wrote a number on a sheet of paper and handed it to me. It was about 30 percent off the original price. I showed it to Peter, who nodded in approval. I was ecstatic but maintained my calm, as if I did this sort of thing every day. Why hadn't I thought of this before? I thanked him and we shook hands. His hand was damp and he transferred little black jaguar toes to the heel of my palm. The manager then instructed Moe to show us to our room and disappeared.

In exchange for the discount I promised to mention the hotel, which I would've done anyway. I made similar deals with dozens and dozens of places throughout the trip. Acquiring those discounts was one of the only ways we had to shave costs from housing, our greatest expense, and on a personal level, it felt great that I could contribute something tangible to the cause.

The hotel itself was less than stellar. There were holes in the mosquito screens big enough to pass birds, the toilet wouldn't work, we had no towels, and the shower was frigid. To be fair, it's not easy to run a hotel in the middle of the jungle, where everything is powered by generators and maintained with trucked-in supplies. We may have been staying in a rat nest, but at least we paid 30 percent less than everyone else. As the midday temperature steadily rose, we changed into shorts, slapped on sunscreen, armed our hip packs with notebooks and cameras, and got ready to explore the ruins. "Good work, Devil Boy," Peter smiled. "Maybe we'll keep you around."

The ruins were in very good shape, with samples of the original plaster and wooden crossbeams still in place. Unfortunately vandals had been everywhere—names were scratched into the white stucco in blue and black ink, some of them filled in with moss, making the letters green. The temples were ensconced in the thick Guatemalan jungle and the ancient rocks, sculpted by human hands and eroded with time, thrust skyward from the earth, poking above the foliage. Tall, drooping trees and tropical vines dangled to the ground, and monkeys and birds made the perfect jungle racket in the background. On one temple we rose above the canopy and the blue horizon lay miles away in all directions. When viewed from above the trees, the caps of the temples—white pyramids floating in the green—were the only indications that humans had been here.

The animals paid little mind to the tourists. We saw coatimundis, howler monkeys, and several species of ants and birds, all going about their noisy business. A giant wasp, over two inches long with brilliant, iridescent blue wings, attacked a small tarantula. She carefully circled the spider, stinging it several times, and then flew off while the poison took effect. She came back after a while and fussed over her prize until I got bored and walked away. The wasp presumably intended to inter the spider in her hole, in this state of living immobility, to provide her larvae with a warm meal when they hatched.

"Look, Devil-o!" Peter shaded his eyes with his hand. "Little hotties, ten o'clock." A pack of Australian teenagers lay beneath a tree, languidly stretching tan legs on the grass and flopping their arms behind them. I couldn't really make them out clearly in the distance.

"I don't know . . . they look a little young," I said.

"Don't worry, Danger Boy, they are old enough," Peter said assuredly. His eyes got a wistful, faraway look. "Old enough to be food for the dragon." Looking at the expression on Peter's face, I was struck by an image of Nabokov, the lecherous old writer, laughing maniacally and zipping along on a motorcycle after young Australian girls. I pushed the thought from my head.

The final event on our tour was the climbing of the steps of temple five. Well, it was not actually the climb that was noteworthy, but rather who was at the top of the steps when I got there. It was a woman, and she was *it*. She was charming, outgoing, vivacious, beautiful, intelligent, funny, interesting, and very friendly. I gathered all this in about the first two seconds of looking at her. Her name was

Elena, and she was a mix of Spanish and Irish, with dark hair, a light olive complexion, and freckles. She wore a little orange tie-dyed sundress, hiking boots, a small backpack, and mosquito bites all up and down her legs.

I was smitten, struck, numbed, and titillated all at once. What is it about some women that can hit a man right in the retard button, sending him from zero-to-moron in a matter of seconds? She didn't seem to notice my temporary idiocy, or at least she didn't mind it too much, because she was perfectly charming as we chatted briefly. I gave her a business card (only 499 left to get rid of) and wished her well. Fortunately for me, that wasn't the last I saw of her.

As the cool, late afternoon breeze blew through the ruins, I decided to head back to the room for a shower. Again I saw Elena, this time at the Jaguar Inn bar, and she invited me to have a beer with her and an older gentleman. He was actually her father, an Irishman in his late sixties with a wealth of stories from his adventurous life. He'd met Elena's mother while riding a 500cc Triumph motorcycle around Europe. While in Spain he was smitten by the beautiful woman from Valencia and together they raised five children. Elena's dad gave me practical advice on organizing and participating in mountaineering trips, which he still did. "It's fun to get a diverse group together," he said, "as long as no one arrives home with an ice ax buried in his back."

Elena worked with an international peacekeeping organization in Guatemala, in a city not far from Antigua, and planned on working there for at least another year. She was twenty-six, educated, and had one of the quickest and most sincere smiles I've ever seen. After an eternity of group discussion, after we'd moved to the hotel next door when the Jaguar Inn bar closed, and after we polished off all of Peter's remaining Belizean rum, I was finally alone with this girl, this object of my complete attention and warped imagination.

I loved to hear her speak—in English she had the brogue of a Dubliner, and in Spanish, distinctly Valencian tones came to her voice.

We sat alone together in the back patio of the hotel, and since it was well after 10 P.M., the generators were shut down and all the lights had been turned off. There was just the thinnest sliver of moonlight and scattered stars to talk by. I closed my eyes and listened to every waver of her voice, knowing she couldn't see that my eyes were closed—God forbid she think she was putting me to sleep. She was having quite the opposite effect, in fact. Her voice was maddening. Our conversation covered everything from the metaphysical to the mundane and the whole time I was giddy. "My hair's dried out," she commented in an off-hand, drunken way. I snapped out of my Irish-lilt-induced trance, reached out and felt her hair, then pulled her close and kissed her mouth. Her lips were incredibly soft. We kissed again and embraced. Then, while still seated, I reached over and lifted her off her chair and placed her on my lap. She kissed me passionately again and again. We had a very unusual sort of familiarity and instant comfort around each other, one that generally only comes after spending a great deal of time with someone. Things felt wordlessly natural.

She asked me to stay (she and her father had taken separate rooms), and I responded by sliding my hand beneath her skirt and tearing off her panties, and then I gently placed her back into her chair and kissed my way along her legs. Her skin was salty from the day's explorations of the ruins. We quickly gathered our things and held hands back to her room in the darkness, fumbling and trying to close the blinds without falling over the two beds.

It was oppressively hot, and we had no water. We had sex once, and it took at least an hour and a half. My skin felt like smoked jerky, so I wet a towel in the bathroom and squeezed the water over my neck and back, then did the same for her. We both felt a bit sick from all the rum, so we intermittently slept and had sex again. Our bodies were almost choreographic in the precision with which they fit together— like moving puzzle pieces. We slept until the rays of the sun woke us up, then we had sex one last time. I must've lost twelve pounds of water over the course of the night.

I said good-bye in the morning, as she lay naked, facedown on the bed, just watching me leave. I looked at her, all the sweat pulled from her body and long since dried, watching me with half-shut eyes from the messy, dawn-ray-streaked bed. I never asked Elena what she was thinking at that moment. I'm sure it was probably "Good, now I can finally sleep," or "Man, I could use a glass of lemonade," or something along those lines, but I like to think that she had the same confident feeling I did, which required no words and assured me that we'd see each other again. In my mind there was no doubt I'd see her again.

I was so sure of this feeling that I didn't even bother to get her e-mail, phone number, or address. I know it sounds ridiculous, but at the time I just walked out of there without even considering how I might initiate the future communications that I felt so certain would come to pass. Luckily for me she'd exchanged e-mails with Peter earlier, and I had a way to contact her.

Outside my hotel Peter and Robert watched me approach as they prepped their bikes to ride. Great. A nice early start at seven-freak-ing-A.M.! Don't these bastards sleep? They waited for the Jaguar Inn restaurant to open while I packed up my clothes left wet from the incomplete laundering I'd started the day before. I packed like a zombie—like a hungover, dehydrated, sex-depleted one. If I'd been in my right mind, I'd have gone back and asked Elena if she minded if I came to visit her where she worked in Guatemala. I might've asked her if I could stay with her for a while. Perhaps I didn't want to seem to forward. (Isn't ripping off a girl's panties the first time you meet her forward enough?) Perhaps I couldn't think straight. Perhaps I'm just an idiot. Regardless, I didn't go back to talk to her.

That was an obscenely early time to be riding. I felt tired, hungover, and today, very lonely. There's a strange alienation that all motorcyclists must, at one time or another, feel. The sensation is partly due to the solitary nature of being on a motorcycle and partly because, as a mobile pastime, motorcycling requires you to be constantly leaving places where you've just arrived. It's even lonelier when you hop on that bike and leave an incredibly attractive woman (who also happens to be naked on a bed) behind. And when I tossed in the idea of the romantic repetition of history (Elena's dad met her mom on a trip not unlike mine, many years ago, married, had five kids, etc.), this situation was depressing the crap out of me. Even more depressing was the fact that Elena had a boyfriend back in Europe—how alone each of us really is, I thought. Elena had her thing, I had mine, and Elena's boyfriend had his. How pitiful everyone's states of aloneness seemed. Elena's parents broke up fifteen years ago. Even the most romantic stories can turn depressing with time. God, somebody stop me before I shoot myself.

An unfamiliar road is not the best place to dwell on such concerns. Reality is a near-death experience waiting to happen. The road to Rio Dulce, our next destination, was a combination of treacherous rocks covered with gray dust and scattered patches of pristine, jet-black asphalt not more than a month old. One moment we were dodging stones the size of footballs, the next we were gliding on racetrack-quality pavement. I decided to worry about living and focus on the ride at hand. We came upon a long line of vehicles waiting to pass a roadblock. A yellow bulldozer belched violently, plowing fallen rocks off the side of the road. The big stones clattered down the cliff side, smashing to the ground far below. We scooted up to the front of the line and were the first ones across the cleared road. The road worsened, becoming more rocky and dangerous. At one point it took an hour to travel thirty miles. Several hours later we made it to Rio Dulce, where I could finally drink enough water and get some rest.

4

Moto Monks and Border Bastards

➤ IN BELIZE, WE'D GOTTEN a recommendation to check out a place called Bruno's Marina and Restaurant, a guest house located just under the bridge in the town of Rio Dulce, Guatemala. Bruno's hostel was a hidden oasis of cleanliness in the desert of ugly that was Rio Dulce. The neighborhood was less than appealing, but the hostel had a beautiful swimming pool, nice foliage, and a great view of the water. I worked out a cheaper rate for our room with Bruno, in much the same manner as I had in Tikal. Our quarters were excellent: a large, two-bedroom pad with a kitchen, and a spacious living room featuring comfy couches. We did laundry for four dollars and then we ate and spent the rest of the night enjoying the pool.

The following morning we took one of Bruno's tour boats downriver to Livingston. Our captain was a skinny fellow who insisted we call him El Negro. He wore a faded black shirt that read, in English, "Never trust anyone over ~~thirty~~ forty." He seemed friendly enough, but we exchanged questioning glances when he topped off the gas tank with a lit cigarette in his hand.

On our way to Livingston, El Negro took us to the Castillo de San Felipe, a restored fort once used to defend the mainland from the coastal attacks of pirates with names like Pegleg Anthony Shirley, Diego the Mulatto, and the de la Costa Brothers. The castle had purportedly been the set for two Mexican-produced movies in recent times: a pirate adventure called *Isla Raratonga* and an adult adventure of a different sort called *Pecado*, or Sin. Another feature of the fort was the half-mile-long underground tunnel leading to the town. Probably used to access food and supplies when the fort was under siege, the tunnel was unfortunately closed off because of all the decomposing tourists that were being found inside; apparently they were getting lost in the catacombs and dying with some frequency. At least that's what our guide told us. And I'm sure El Negro wouldn't mislead innocent tourists.

Our tour group was six in total, three motorcyclists, two Canadian students in their early twenties, and our chain-smoking captain. Our vessel was an azure blue fiberglass job with a navy canvas parasol. We stopped for gas at a floating gas station—just a little pier on the riverside with a pump affixed to it, and the attendant took our jerricans and filled them. El Negro puffed away at his cigarette with the engine running while he fumbled with the gas, and to make matters extra interesting, our floating pump attendant did all his financial transactions with a pistol crammed into the front of his shorts.

We then visited a "nature preserve" to hike the acclaimed tourist trap ecotour. In theory it would be interesting to see what's inside of a rainforest in Guatemala, but this heavily trodden path, which briefly skirted a stretch of the river, wasn't worth the twenty-quetzal entrance fee, in my humble opinion. There was a "museum," a grass-roofed shack with no walls. In the museum were some photos of animals we didn't have a chance in hell of witnessing on this road most traveled, and a few photos of plants we could see only because the poor things couldn't uproot themselves and scurry away.

After this fiasco, we continued on to Livingston, a somewhat isolated city, inaccessible by land. The only way in is by water, yet it has

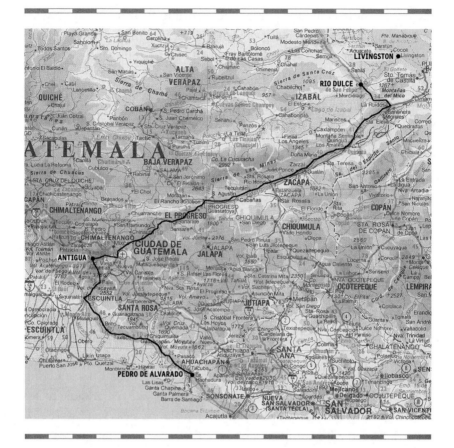

a surprising number of nice cars and motorcycles that have been ferried in. Livingston also lacks electricity on occasion, but despite this,
there were signs offering Internet access and e-mail. Amazing—a town
without roads or regular electricity has the World Wide Web.

The town was supposedly founded by blacks who had escaped
from Guatemalan slavery. I mostly saw white tourists. For a place with
no roads going in or out, there were a hell of a lot of tourists. Our
group decided to eat together at a local restaurant. I had the *tapado*, a
traditional seafood soup made with coconut broth. It tasted fantastic,
but I was dismayed to find that all the seafood in my soup had been
thrown in whole: shells, heads, scales, and all. There was a whole

perch, a whole crab, and three whole shrimp floating in my bowl. I burned my fingers dissecting the boiling hot creatures, probably much to the amusement of the cooks, whom I'd bet make it that way just for the tourists. As I was finishing, I found a perch eye floating in the broth, so I popped it in my mouth and ate it. The orb was very salty, and at first, watery. Further chewing revealed a surprisingly sinewy texture. Who knew eyeballs were stringy? I find it useful to have a catalogue of such experience for comparison or analogy in future conversation. For example, when at a dinner party and someone comments: "My, this onion dip is very salty," you can add: "You are so right. And did you notice that the little chunks in it taste exactly like perch eyeballs?"

We headed back to the boat after wandering around the town. On the way back, for a small fee, El Negro took us to what he called a manatee-infested mangrove swamp. Without a manatee in sight, we cruised around wondering when our lying captain would blow us up with his Marlboro. He dropped his cigarette twice, each time narrowly missing the open mouth of the gas can.

Back on the road, we cruised along to Guatemala City, dodging huge semis and tour buses all along the way. It was remarkable to see all the guns people carry openly in Guatemala. At a gas station we saw a truck loaded with corn, and on top of the corn were four guards with twelve-gauge shotguns. Finding this curious, I questioned the guy at the gas pump. He claimed the guards were there to discourage people from hopping on the truck for a free ride. Could the stowaway problem on corn trucks be that serious? I asked him why not use just one guy for that job, but he just smiled and shrugged. Peter laughed it off. "That guy doesn't want to tell you about all the land piracy that happens around here. I bet these trucks get hijacked all the time, and then the stuff they carry gets resold."

The guns were everywhere. After that gas station I started noticing lots of trucks with armed men atop them, and every bank in Antigua had security guards (usually two per exit) with shotguns, pistols, batons, and bulletproof vests. We were frisked from heel to head when entering a crowded nightclub. There was even a shady-looking tough walking around one of the ruins we visited with a .45 wedged in his pants. He was so skinny that his pants could barely support the weight of the gun around his hips. I don't know if I was more scared of being shot or flashed.

Robert was the master on the road. He passed trucks and speeding buses, on seemingly blind curves without enough time. I tried to repeat his actions when possible, but I sometimes found myself cheating and passing slower trucks on the inside, riding along the gravelly berm near the edge of the road. I stopped doing this when we blew through a falling rock zone and I noticed a boulder the size of a small car lying right where I might've passed. Hitting one of those can really be bad for the old complexion. Peter was riding like a granny, and with

good reason, because I almost got myself killed trying to mimic our bearded leader.

At lunch Robert spazzed out and stomped a massive spider when it tried to scurry up his leg. Robert 3, Wildlife 0. (He was up to three because a bird had smacked into his headlight the day before.) We couldn't even name the spider to wish it good-bye, because we'd been informed that "the only spiders that have names around here are tarantulas—all the rest are just 'spider'." Besides, it was unrecognizably squashed. By now Robert had killed so many animals that I suggested it was time to start commemorating them on the side of his bike, like a fighter pilot records the enemy planes he's downed. I had little animal stickers I'd brought as a gift for kids I met, to reward them if they watched my bike for me while I bought gum or something, so I gave Robert a bird, an iguana, and an ant (I had no spider stickers) to decorate the fairing of his BMW.

Speaking of Robert's BMW, it was soon going to acquire a name. Because of its avian appearance up front, Peter started calling it the Vulture. With its huge tank like a thorax and the long fender up front, I thought it looked a bit more like a giant mosquito. As you can probably imagine, Robert didn't take too kindly to the nickname. Peter began calling it the Condor instead, which seemed to satisfy Robert. The only bike without a name was mine.

It was 106°F and very dry. I felt sick and my sinuses burned as we rode. Even more sickening was the poverty in Guatemala. On the highway into Guatemala City were cardboard-walled shacks built onto the sides of the hills, with old hoods of cars or sheet metal for the roofs. Some hovels were still under construction. There'd been a recent mudslide on these hills; over two thousand people were killed. But the impoverished locals saw no other recourse but to build anew, presumably hoping and gambling that the tragedy wouldn't be repeated while they and their children lived there.

We were soon bumping along on the lovely cobblestone streets of Antigua. The afternoon sun was still warm, and Antigua was a beautiful wash of pastel-colored houses overshadowed by volcanoes. We stayed in the Hotel Convento Santa Catalina, an old converted abbey with an enclosed archway over the road. The arch was built in the late seventeenth century to allow the cloistered nuns access to the expanded quarters of the abbey across the street. They couldn't be seen in public, so they had to avoid the streets and any other public areas. The hotel had spacious, well-appointed rooms directly connected to the patio. The central area was well maintained and featured a fountain and a garden. Our room had couches, a skylight, and a huge bathroom with two sinks.

There was no parking on our street, so we rolled the bikes inside past the lobby and around the tables of the restaurant and stored them in a walled enclosure in the back. We again managed to get 30 percent off the cost of our room, and by now it was starting to feel expected.

The next day we sent mail, visited museums, and took in the city. Semi-ruined churches were everywhere. After the earthquakes that wrecked them had subsided, they were often left as they stood, in shambles, because in many cases there wasn't enough money to repair them. Sometimes the churches were in the midst of repairs when they were leveled again by another quake. Native street vendors sold hand-made clothes and crafts in the market. The women wore traditional multicolored fabrics and had babies slung over their backs. "Buy something, sir, good price," was the universal cry, and men with stacks of flutes in small baskets wandered around playing them. The same goods were all over the market, wooden bowls, stone ashtrays, knives, and miniature Mayan temples.

We split up, and when I later came back to the room, I caught Robert off guard in the bathroom. He'd bought some more dresses and was holding one up in front of himself in the mirror. He looked at me in the reflection, frozen for just a second, then he slowly lowered the dress and turned around.

"I'm just comparing the relative size to see how they'll fit Sandy," he said.

"Of course. No need to explain." I smiled. I made a mental note—never surprise Robert in the bathroom.

Peter showed up later and excitedly insisted we follow him to an amazing place he'd just toured. Called the Casa Santa Domingo, it was one of the many scenic places former President Clinton stayed during his whirlwind Latin American tour. The site was a monastery at one time, but it was covered over and buried by the monks who had lived there after an earthquake partially destroyed it many years ago. The holy men knowingly entombed treasures of art and metalwork, but the reasons why are not clear. The incredible artwork included gold and silver chalices, a three-foot silver sculpture of the archangel Michael (complete with flaming sword), murals, paintings, and a sculpture of the Christ child envisioning his own demise—which none of us had seen depicted in any form.

The Casa Santa Domingo was part museum, part church, part hotel, and all class. Out back lay a glittering pool with parrots nesting nearby. Plants and freshly cut flowers decorated every corner. The hallways were lined with hollow stone cubes filled with water and delicately floating rose petals. Mass was performed in the rear of the grounds, where a refurbished two-story mural portraying saints and other iconography rested behind the altar. Supposedly it's the new hip place to get married, and all the wealthiest Guatemalan families were trying to get their children hitched there.

While we were out, someone left a note on Peter's bike. An American motorcyclist had written it, stating he wanted to meet us. His note included the address where he stayed, but the other guys weren't interested in tracking him down. I was always game for finding more freaks like us, so I went in search of his hostel. His name was Jack, and he was about twenty-seven years old, with brown hair and rugged features. He rode a '97 KLR like mine, with aluminum panniers and just a few less miles. I invited him to come back to the hotel to meet the others.

Jack was on a tight budget, so tight that he wouldn't even allow himself the luxury of a beer, so I bought him one, which he gladly accepted. Robert celebrated the meeting by opening a fresh bottle of rum and mixing each of us a tall Cuba Libre, which was fast becoming the official trip drink. Peter brought out a bag of tamarinds, a small, sour fruit in a brown pea-shaped shell, and taught us how to crack them open and make our teeth sore from the sweet-acidic pulp.

Jack had ridden from Colorado, and for a while had even cruised with Birgit and Sam, the couple on BMWs we met at Edzna. Jack said he started the trip with a budget of fifteen dollars a day, but he'd now scaled it down to twelve. "Yeah, but the other day I finally caved in and decided to treat myself," Jack confessed. "I bought some sugar to sprinkle on my oatmeal in the mornings." Peter, Robert, and I looked at each other in shock. Was this guy for real? We were in the presence of a true moto-monk, a man who rationed twelve dollars per day in the most spartan of manners, while we probably blew twelve bucks a day just on rum. I, for one, was a little ashamed of how much I was spending, so I neglected to mention our alcohol budget. What discipline. We also found it amazing he managed to use so little gas. Jack's gas costs were low, he said, because he only rode about one hundred miles per day.

Like me, Jack planned to be in Ushuaia for the year 2000 party. I hoped to see him there, but in the end he never showed. I tried to contact him by e-mail but perhaps I noted his address incorrectly. I hate to think the worst, but I never heard from him again, and trips like these are dangerous. I don't know what happened or where he ended up, but I hope Jack the ascetic motorcyclist is well and somewhere enjoying a nice bowl of plain oatmeal with sugar. And if you see him, for God's sake buy the man a beer.

I stayed up late that night writing e-mails, and I even sent one to Elena. All day I kept having mental flashbacks to the smooth bare skin of her back, legs, and neck, as she lay on her stomach on that bed back in Tikal. I was overcome with a terrible desire to drive to her town to see her (it wasn't far from Antigua), but she wouldn't be back from her vacation with her father for another week.

The morning meant moving on, so we left town on an incredible paved, winding road, followed by a crappy dirt one overlooking steep precipices where people had thrown trash, junked cars, and offal down below. An hour and a half outside of Antigua we had a problem. Peter led us down a steep, one-lane dirt road when a Cherokee 4x4 flew around a corner, coming right at him. By the time Peter was in sight the driver couldn't stop, even though he was traveling uphill, and he swerved and skidded all over the road as he lost control of the Jeep. Peter was forced aside and lost traction in the loose dust and rocks on the road edge. He went down, injuring his calf underneath the Virgin Queen and crushing his right ring finger when the brake lever clamped on his hand.

Peter managed to get up, but the Jeep driver never stopped to see if he was all right. We were too far behind to see any of this, and when the Jeep passed Robert and me, the driver just smiled and waved calmly, giving no indication of what had transpired. The asshole left Peter fallen on the side of the road, essentially pulling a hit-and-run. By the time we reached our comrade and figured out what happened, the Jeep was long gone. Peter's finger was sore but unbroken. He pulled himself together and we continued down the road.

We made it to the Guatemala/El Salvador border, located just outside Pedro de Alvarado. We managed to survive the great staged border event, which was perfectly orchestrated for our benefit by all the characters at the customs, police, and immigrations offices. They figured us for what we were—(relatively) rich tourists—and quickly dedicated themselves to making our lives hell by wasting time, slowing internal processes, and delaying us so we'd have to ride after dark, which we were dead set against. They knew that if they could pull some sleight-of-hand and make our passports or vehicle titles disappear, we'd have been under their control.

One man, impersonating an official, followed us to our bikes, had us open our bags, and proceeded to enter our customs information on bogus forms, wasting about a half hour of our time. Back inside, the guy disappeared with our "necessary paperwork" and we had to do it all over again with the real official. After that we were separated, and while I sat alone with our jackets, helmets, and other gear waiting for Peter and Robert to return, another official came rushing in, all panicky, and told me my friends needed my help in a hurry. "Right now!" At first I was shocked, ready to rush to their aid, but when I stood and quickly started gathering the gear he said, "No, no, you must go right now!" Something in his voice gave him away. I calmly sat back down, eying him with my arms folded across my chest, and waited for my companions to return. He made a few more attempts to convince me, but by then he could see I knew his game. He wanted me to leave our gear unattended so he could steal it.

These were some of the many tricks used to frustrate tourists at borders. The idea was to anger the traveler such that forking over large sums of cash appears to be the best, and sometimes the only, way to get out of there. This crossing was also our first experience with *tramitadores*, or processors, the little parasitic paper-shufflers who live off the tourists and the system, but are supposedly there to make your life easier by doing all the legwork. All they ask is that at the end you reward them with a small tip—usually about five dollars per bike. But that's only if you know how the nefarious system works.

If you don't know the system, the tramitadores will suck you dry, as the Moonriders discovered just a year or two before us. The Moonriders were a group of a half-dozen men on KLR 650s who did a trip similar to ours, but their ride was organized for charity. They had the best of intentions, but according to their trip account they were taken at virtually every pass. They ended up forking out thirty dollars per bike in order to get through some of these borders.

We discussed the issue of paying for a tramitador and decided they were a necessary evil. "But there's no way in hell I'm handing over as much as the Moondorks." Peter said. Unfortunately, bikers like the Moonriders help set a bad precedent for others that come after them, because these frontier vampires now believe all motorcyclists could be made to squirt cash when squeezed. Considering that the average daily wage in El Salvador is about two dollars, we felt a three- to four-dollar tip was more than adequate for twenty minutes' worth of running paper.

Are the tramitadores overpaid? Sure. But the fact is that they do know the routine—a complex system of stamping, photocopying, and bustling around that none could hope to figure out alone in one day. The separate offices are unmarked and randomly scattered about the border complexes, and some of them look like simple huts that a street vendor might use. You can never tell where to go, and in case you guess correctly the officials might just misguide you to a different office or ignore you altogether, unless your tramitador leech is firmly attached. Frustration is all you're left with as everyone keeps closing their window when it's your turn in line. Until you get some pimply kid in a baseball cap to follow you around, you're probably going to be stuck there.

The worst part about the tramitadores is that you can't trust any of them. They look innocent enough, but if you take your eyes off them for a second, your valuable passport, vehicle title or registration, and other papers could disappear and later get sold to someone that wants to be a citizen of anywhere else. And then someday in the future when the authorities track you down for writing bad checks, robbing banks, or murdering a cop in a drug bust gone wrong, you'll realize that it was an illegal alien using your stolen passport. For that reason we always insisted on personally carrying our own IDs and bike registrations. My documents never left my sight, and I only surrendered them to someone who was going to stamp, verify, copy, or perform some other official business with them. If at all possible, tramitadores did not physically handle anything of mine.

Finally we finished the hellish border crossing, after three and a half hours, immeasurable aggravation, and a liter of sweat from each of us. We asked our teen tramitador how much he wanted for his "help," and he simply said "Thirty." Of course he meant dollars, and probably per bike, but we gave him thirty colónes total, or about three dollars and fifty cents. He was fuming, we could tell, but we just smiled "you said thirty, right?" The little bastard and his friends tried to fleece us, but we were done and there was nothing they could do about it. I'm sure that the other participants in the "opera of tourist theft" were disappointed to hear how small their share of the take would be. Come to think of it, they probably thought the kid was lying to them when he said how much we gave him. They should know better than to trust those sneaky tramitadores.

That border crossing experience was about as bad as they come. And even that one wasn't so bad. The key was just being calm and observant. No matter what your strategy, border crossings are always easier if done in a group. The next one I faced, between El Salvador and Honduras, would be my toughest since I'd have to do it alone.

5

Tramitadores in the Mist

➤ THE TOWN WE ENTERED on the El Salvadoran side of the border is called La Hachadura, or hard ax, which was appropriate enough given the tough, shady look about the place. An hour or so of sunlight remained, which we hoped was enough to find somewhere to stay, preferably far away from there. Border towns are generally unclean and unpleasant at best—at worst, they're completely unsafe. All manner of predators haunt towns like La Hachadura, surviving off the incautious traveler.

The coastal Route 2 highway was beautiful and fairly well paved. The roads were fun, incredibly twisty and hilly, and featured scenic views, interesting tunnels, and even a few switchbacks. For those who don't know, a good switchback is one of the things that keeps a motorcyclist riding motorcycles. Taking a few sequential switchbacks at speed is nothing short of a purely legal high. Imagine speeding into a curve, leaning deep as you turn to fight the gyroscopic pull that wants to set the bike upright, and then quickly hefting the bike over and slinging your weight to the opposite side of the saddle to take the alternate curve, and then doing it all over again. Switchbacks on a motorcycle are like horizontal roller coasters. Night was coming, and except for the time crunch we were having a great time. That is, until I negotiated a beautiful, slightly technical, decreasing-radius curve to find a huge-ass cow standing in the middle of my line. I panicked but managed to avoid it and all its other bovine friends. Then I suddenly noticed that the view of the ocean from the mountain roads was breathtaking. Maybe the view didn't deserve the praise; I was already out of breath from being scared shitless by all the beef wandering the road.

Evidence of the wars here was everywhere. Bombed-out bunkers still littered the hills and the traces of a few exploded bridges were visible. The sun was setting fast, so we pulled into a trashy-looking place but decided against it, pressing our luck a little farther down the road at another dive called the Cabana de Don Chepe. "What do you guys think?" I said as we stood beside our bikes, helmets in hand. Don Vincente, the chubby, slick-haired general manager, smiled and discussed our options. He offered two rooms, relatively secure parking, and his significant other, Vincenta, would prepare dinner for us in no time. The hotel also had a pool and a dog, both of questionable cleanliness. The rooms were so inexpensive we didn't even bother trying to deal. The only question was whether or not we actually wanted to stay there.

"It is getting kind of late," Robert shrugged.

"You know this is a No-Tell Motel, don't you?" Peter said.

"A what?" we asked.

"A No-Tell Motel. People come here and pay for rooms by the hour, after work or whenever they have time, when they don't want to risk being caught taking a lover somewhere in town." Peter looked at us pityingly, clucking his tongue at our naïveté. "Why do you think he's so surprised to have us here?" It's true, Vincente did seem confused when we showed up—and the rooms were a bit shabby for a place that appeared (from the outside at least) to cater to tourists.

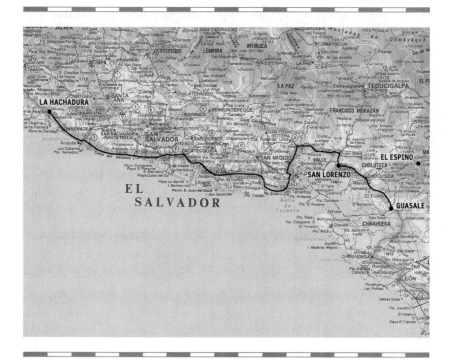

In the end we stayed, despite the unclean appearance. In fact, the rooms were real rat nests. Literally. So we Roe Sham Boed to see who'd get a rat nest all to himself. Peter and I swore out loud. Damn that stone!

Doña Vincenta made a wonderful meal of fried fish, potatoes, rice, and salad. Cold beer and sodas leveled off the food, and we adjourned to the rooms to relax. The evening was still hot, so Robert and Peter were going to take a swim. The pool's green tint was a turn-off, and I decided to stay in my room and catch up on some notes. I settled down to write and a loud chirping came from under my bed, or rather, from inside my bed. Apparently there was a grasshopper living in it, calling out for a lady friend, and when I smacked the mattress he'd stop his racket. There'd be a few moments of silence and then the chirping would begin again. I soon gave up doing anything productive and went outside to see what was going on.

Peter and Robert were swimming away in the nasty pool. Joining them were two men in their thirties, and two women in their late teens. The men introduced themselves, but I sat quietly in the background while Peter talked with them. They gave off a strange vibe, and perhaps Robert felt it too because he also kept his distance from the group. The elder of the two claimed to be a lawyer or a paralegal. He said that the younger man was a former airborne infantryman in the El Salvadoran army during the war in the eighties, but I didn't hear what he currently did for a living.

That ex-soldier definitely creeped me out. The men had introduced us to their companions, two attractive young women who couldn't have picked a more unsavory pair to associate with. Peter said that that type of woman is what Latinos call a *zorra*—not quite a prostitute, and definitely not the man's girlfriend, but something in between. Vincente just referred to them as women of *mala vida*.

I went back to the room and climbed into bed with my cricket, and we slept fitfully together. He pined loudly for his lover. I felt his pain. We'd blown through Guatemala and suddenly that very cool country, and the very cool woman that resided there, were both long gone. In the morning we'd enter Honduras, and the following day we'd be in Nicaragua. What can you possibly learn about a country in just one day? The map looked wide open, but this rigorous schedule was suffocating me. Every day was a race. I envisioned this trip more as a leisurely stroll through Latin America, not as a 72 MPH, ass-blistering burn down the highways.

The next morning Don Vincente told us that the ex-airborne guy freaked out in the middle of the night, argued with his buddy, argued with Vincente, and then peeled off down the road, leaving his three companions stranded. Vincente was kind enough to call a cab for them, and they repaid his kindness by stiffing him for the cost of the rooms.

The weather was still hot as we continued to move south, but it wasn't as torturous as it had been in Mexico. We cruised along nicely, and when we finally stopped for a drink I couldn't take it anymore. We just kept zipping along and all I could think about was how much further we were getting from where I wanted to be. Plus every pain-in-the-ass border I had to cross meant another pain going back. After much internal debate I made up my mind. Now was the time for me to split up with Robert and Peter. When we pulled over under a shade of trees near a gas station I let them know.

"Are you sure you want to do this?" Robert asked.

"No," I said, "I just don't want to go so fast through Central America. I'd also like to go back and see Elena, but I can't get in touch with her. I sent her an e-mail, but she's probably still vacationing. She mentioned a few more places she wanted to visit with her father."

"Are you sure that she wants to see you again?" he asked. Ouch. Although not encouraging, it was a good question. How silly would I feel if I rode back up to Guatemala and she slammed the door in my face? I wasn't really worried that was the case; after all, I mentioned I'd be in Argentina for a few months later on, and she suggested the possibility of coming down to visit me there. But on the other hand that might've just been afterglow chatter.

"Why don't you check your e-mail again?" Peter suggested. "Then you can decide what you want to do."

We found a local college that had e-mail and we convinced the nice people in the administration building to let us use it. Peter and Robert grabbed lunch in the cafeteria while I was busy. I found them finishing their meals in the dining hall.

"No message. I guess I should probably just ride on and see what happens." We mounted the bikes and pulled off down the road. About six miles later I was flipping out again. This was ridiculous. I was going to be a pain in everyone's ass until I settled this once and for all. I signaled them to pull over and gave them both a hug good-bye. It was pretty sappy and melodramatic—we were bikers, damn it!—we should've just slapped each other on the back and butted our helmets together. As simple as that, we parted ways and I began riding back the way we'd come.

I rode for about an hour. This was great! No worries, no commitments. Wherever I point the wheel is where I go. So this is what it feels like to ride alone. Perched high up on my seat, the wind blew steadily over my windscreen, splashing gently against my helmet. When I leaned my head slightly to the left, eddies of air whistled across my helmet just so, making a tiny sound like the crying of a kitten.

"Are there a lot of kittens roaming the streets of El Salvador?"

"There are strangers everywhere and they are staring at me."

"Was it unwise to change nine months of planning in a moment's notice?"

These are the sort of thoughts that can enter your head when you're in the middle of El Salvador, on a motorcycle by yourself, and you just narrowly miss dumping your bike behind the truck you were tailgating because you weren't concentrating on the road.

Obviously this wasn't for love, right? I didn't know her well enough to love her. Yes, she was fantastic in bed, but was that why I turned around? Doubtful. I couldn't tell, it might've been love in time—it was a glorious seed, but who knew what, if anything, would bloom from it? But there was more than just the girl, I reasoned; I needed more time to get to know Central America. Without a doubt, a country a day is too damn fast. But now I was alone. If I wrecked or had a problem, I'd have to solve it alone. How would I explain this to my family? They were already worried enough thinking I was in a group. I felt confused, foolish, and unsure.

Quiet reflection is the best reflection. I pulled into a restaurant and had a sandwich and a cold drink. Then I had another cold one. Within a half hour I'd decided. Why split up with the guys? I could come back to Central America later, on the way back from South America, and I'd take my time then. Elena and I would meet up later in Argentina. If not, then I would see her someplace else. It was a bad idea to mess with nine months of trip planning on a whim.

So I turned around—again—and headed back for the border of Honduras, following the trail of Robert and Peter, who were now over two hours ahead. I'd made up my mind—again—to stick with them for the duration, so I rushed to the border to find them before dark.

I needed cash, so I stopped at an ATM. All the machines I tried on this late Saturday afternoon weren't working for some reason, and the banks were all closed. I scored a cash advance at a supermarket customer service desk, but it was barely enough to get across the border.

The El Salvador border with Honduras was no less chaotic than the last one I saw. The only difference was that now I was by myself. Nobody shared the burden of watching the bikes, the tramitadores, and the eight-year-old street beggars that were always underfoot. I no longer had access to the sacred GPS or to Peter's Spanish fluency— which was extremely useful for disarming fast-talking border jerks.

Worse still, I was unknowingly being scammed. A tramitador named Paco had latched onto me. He was about fifteen years old and wore the hopeful beginnings of a mustache and a red baseball cap. He waved me down roughly a mile and half from the border, claiming that Peter and Robert had told him to wait for me, and that they'd asked him to help me get across the border if I should come along. He described them perfectly and even knew what countries they were from. Perhaps he just guessed what I wanted to hear. Maybe his time spent fleecing tourists had refined his ESP skills. Who knows, but I had no reason to doubt him. Except for the fact that you should never trust anyone you meet near a Central American border.

So Paco climbed onto the back of the bike and we rode to the border together. I realized he was up to something when I asked how much they'd paid for his services. "About thirty dollars each," he said. I laughed in his face. Robert, Peter, and I had repeatedly made fun of the tourist that pays out the nose at borders and I knew there was no way he was telling the truth. This kid was lucky if they'd given him five dollars for both bikes.

We argued over this at the border near the immigration building while a shoeless urchin pawed the KLR, offering to watch it for me. I told him to get off my bike and he just laughed and ran around while other kids took turns climbing on it. Then my tramitador friend began to squeeze. At the emigration window he tried to pay my fee in advance, on the premise that he'd cover all my costs at the offices up front, and then simply collect the total from me when the work was all over. I immediately jumped in and paid the fee myself, which was ten lempiras. I realized he'd tried to hand over twice the actual amount to the official, who was in cahoots, so that I'd have to reimburse Paco twice as much. Obviously they planned to split the profit between them. This kid was damn slick. First I looked at him in disbelief, and then I became angry. Very angry. I was frustrated, hot, and tired, but I struggled to maintain my calm. I needed my wits to get out of here, I decided, and this little man wasn't going to beat me today.

Ideally I'd have ditched that thief and gotten another, but I really had no choice. Once a tramitador has staked you, the rest disappear or ignore you (must be part of their code), and the officials weren't going to help me without one of them around. Besides, what good would it do? They were all the same. So there I was, sweating in my gear, afraid to lose sight of the bike lest some little street rat deflate my tires, cut my fuel line, or run off with all my important papers, and meanwhile I was being assisted by Paco the tramitador from hell. Actually, when I thought about it I was kind of impressed. He must've made a killing here.

Suddenly a man was approaching me, and people were quickly moving out of his way. He was as tall as me but more muscular, about ten years older, and he moved with a very intent gait and glare. He was swarthy, grease-covered, and wore a faded blue pinstriped mechanic's overalls and a filthy baseball cap pulled down over his beady eyes. He looked like a man out for blood. Great, I thought, this guy is going to knife me because he doesn't like my haircut, and all these border vultures are going to feast on my remains. I squared up against him, head down and eyes up, hands loosely at my sides. I was instinctively getting into a position of general readiness. In an instant, I'd resigned myself to the fight I was certain was about to occur.

"Where are you from?" The mechanic said in a gruff voice, in English.

"New York," I said, carefully keeping my distance.

"Don't drop anything from your pockets," he glanced around behind him, "because you'll never see it again." He took a step forward and leaned in close, as if to avoid any eavesdroppers that could've been following our conversation. "I'm from Nicaragua, but now I'm stuck in this bullshit border, and one of these little fuckers has run off with my papers." He took me off guard. Maybe his anger wasn't going to be directed at me after all.

"What are you going to do?" I asked.

"Find him, kick the shit out of him, and then get out of this hell," he said. What a charmer—I was starting to like him already.

"Where did you learn your English?"

"I lived in Mississippi for a few years," he said, "but I also speak French and German." In Spanish I told him that was impressive, and he replied in English "I know it's impressive, but don't talk in Spanish because the less these guys know about me the less they can rob me. If they think I'm just a poor, stupid mechanic, they won't charge me as much to get out of here."

His name was Marco, and we formed the kind of friendship that two strangers can form in a stressful situation. I watched his stuff while he did paperwork, and he helped me not get screwed by the exchange rates of the money changers. Half the time I was unsure about him, and thought he might've been in league with all those border bastards, just one more clever ruse to get my money. I also considered the possibility that he was befriending me in an effort to lower my defenses so he could rob me later. Who could tell?

Eventually I decided he was OK. He had a tough road ahead of him; he'd come all the way from the United States trailing two wrecked cars and a partially disassembled Gold Wing behind his little red Nissan pickup. I actually felt sorry for him. His paperwork was a nightmare—he only had replacement titles for his wrecked vehicles, which were probably stolen anyway. Those officials at the border knew they had him where they wanted him, and they weren't going to let go until he'd had the customary bloodletting. Every border official in every country had given him the same headache, and they all wanted their fair share.

I got through the El Salvador exit and into the Honduran entrance, and Marco arrived shortly after. He had waited at the El Salvador exit for two hours before I got there, and he was going to be at the entrance to Honduras for several more. The proper palms had to be greased. But since Marco didn't want to pay, he'd have to wait until the authorities got sick of looking at him and finally let him go. I eventually made it out, but I used up the rest of my cash in the process.

I said good-bye to Marco, got on my bike, and wished all those border creeps a nice eternity in hell. Fading yellow light turned orange and rose on the horizon. I had about a half hour of sun, and I kept hearing the number one rule of the international motorcycle traveler: Never Ride at Night. I also heard Marco's last words of advice: "Don't stop for anything. If you see a guy laying on the road, blocking your path, duck your head low, accelerate hard, and just run him over."

"Come on Marco, I'm not going to hurt anyone," I said, laughing at his suggestion.

"Do you want to be hurt?" He looked me in the eyes, deadly serious, and I could instantly tell that he'd seen a lot of unpleasant things in his life. "If you stop for someone, even if they look injured, they'll suddenly get better, get up, kill you, and take all your stuff just because you were a 'nice guy.' Promise me you will not stop."

I was hearing these words when I realized I might never see him again and I had no way to show my appreciation for his help. So I turned and went back to the border, riding up to where he was perched on the vehicle parts stacked in the back of his pickup.

"What's wrong?" Marco said.

"I forgot something." I opened up my top case and pulled out the rarely used folding camp chair I'd been carting around. The chair took up too much space and I needed to unload it—earlier on I'd decided to give it to someone cool I met along the way, but unfortunately I'd forgotten all about it as Marco and I passed time with the delightful border folk. "You can use it to sit on top of your junk," I suggested.

"Man, you drove back here to give me this? You're crazier than me." He seemed flustered by my gesture.

"You're a good guy and I wanted to give you something," I replied.

"I am not a good guy," he said, his eye never wavering. That stopped me short for a second. He spoke in a sincere, terse, and unapologetic way, as if he had done something (or things) terribly wrong in his life, and had resigned himself to what he'd become. His words carried weight—he obviously believed what he was saying and he didn't speak in a way that allowed for polite refutation. He wasn't a bullshitter and he had no intention of dissimulating just to graciously accept my gift. He was hardened beyond that kind of social posturing.

"Take it anyway," I said.

"You better get out of here or it's going to be night," Marco said. He kept the chair.

I spent the rest of the daylight following the trail of my two estranged companions. I stopped at a hotel where the owner had talked with them, but they'd decided to move on. I rode as far as I could, ending up in San Lorenzo. Night had fallen, and I was sure that at any second I'd see someone playing possum, lying across the road in ambush. Stopping at the next hotel, I found it was completely full. But I begged and managed to get a spare room used by the hired help.

The place was the Gran Hotel Miramar Inn Plaza. The manager was more than kind. She hooked me up with my room and dinner for a

great price, a lifesaver because I had used most of my money crossing the border.

There was probably not a worse country in which I could've chosen to suddenly become a cheapskate. Just a few months before, a small tropical storm in the Caribbean flared up into a hurricane and devastated many parts of Central America, particularly Honduras. Hurricane Mitch, as it was known, was the fourth largest hurricane ever recorded in the Atlantic and was extremely deadly, killing over seven thousand people and leaving an estimated one million homeless. Honduras lost 80 percent of its agriculture and 94 of its bridges in the disaster, and now relied heavily on tourism for income. And here I was renting the cheapest possible room and paying the least I could for food. I also planned to leave very early the next morning for Nicaragua. I wasn't going to eat breakfast because I needed all my cash in case I had a problem and couldn't get money out of an ATM. Honduras was obviously still suffering from the effects of the hurricane, despite the recovered tourism industry. Roads looked washed out, and the police directed traffic in a few places where major bridges were detoured. I promised myself I'd come back and make it up to Honduras another time.

Right now I wanted to find Robert and Peter. Assuming they hadn't tried to cross two borders in one day, I knew that there were only two likely roads they'd take into Nicaragua the following morning. Both of them diverged from Choluteca. I suspected they'd take the southern route, which ran closer to the coast. My plan was to rise very early, beat them to the border, and then just sit around and wait for them to show up.

The ambient temperature in my room was about 95°F, and I was sweating in boxer shorts with the fan full on. I kicked the dead cockroaches out of the tub and had a refreshing icy shower. There was no air conditioning, but there was cable, so I watched TV and sweated for while. I slept with the sounds of the whirring fan and of rats scraping on the tin roof above me.

By 5:15 A.M. I had showered, packed, and loaded the bike. I rode straight to the border at Guasaule, where I was almost certain they'd cross. There was a possibility I'd guessed wrong, and that they'd elect to cross at El Espino in the north, so when I got to Guasaule I spoke to the border administrator. He kindly phoned El Espino to have them keep an eye out for two bikers on BMWs. I arrived at 7 A.M. and it was going to be a long wait, surrounded by the same type of people that I'd learned to hate so much at the El Salvador border: tramitadores.

After the initial half hour of pestering by every tramitador in town, I managed to convince them all that I was not going to go anywhere until my friends showed up, so they should just relax and wait. They asked me all sorts of questions—about my bike, the United States, my trip. I got to know two of them pretty well: a skinny sixteen-year-old, the resplendently named Hensy Adalid Funiz Mendez, and a pudgy, unshaved guy of about twenty-four named Richard

Nixon Escalante. Richard's parents were admirers of the ex-president, who they felt had done a lot of good things for Honduras.

With these guys all gathered around with their respective guards down, I slowly learned how the border system works. There's usually a head tramitador, who oversees the operation of the underlings. He typically answers to the border administrator, who, in turn, decides which members of the local populace get to be tramitadores, which is a highly coveted position with lots of perks. Getting the job usually requires several recommendations from notable people in local government, or you need to be a close friend or relative of someone who works there. Depending on the border, all the officials, including the cops, are in on the deal, and it can be a real nightmare getting around the system. We'd been very lucky in our stubborn ignorance and had gotten off pretty lightly. Most people just can't take the hassle and fork over the cash.

The best weapon is patience. Find a tramitador that looks relatively trustworthy, negotiate a price for the processing beforehand, and then keep an eye on your papers and pay for everything yourself. Follow that general guide and be prepared to wait, no matter what happens. To be patient and calm, acting as if you have all day, is the one countertactic that drives them crazy. If they see you're not fazed by delays and that nothing they do frustrates you, they in turn become frustrated, and will soon tire of the sight of you. Eventually they'll decide they'd rather find someone easier to swindle, and that's when you will have won. But that can take a long time.

A tramitador's dream is the "miracle tourist," a rich old European or North American with no clue of the border system nor the Spanish language—a person that gets so flustered by all the grubby little beggars, vanishing paperwork, and endless delays that they'll pay anything to get out of there. As for the beggars, they are actually the children of the local vendors—their job is to wander around all day looking for handouts. Their parents dress them in rags and bare feet, and they desperately need a bath. This is all part of the ploy to make people pity them. Did I mention their acting skills? Oscar worthy.

After I'd been there for a while, a brown-haired boy of four came up to me, asking for some money. "What for?" I said.

"To eat," he said.

"Why don't you go ask your parents?"

"They're dead. I'm an orphan." He let out a few sobby little gasps.

"Really?" I laughed. "Are you sure that your parents haven't come back from the dead? Could that be them watching us from that fruit stand across the street?" He didn't even look—he knew exactly where I was pointing. The other kids around laughed because I was right. Discouraged, he wandered off and sure enough, he came back soon after eating a ripe, peeled mango as big as his head, the juice mixing with his filth, dripping down his little arms in dirty rivulets.

The other variety of street rat, also not orphaned though they'll swear otherwise, are "the watchers." They approach your vehicle and offer to watch it for some small change. Usually there are about twelve of them, climbing all over your stuff, and it can be quite depressing to see them fondling your precious ride with their grimy fingers. They flipped switches, sat three up on the seat, and one kid even turned my mirrors so that he could check out his teeth. They leverage the fear that if you don't pay up, they'll do something unpleasant to your bike when you aren't looking.

I learned from Hensy and Richard Nixon that if they actually did do something to a tourist's vehicle, the administrator would fire them, and if they were old enough, he'd quite possibly have them thrown in jail. A border administrator generally doesn't mind people trying to get handouts (beggars and watchers are usually selected by him as well), but if they actually did anything to a vehicle, he'd hear no end of complaints from the tourists that pass through, and eventually it would get back to his boss. Ultimately, the border officials don't want to discourage the tourism industry—just leech off it a little. The clearest proof is that I've since left my bike unattended at several borders, and never had so much as a pen stolen from my zippered tank panniers.

I sat on the curb waiting, and all the tramitadores, watchers, and beggars gathered round and waited with me. The little mango boy had claimed me as his new big brother, and sat down next to me with his head against my jacket. I envisioned his future career: homeless orphan first, later upgrading to street rat at about six to eight years of age (depending on how long he could stretch the cuteness quotient), finally culminating in the glorious graduation to full-fledged tramitador bloodsucker. If he was really good at his job and politically savvy he might become head tramitador someday. I realized I could nearly write a book just about my experiences in their world—in four short hours I'd been accepted by the community, welcomed as one of them. I couldn't help but feel a bit like Dr. Jane Goodall after her breakthrough with the chimpanzees, or that special sense of closeness that Dr. Diane Fossey had with her gorillas.

The characteristic grumbling of horizontally opposed motors approached. Abruptly, the calm that had settled on the tramitador community was over—Robert and Peter were coming. My crowd of calm paper shufflers and youthful vagrants changed into a swarming hoard of jabbering hyenas that surrounded the bikers, dollar signs flashing in their eyes. Careful not to run anyone over in the chaos, my former and future companions pulled up next to me and took off their helmets.

"I read on the Internet that you guys were looking for a riding partner," I said. "Does the offer still stand?"

"I knew you'd be back, Devil-o," Peter said happily. "Santa thought you were a goner, but I knew you'd be back."

"Hey, glad to hear it," I said. "By the way, can either of you loan me a few bucks? I'm a little strapped right now." From the looks on their faces I could see it was just as though I'd never left.

6

Riding the Whore of Babylon

➤ SO AFTER OUR BRIEF, bittersweet separation in El Salvador, my motorcycling buddies and I were on our way, reunited, ready to face the trials together in Nicaragua. Robert and Peter cried from joy to have me back. Actually, only Peter was crying. Well, he really just had some dust or something in his eye, and was rubbing it with the back of his hand. Clearly, the guys were just afraid to express their true emotions in front of all the locals. They had their game faces on; there were many border frustrations ahead of us and we turned our attention to overcoming them.

Contrary to our expectations, we breezed through the Honduran border in under forty minutes, even though it was officially lunch hour. We got out of there quickly, at least in part, because everyone now knew me and they weren't really messing with us. Only the policeman down the street, whom I hadn't met, was reluctant to let us past the frontier gate during lunch hour.

We got to the Nicaragua side to find Marco and his rolling junk heap in the parking lot. We had a brief yet warm reunion. I bought him a cold soda and he swore some more about all the jerks that were jerking him around. "All these fucking jerks are jerking me around!" he said. "This is my own fucking country, and it's full of fucking jerks!"

We left the border after 1 P.M. and rode hard all day through Nicaragua. About midway to our planned stop, Hotel Monte Limar, Peter and I followed Robert and we had a perfect view as a young bull suddenly came bucking out into the road in front of him, almost as if someone had smacked his backside to make him charge out at just the right moment. If someone did that to give us a scare, it worked. We cringed at the squealing sound as Robert's butt cheeks clamped down hard on his saddle and every rubber molecule in his tires strained against the road. "If my bike didn't have an antilock brake system, I'd have hit that cow for sure," Robert told me.

Shaken by the near miss, we pressed on. The evening encroached, and we pulled in for the night as the sun's light faded and the street lamps surrounding the Hotel Monte Limar sparked to life. Robert really outdid himself this time. He'd found us a five-star joint with all the meals and drinks you could force down for under fifty dollars a day, and it was, by far, the nicest place we stayed during the entire trip. Because the season was coming to a close we practically had the grounds to ourselves.

The hotel consisted of different clusters of small buildings with stone paths between them. The complex itself was located on the Pacific shore with a fantastic volcanic sand beach. In the middle of the site was the enormous turquoise pool, which featured a bar in its center. To the right of the pool was the giant lawn chess set where we eventually spent most of our time.

We passed three days playing chess, drinking, and swimming in the ocean or the pool. Ours was a difficult choice each day, and sometimes we had to compromise and swim in both the ocean and the pool.

Who was I kidding? For the next three days we ate ourselves into digestive stupors and had decent buzzes before two in the afternoon. There was no denying the truth—we were officially posers. I expected

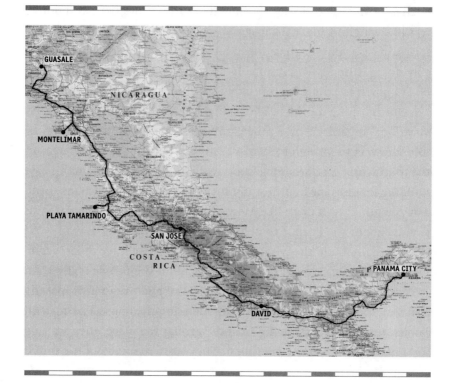

my trip to be one of hardship, adventure, and sacrifice, of traveling to places with little food or gas, not five-star international resorts with pools bigger than my entire high school. This wasn't adventure travel. Ed Culberson would've laughed himself silly at us. My moto hero, Emilio Scotto, probably wouldn't have been caught dead on the same highway we rode. How depressing. I'm supposed to be surviving exciting trials and difficulties on the journey of a lifetime, but my biggest problem was that the hotel's giant chess set was missing a rook. Of course, after liberal doses of complimentary alcohol, I noticed that these worthy concerns melted from my mind the way salt dissolves from the edge of a margarita glass.

Speaking of chess, Robert and Peter have many skills, but the game of kings is not one of them. Those two struggled over a six-piece exchange on that ridiculously huge board for more than an hour. It was like watching giant Galápagos tortoises having sex. Galápagos tortoises, in case you can't imagine, do it slowly—painfully slowly—look silly doing it, and will occasionally do it completely wrong (males have been known to hump appropriately sized rocks).

One morning on the beach I met a tall chubby guy on a "charity vacation," organized by a relief group he'd read about. The idea, he told me, was to take a group of vacationers to impoverished areas of the third world, perform some good work for about a week (in this case building low-income housing) and then the traveling Samaritans spend a day in luxury at a place like Monte Limar before going home. He was excited about the chance to help others while traveling abroad. "We don't actually build the whole house," he said, "we leave them incomplete on purpose. We put up three walls and if the people really want to live there they can put up the fourth wall and the roof. Hopefully that way they'll be more committed to making the house a permanent home, instead of just moving in and trashing the place, then waiting for a new free house to come along. They need to invest a little into it as well."

We left early on the morning of April 20. I realized I'd made the right choice by sticking with the plan. Intermittent powerful winds were blasting across the landscape. Each year the winds are the first indication of the seasonal rains to come. If I'd gone back to Guatemala, I'd most likely have been trapped there as the swollen rivers became nearly impassable, since most bridges in Central America were destroyed or under repair from the previous years' El Niño storms and hurricanes.

As we rode on that sunny, blustery day we passed the beautiful Lago Nicaragua, which featured large lake sharks and the twin peaks of the Concepcíon and Madera volcanoes. In Grenada we stopped for lunch, and I wanted to stay there for the night to check out the old city, but we had to make up lost time.

At the Costa Rican border we stamp, stamp, stamped our way through clusterfuck heaven. The strangest thing was that this border didn't require tramitadores to get the paperwork done. There were still a few brats in baseball caps running around, but they had no power here because the border officials permitted tourists to do their paperwork alone. I almost missed the little bastards. Happily we exited, ready to continue down the main road. Some burly men in army fatigues doused our motorcycles with insecticide and we were on our way.

Our first stop would be the Playa Tamarindo, a beautiful beach resort on the western coast. We puttered nicely along the road, which looked like a normal paved road in every way except that it was a rusty red instead of black. We were making good time when Peter hit a rock as big as a tissue box. He was passing a truck and the driver frantically waved in attempt to warn him about the obstacle in the road, but Peter thought he was just being friendly. So, in Peter's words, he waved back "with a big stupid grin on my face and nailed the brick. I just nailed it." The rock then shot out from under his back tire, right at me, but luckily it bounced out of the way. We stopped at a gas station to inspect the damage to his bike; the rim was badly bent, but it wasn't leaking air so we could continue. "She's the Virgin Queen no more," Peter sighed. "Now I'm riding the Whore of Babylon."

We continued as the streets darkened. Visibility for driving is said to be worst during the hazy moments of dusk, just before the sun fully sets. I'd agree, since I nearly hit a person in a wheelchair, who for some unknown reason was cruising right down the middle of the busy street. Cows and dogs I could handle, but that was a new one that frightened the hell out of me. Night soon fell, and for the first time on the trip I found myself leading the group. I was suspicious to be given this opportunity at night—perhaps they wanted me on point so I'd hit any upcoming road dangers first, thereby giving them fair warning? Although still dangerous, the risks of night driving were lessened in Costa Rica because banditry wasn't really a concern. The main dangers were obstacles: potholes, fallen logs, animals, and now, paraplegics. Honestly, I didn't mind being the sacrificial lamb; it was nice not to inhale other people's dust for a change.

Around this point on the trip I stopped trying to use maps. Robert had made copies of almost the entire route for both Peter and me (even highlighting the roads we were to take), but I'd left home just before mine arrived. I'd been making copies of Peter's or Robert's maps at various stages, but now it seemed pointless. I enjoyed cruising along, taking in the scenery, and letting those guys worry about getting us wherever we were supposed to be. A frivolous attitude some might say, but then again, most of those people would find motorcycling Latin America too frivolous for their tastes anyway. For my part, since it was all new to me, it didn't really matter where we went. I was just enjoying the ride. I was never in any danger: Robert had a GPS and maps, Peter had copies of Robert's maps, and if by some chance I got separated, I always found my way by asking directions. If things became very dire I did have some big maps I'd bought in the United States, which were excellent, and although they were impractical for daily use, they were perfect for tracing the overall route.

Bad roads are made worse with poor visibility, and after taking a beating along some poorly lit back roads we arrived at Playa Tamarindo about 8:30 P.M. Thomas, the manager of the Hotel Tamarindo, was incredibly friendly and generous. Peter and Robert were so happy with our discount that they offered me the extra room as a reward, forgoing the normal Roe Sham Bo settlement.

Back in my room I was having an allergic reaction to something. My left eye was swelling shut and a rash was spreading along my arms, especially in the crooks of my elbows. It had even spread to my stomach and hip. This troubled me because I've never been allergic to anything. In terms of health, up to this point in my life you might call me a lottery winner. I've never even gotten chicken pox or measles. I'm not unbreakable, but for a guy who was dropped onto a busy road out of the back of a moving bus when I was three, I guess you could say I've been lucky when it comes to general wellness. So this spreading rash thing was an unhappy development.

Dr. Hermes Quijada treated me in the morning for about thirty-eight dollars. He suspected I had scabies, a common name for rashes caused by a tiny mite that burrows under the skin of the host, where it feeds, reproduces, and lives out the course of its life. If left untreated, entire generations of the mites will prosper subdermally while the host futilely scratches himself skinless. Peter suspected I got it from one of the tramitadores or beggars I'd shaken hands with; and suddenly his strict policy of not touching street people was making a lot of sense. Those damned tramitador punks were still messing with me!

While enjoying a postlunch beer in the afternoon heat, it occurred to me that the microscopic things currently calling my cutaneous tissue home were going to indirectly receive the benefits of the very meal I just ate. I found that repulsive. I didn't approve of these nasty creatures coming along and trying to steal from me. If it weren't for the benefits of modern medicine there would've been little to do about it. To a Costa Rican making four dollars a day, having parasites raising kids and paying mortgages in their flesh may be less painful than covering Dr. Quijada's fees to get rid of them.

Once again we were moving, ever moving. The next day's beautiful mountain ride was to Quesada, and the day after we continued on toward the capital. I was in awe of the Costa Rican scenery. Flowers littered the roadside in magentas, turquoises, violets, and oranges, with startling richness and a depth of color that bordered the surreal. Bright blue butterflies wafted by as we zipped around endless switchbacks and roller-coaster hills. This was a motorcyclist's paradise.

We stopped in Zarcero, a town famous for its sculptures made of bushes. The town's center boasts a twin-tiered pink church, the Iglesia Patron de Alfaro Ruiz San Rafael, which is surrounded by a huge garden with fountains, flowers, and enormous shrubs in plasmatic shapes. Some of the bush sculptures were more clearly defined, and had shapes like a dancing pear or a monkey on a motorcycle, while others were just amorphous interconnected blobs.

I met the artist and founder of the garden, Evangelista Blanco Renes, outside his small workshop. As we spoke he busily worked on an unattractive painting. He couldn't even waste the time to look at me as we spoke. Thirty-five years of hard work and creativity had been invested in his topiary menagerie, and at the age of sixty, Evangelista had no plans to stop anytime soon. He was a curt man with a pockmarked face and dyed hair and mustache. He appeared to have little time for inquisitive foreigners, so I left him to his work. Some might say he was rude, but I gave him the benefit of the doubt. Maybe he was just trying to finish his repellent painting and make it to his hair-dyeing appointment on time.

We continued to Sarchi, a place famous for brightly painted ox-carts, so we popped into a factory by the side of the road to see how these regional treasures were made. The owner, Juan Carlos Alfaro, came out to meet us. His grandfather built the factory seventy-four years before and the entire operation still worked in the traditional way, completely free of electricity. All of the machinery in the barn like building was powered by the Senior Alfaro's clever mechanical creations, which transformed the energy of a local stream (via a waterwheel and a deceptively simple system of ropes, levers, and pulleys) into mechanical force for drill presses, sanders, table saws, and other tools. The factory itself was a wonder of creativity and human ingenuity.

The painted oxcarts were exquisite. Brightly colored and ornately detailed, they varied in sizes from a large wheelbarrow to a small truck. We followed Juan Carlos as he proudly displayed the inner workings of the shop and the traditional crafting techniques handed down unchanged from his grandfather's time. "The large cart wheels are made by placing sixteen triangular blocks of cocobolo negro, the most dense of the Costa Rican hardwoods, into the shape of a circle around an iron hub." He pointed to a large round wheel in the middle of the factory. The triangular wooden blocks that formed the circle were fitted together like pieces of a pie. "The outer rim of the wheel is then put in place while still red-hot, and then quickly quenched. As the metal cools, it shrinks into place around the wood, compressing it and forming an incredibly tight circle, which uses no adhesives, dowels, or fasteners." The secret to the strength of the wheel, he told us, was the exacting tolerances used, the quality of the materials, and the time-tested process. "These days the quality of the cart is judged almost solely on the aesthetics of the paintings and the overall beauty of the cart," Juan Carlos said. "In my grandfather's day, the cart was judged by the sound the wheels made when struck—the painting was just a decorative afterthought."

We bid Sarchi good-bye and wound up and down the wild hills to San José. Coming into the outskirts of the city, the heat of the sun forced thick clouds to pour off the nearby volcanoes like whipped cream off hot apple pie. We spent the night in the capital uneventfully, and the next day we were on our way to Panama. I could've easily used all my film trying to capture the indescribable beauty of Costa Rica. The lushness of the greenery reminded me (of all places) of Ireland. Every inch of available soil was just packed with growth. The nice paved roads that led through the city soon gave way to dirt and then to mud, as a light rain moistened our way up the mountain pass.

We climbed the Cerro de la Muerte (Mountain of Death) into a real rain forest, full of menacing fog and slippery clay mud switchbacks. We rounded a corner and encountered a landslide in progress, so we were forced to stop and wait it out. As we ate mangoes by the orange cones blocking the road, I listened to the sounds of the falling earth. Out of the fog, rocks the size of microwaves, human heads, and baseballs came tumbling down before us. Occasionally a boulder as big as an engine block would fall from the Mountain of Death, bouncing and crashing, and I couldn't help but wonder what a force like that would do to a bike and rider if caught unaware. The sound of the landslide was remarkable—a combination of crinkling paper, hard summer rain, and ice clattering into a glass, with the occasional staccato thudding of a large taut drum thrown in. The fog cleared enough to reveal two massive earth moving machines high above us on the hill. They were the source of the landslide as they repaired a road higher up the mountain.

As we made our way to the Panamanian frontier, it began to rain. The first official rain of the trip was heavy and monsoonlike, but I didn't mind. As we arrived at the border, a man nearby in a black pseudouniform with a "police" patch on it closed the Bible he was reading and approached us. He wore military boots and a crew cut, and asked us our origin and destination. We started to take him seriously, but closer inspection of the badges on his fatigues revealed embroidered words like "official" and "security." He also wore a T-shirt with an iron-on Slayer decal. Peter was the first to realize he was just some fruitcake and walked away, no longer willing to even acknowledge his presence. Robert followed Peter, so I politely excused myself and the man went back to his reading.

Aside from the freak, the border was remarkably civilized and boring. After signing all necessary forms and paying all fees, we were done in half an hour. We'd survived the worst that the Central American borders could offer. The rest of our border crossings would become simpler the further south we went.

Panama was almost instantly distinguishable from Costa Rica. The scenery seemed to change just by crossing the border. The land became flatter, dryer, less lush. The rain, on the other hand, was completely unaffected by the international boundary and continued to pound us all the way to David, where we pulled in for the night, wet and miserable. The Gran Naciónal Hotel had possibly the rudest people we'd met to date—the desk attendants offered no help in any way and scrutinized us as though we planned to leave without paying. One sure way to deal with rude people, I have discovered, is to drink them off your mind. And that's exactly what we decided to do.

Things rapidly went downhill from there. After sampling several bars, we were soon lit up like votives in the church of insobriety. I decided I needed to eat and left the guys downing their umpteenth Cuba Libre. I didn't realize how unsafe it was to wander the streets at that time of night, especially given my condition—I couldn't have defended myself from a Girl Scout with a bad cold. Fortunately this part of Panama was not currently a hotbed of a criminal activity, and my failure to recognize the stupidity of being a drunken gringo on a Panamanian street at 4 A.M. went unpunished.

Hunger was the only thing on my mind, so I found the only place still open and ordered some meat I thought was beef, and told the server to cook it quickly, because I was in a hurry. The dish turned out to be pork (undercooked, just as I ordered) with a side of slimy fries. For the love of God and all that is good on this green rock I cannot tell you why I ate it, but I did. By morning I'd thrown up three times. Worse still, it was now 8 A.M. and Robert and Peter were getting up. They'd drunk more than I, and inexplicably seemed fine and ready to roll. The last thing I wanted to do was get near that bike. The good news was that at least I didn't have a hangover—but the bad news was really bad—the reason I wasn't hungover was because I was still drunk.

All my efforts to delay leaving were wasted. "Looks like you can't hang with the big dogs," Peter said. "You just had to have your little adventure with the rat meat off the street."

"You know what the trouble is with this new generation?" Robert smiled at Peter. "They're weak."

Heartless bastards! Just because their livers were so hardened that alcohol no longer affected them was no reason to make the rest of us suffer. I'd just spent three hours barfing up the trichinosis surprise, but these guys didn't care what I went through. I'll show them, I decided. I could ride all day, regardless of whether or not I was drunk. What the hell was I thinking? Clearly I had to find some new friends because these guys were going to get me killed.

By the time we'd showered, packed, prepped the bikes, and eaten, I wasn't drunk anymore. But I nodded my head and wrestled my lids open the whole time we rode. I felt so nauseous and hungover that I couldn't even drink water to rehydrate. You know you're really sick when you can't even keep water down. I passed a car with two young women in it. As I slowly overtook them, the passenger leaned past the driver and took my picture. That's it, ladies, get my good side, the one with dried vomit on it. I could barely stay on the road. If I didn't stop myself soon, some hard roadside object was going to do it for me. One hundred and thirty-eight miles after we started I'd had enough. "You guys go on ahead," I said, while forcing down gulps of bottled water at a gas station. "I quit. I don't care what you do. I'm staying in the next town."

Robert hoped to make it to Panama City that day, but he was satisfied to spend the night in Santiago de Veraguas. In fact, they both seemed to find this change in schedule amusing, and they probably stuck around just to have more fun at my expense. We got two nice rooms at the Hotel Camino Real for sixty dollars. I managed to score a single room to myself with a well-timed paper, defeating both their rocks in one shot. Thank God for small favors.

By midafternoon I felt better. The big dogs, on the other hand, were looking ripe and ugly. They were both wrecked and needed to crash early—perhaps their ancient livers still showed a faint sparkle of enzymatic function? Maybe they did not piss 80 proof as they'd have the world believe.

Next morning we continued toward Panama City, noticing that in general the roads were orderly and well maintained. Just outside the city, the highway led onto a beautiful suspension bridge.

The roads and buildings outside Panama City looked so much like United States constructions that we almost forgot we were in Latin America. That was until we were pulled over by a cop for passing on a double yellow line. He waved us over to the side of the road as we neared his position on the top of the hill. He was short, thin, hard featured, and serious looking. He wore a beige uniform, neatly pressed.

The officer asked for our licenses and examined them. "I'll need to keep these in lieu of your appearance at trial." Funny how the concept of due process had not made it down here along with all the United States-style lamp posts and shopping malls. He didn't mention that we could just plead guilty and pay the fine in town. Instead, he made it seem as though we'd have to stay in Panama for a month, which he obviously knew we'd find unacceptable. He was making it very clear that we suddenly had a problem, and he waited patiently while we came up with a reasonable solution. We actually found thirty reasonable solutions, ten of them from each of us. Our seasoned swindler then oh-so-subtly accepted our payments with a handshake and a smile for each of us, so no passing motorists would witness the transaction. After forking over the cash, we put back on our helmets and rode into the city.

That was my first experience with a cop bribe. I should've let that slimy pig keep my license; it was just my backup anyway. I carried the old one with me and handed out to anyone that asked for ID, just in case something like that happened. I was concerned I might need the back up later if I lost my real one, but it would've been so gratifying to just smile calmly and say "OK, you hang onto my license. I'll stay here and wait for my trial. I don't really have anywhere else to be right now anyway." Then of course I would've just left town and let him keep it as a souvenir. I soon learned that a cop bribe is like getting a shot. The first couple sting a little, but after you've gotten a few you hardly notice them anymore.

7

The Quest for the Kawasaki Dealer

➤ NOW IT WAS TIME TO FIND Juan Villarreal, our motorcycle contact in Panama City. We'd talked with him on the Internet, and he'd offered to put us up while we were in town. Juan was a captain in the United States Air Force. I had first heard of him back in the States while researching this trip. I often checked out a Web site called the KLR Dual-Sport News, a place for fans of the big Kawasaki thumper. His was one of the names that popped up now and again on the KLR News List to debate issues like what tires to ride on, what brand and quantity of oil to put in the crankcase, and which aftermarket bash plate was the best for the KLR 650. Peter heard about this list later on when we were all at Juan's apartment. He burst out in his infectious high-pitched laugh and expectorated one of his classic satirical comments. The Internet group was forever after known to us as the KLR Dork List.

Although I know and like several of the list's subscribers, I had to admit that sitting around debating whether an extra .3 liters of oil was going to hurt the engine was a little silly. Oh hell, they'll probably be the first to tell you they're moto-dweebs. But they're well-meaning moto-dweebs, full of useful information, and occasionally you can find some really cool people among them who will sometimes let you crash with them when you're in town, like Juan Villarreal.

Juan met us on his bike just inside the city limits, and led the three of us to his apartment. He was trim, of medium height, and had tanned Latin skin. As a military man he wore his hair short and neat, and as a macho man he wore the sleeves of his T-shirt rolled up around his arms. His huge pad had two guest rooms and laundry facilities. Aside from the obvious perks of the place, Juan told us he was fortunate to live in the same quadrant of the city as the president, and was therefore less likely to lose electrical power in a blackout, or to have his daily electricity rationed should the Canal need it. Juan didn't plan to stay in Panama much longer. The Canal would shift to Panamanian control in a matter of weeks, and the United States base where he worked was shutting down. Until then, he offered us full use of the apartment, which served as our center of operations in Panama City.

Time passed quickly in Panama City because our days were loaded. We planned on shipping the bikes past Colombia to Ecuador and had to schedule flights, handle some minor maintenance, and make shipping arrangements. We also bought some last-minute supplies before we hit the southern continent. Finding a shipping agent was our top priority. We weren't going anywhere until the bikes were packed and stacked somewhere in a warehouse, ready and waiting to fly. Peter found a shipper named Servi-Carga, and after the initial phone interview we headed downtown to check them out. After a couple painless hours we'd arranged to ship our bikes for three hundred dollars, not including the fifty dollar crating charge for all three bikes and any applicable taxes and surcharges. Once again, the deal I worked out at most hotels was useful here; we discounted our shipping costs by as much as 50 percent. All told it was very reasonable price for more than 1,200 lbs of motorcycles.

Having settled the shipping on our first try, Robert and Peter decided to find a BMW dealer for a bike check up and to repair Peter's rim, which was still bent from that brick he jumped. Their plan was a good one, so I too went off in search of people that could help me with my bike.

Panama City is a confusing place filled with crazy drivers. There are many one-way streets, and it's hard enough to read signs and try to figure out where you are without having to constantly scan 360 degrees for any buses bearing down on you. I decided to take the easy way out and get a cab. The cabbie was an impatient, chubby twenty-

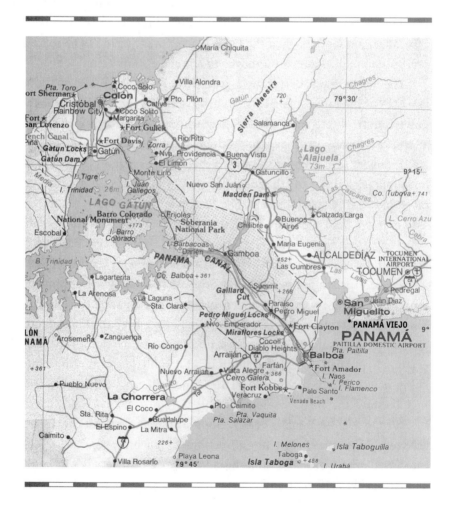

five-year-old who blasted his music (typical Panamanian pop-Latin-Caribbean rhythms with fast, happy beats), honked at all the girls (some of which were of questionable honk-worthiness), and shouted profanity out the window at other drivers (your grandmother's what?). As he drove, he jiggled his many chins to the music and tapped his hands on the steering wheel. I thought he was going to kill us both from excessive speed or at least himself by infuriating other drivers as he cut them off. He squealed to a stop—actually leaving black skids—in front of a gray building. I looked at him questioningly and he wagged his jowls up and down rapidly in my direction, apparently an assurance that we'd reached the right place. I went inside as he roared off, only to realize he'd brought me to a bicycle shop. Crap.

The next cab was driven by a grumpy old boot. He scowled at the world over the top of the steering wheel while he motored cautiously down the street. We made a snail's pace through back roads and empty alleys, presumably to avoid the excitement of other moving vehicles. Hairy fingers worked over the tired wheel as he sat at an intersection for minutes, waiting for the ideal moment to make his bold, arthritic move into traffic. Time passed. The Panamanian sun lazily baked the skin of my neck. Time slowed further. Heat. Slow. Tick. Tick. I became a melting timepiece from a Salvador Dalí painting. I was sure we'd arrive after the dealership closed. I said as much and my driver replied: "The world turns at only one speed, Son." Well thank you very much, Copernicus, you swarthy, grizzled bastard, but I happen to be in a hurry. This was insane. The first driver may have been on a mission to commit murder-suicide, but at least he'd have put me out of my misery quickly. Finally we pulled up in front of a big glass building with shiny new motorcycles inside. "This is more like it," I thought. "He may be slow, but he got me here."

Wrong again—Yamaha dealer. Double crap. But at least they were able to give me precise written directions to reach my Kawasaki people. Third one's a charm, I thought, and stepped into yet another taxi. The driver was efficient and courteous, taking my written directions in hand and speeding us on our way. Viewed from above, Panamanian traffic must look somewhat like a microscopic examination of blood cells moving in a vascular system, never truly stopping (even when backed up), gently brushing past one another in harrowing near-misses, and always pushed in mishmash surges through the city's arteries by some unstoppable, unseen force. My driver handled the fluid chaos with grace, occasionally waving other drivers in front of him and smiling as he paused for passing pedestrians. His behavior was definitely unusual. I asked him why he was so polite and courteous in a place that outwardly seems so unfriendly—especially to foreigners— and extra-especially to Americans.

"Well . . . ." He paused to consider the question. "Regarding your people, it seems your country has a history with us. And my countrymen have very long memories. I think many of my people resent that the United States has such a great control of our country— because of the Canal."

"Are you happy that the Canal is reverting back to Panama's control?"

"Of course. It is a big responsibility that I hope we are ready for." We swooped into the oncoming traffic lane to pass a slow truck, and he turned around and took a quick look at me in the back seat. "I couldn't tell you were a United States citizen. I thought you were from South America." I smiled at his compliment to my language skills. I guess my Spanish was improving. "To answer your original question, I suppose I'm polite because that is how I was raised and educated." He told me he was actually a teacher but he drove a cab because he needed more money to support his large family. "Isn't that funny?" He laughed as he looked in his rearview mirror at me, two squinting eyes and a dark cheek crinkled in a rectangle. "A teacher must become a cab driver in order to educate his kids!"

We arrived. I wished my driver well and he sped off. Finally I was to meet my Kawasaki benefactors. One major perk of my Kawasaki USA sponsorship was that I usually had free service at any Kawasaki dealer in Central and South America. All I paid for was parts. Miguel Duran and Edward Burgos were two men that worked at this one: both were short, stocky types with muscled forearms, square jaws, and honest faces. Each spoke perfect English. Edward was the service manager and he worked for Miguel, a higher-level manager. Although their faces didn't look alike, they seemed as if they'd be completely interchangeable if only they exchanged their clothes, or swapped heads. "Of course we'll help you; our pleasure. Unfortunately, we have to close the shop now. Can you come back tomorrow?"

That night Juan prepared a fantastic steak dinner in honor of our stay. Twenty minutes of scarfing left us fat-bellied and content, splayed across his couches. When pressed, Juan told us stories about his job with the Air Force as the navigator on a KC-135 refueling plane. When not actually navigating, he'd often watch the boom operators work the long fuel tubes that dangle from the back of the plane. The operators have a tough job, manning the controls and looking into a screen as they try to fit the snaking pipes into the female ports of the planes that come to refuel.

"Everything that could possibly go wrong has," Juan said. "Planes sometimes need to refuel under the cover of night, and in the dark it's hard to see the boom. There's no depth perception as the plane approaches, and it's very hard to tell where the incoming plane is just by two little lights." He raised his hands to illustrate two planes flying in tandem, one just behind and below the other one, and off a little to the side. "On the F-15 ground attack models, there's a crew of two: the pilot and navigator. You can see the pilot flying, concentrating, eyes straight into his instruments, trying to keep the plane in the window. And then you see the anxious navigator, two hands and a helmet pressed to the glass, staring at the wing where the boom is connecting. He's completely absorbed, relaying information to his pilot. It's pretty intense." He laughed, settling back into his seat. "There've been times when the boom was dropped incorrectly, and it smashed into the cockpit window and filled the cockpit with fuel. Other times pilots have pulled away, tearing the entire fuel line off the KC-135 and taking it with them, leaving the hose attached and dangling from the fuel port. On models that refuel at the nose that's called a 'unicorn.'"

I'd been feeling very tired the last couple days, and I felt particularly drained that night, so I excused myself early and went to sleep. The following morning I realized why I was so exhausted, and I knew it was time to go to the doctor again. My itching rash from the scabies was not getting better, and I needed to be rid of the microscopic squatters fast because they were wearing me out. The itching was insufferable. I felt like scratching in places one could not hope to scratch, like the inside of my skin and the undersides of my eyelids.

At the local hospital I found a doctor who gave me the prescriptions I needed, one of which was for a topical cream called Eurax. He advised that I take the lotion with me if I travel other parts of the world, since it will work on many varieties of organisms that live on and under the skin. Great, I thought, just in case I decide to make a habit of farming bloodsucking parasites on my flesh.

Having settled my health concerns, it was time to look after those of my trusty KLR. Fortunately I'd left a trail of breadcrumbs to find my way back to the Kawasaki shop, and just before lunchtime I arrived with the motorcycle. Edward and Miguel were right with me; ushering me inside, moving my bike into the shop, and putting an anemic-looking mechanic to work on it straightaway. The skinny wrencher refused to let me in his shop, so I drank coffee from a plastic shot glass while he lubricated the cables, changed the oil and filter, adjusted and oiled the chain, cleaned the spark plug, replaced the brake pads, and put on the new Avon tires that I'd shipped to Juan's house from McAllen, Texas. I decided to meet Juan for lunch and go wrench shopping at a local mall, and when I returned the bike was in great shape. I thanked them all and rode off on my newly tuned ride.

Back at Juan's, I helped him do a valve clearance check on his own KLR. He really wanted the watchful eye of someone who had done it before, and he couldn't have chosen a better overseer. I had a good

working knowledge of what not to do to the bike. The last time I'd checked my valve clearance, I dropped a head bolt into my engine's top end and listened to it clatter and tinkle all the way to the bottom—two-and-a-half hours later I was able to retrieve it.

After dinner at a Chinese restaurant we sat talking. Peter felt sick and was anxious to get to Colombia—he told us he wanted to leave in the morning and that he'd just drop his bike at the airport and catch the first plane out. Robert, ever practical, felt it would be better to sit in on the crating of the bikes, double-check that everything was in order, and then leave the following morning. With some convincing, Peter agreed and went to bed. Juan and Robert decided to go to a strip club. I wrote some notes and went to sleep. Remarkably, for the first time I was the only one up and ready to go the next morning at 7:30 A.M.

Thanks to Peter's dogged phone calling two days before, we secured a 9 A.M. appointment with the crating crew. We arrived at the warehouse, but the craters weren't there yet. So we ate empanadas at a diner down the street while we waited. An old man with burnt-caramel skin came inside wearing black polyester pants and a shirt with pink and yellow cubes on it. You could practically see the alcohol molecules diffusing out of his pores. "Americans don't belong here!" he shouted. "Get the hell out!" He slurred terribly and I could barely understand him, but I sensed that Peter had a few choice words for the guy. He was very disturbing at first, more so because he was skinny as a vine and looked quite sickly. I walked outside to get some fresh air and avoid him.

As I stepped out, one of the huge, painted, omnipresent Panamanian buses roared past. They were privately owned ex-school buses turned into mass transit vehicles. Since they're not government regulated, thousands of them race around, operating on bus routes chosen by the drivers. Customized and decorated with intricate landscapes, still lifes, and portraits of celebrities or friends of the driver in rich blues, oranges, blacks, yellows, and greens, they flash by on the streets like enormous rolling murals. Two fat chromed tailpipes run up past the rear emergency exits and end above the roof, where they billow out black smoke. The names of the drivers or their girlfriends are painted on the sides of the vehicles, and the windshields sport colorful cartoon letters with the buses' endpoints: "Chorillo, Tocumen." Inside the diner we chatted with a couple of those bus drivers while they ate. One smiled quietly and chewed his food while his boisterous friend did all the talking. "I've only been driving for twelve years," the talkative one said between forkfuls. "But this guy," he pointed his knife at his friend, "his mother was knocked up on a bus, he was born on a bus, and he's been driving them ever since!"

We rode back to the airport. Our troubles with the Servi-Carga shipping company were about to begin. As I said, the crew of three was already late, but we might've been better off if they never showed. We emptied the gas tanks and disconnected the batteries, and then handed over the rest to them—until things got out of hand.

They began by cutting up rotted old pallets to make two ends under the tires of each bike. Then they laid a single thin piece of wood across each side of the motorcycles and nailed them to the two ends, and prepared to wrap each individual mess with shrink-wrap. This implied they felt they had provided sufficient support for each of our 400-plus pounds of motorcycle and equipment. This was more than a little disconcerting, and Peter's "crate" looked the worst. He'd removed his front wheel to carry it with him, hoping to have it fixed in Colombia (the Panamanian BMW dealer was unable to repair it). Therefore his front forks rested unsteadily on the half-pallet end, and the Virgin Queen looked ready to topple over any second. Surely our bikes would bounce around like pinballs inside the plane's cargo hold because these crates were going to collapse before takeoff.

I finally had to stop this charade of pseudocrating and intervene. Although I'd never crated anything before in my life, I was sure I could do it better than my assigned "professional." With a mixture of diplomacy and insistence, I sketched out a plan to my crater. Instead of taking offense, he appeared relieved that I was helping, because, he confessed to me, with all the pressure from us owners watching he was having a hard time building his first crate! Together we started with a base from three sturdy-looking pallets. We hammered support beams across the tops and bottoms of the pallets, until we'd fashioned a very solid platform two-and-a-half pallets long and one-half pallet wide. Robert and Peter followed suit and were soon directing the crating of their bikes as well. Robert made a base similar to mine, but Peter's was a bit more intricate to support the wheel-less front end of his bike.

I moved the KLR onto the platform, put it into gear, and hammered wood around the wheels to prevent them from rolling. I placed an eight-inch piece of 2x4 between the bottom of my fender and the tire to prevent excessive spring compression, and then we cinched the whole bike down with ropes in the front and rear to form a single firm unit with the pallet base. Finally we built a wall of cardboard around the bike and bundled it up with black plastic wrap. Our crates weren't pretty, but they'd do the job.

"Damn it!" Peter said as they rolled our fat black parcels into the warehouse on forklifts, "We should've brought a camera. Who knows if we'll ever see them again?"

No trip to Panama is complete without seeing the wonder that is the Canal. We hopped into a cab to do just that. No ships were passing through at the time, but we were able to marvel at the canal's impressive size and learn a few interesting facts from the signs around the site, such as: The lock gates are over two meters thick and hollow—their buoyancy allows them to be opened and closed with less energy; If the material originally excavated to create the canal were placed on a single train of flatcars, it would circle the earth four times; Because of the reclining "S" shape of the Isthmus of Panama, the sun rises from the Pacific and sets on the Atlantic.

But the learning didn't stop there. On the ride back to the apartment, Peter convinced our taxi driver to give us a small tour. While the driver simultaneously prattled away and zipped us through the city, Peter translated, edited, and annotated his monologue from the front seat for Robert and me in the back. "Chorillo is the place where the United States bombed the crap out of Noriega, and that part of town caught fire." Peter pointed out the window as the driver talked and negotiated traffic. "And there's the house where Ruben Blades, the Panamanian singer, was born. That used to be Pasqual Sanchez's gym, which has now been bought and turned into a fish market by the Japanese. The cab driver says he was some famous boxer." The driver pointed at a building, still jabbering away. "There's the Vatican Embassy," Peter said, "where Noriega was hiding while United States tanks blasted rock music at him twenty-four hours a day to wear him out."

Our educational excursion ended with an abrupt slam of the brakes in front of Juan's apartment. Incredibly, though so much had happened, we'd only been in Panama City three days. We packed up all our stuff and waited for Juan to return from work. When he arrived, we overloaded his little car with bags, helmets, and a communal duffel big enough to hold a corpse, which carried all our riding gear.

Juan seemed sad to see us go. We were a hurricane of excitement that blew through his apartment, and I know he would've liked to come along for the rest of our journey. "Together you have a good chemistry," he told us. "The perfect blend of humor and seriousness, dedication and playfulness, energy and calm. You guys are lucky to have founded such a great group." Although it was sometimes hard to see, he was right. Three strangers teaming up after a few e-mails is an unlikely proposition at best, but somehow we were making it work. His words reflected a sentiment we rarely gave ourselves the luxury of feeling. We thanked him and said farewell, then focused on the business at hand.

Servi-Carga would fly the motorcycles to Quito, Ecuador via cargo plane, where they'd wait for us in customs. Then we'd plane-hop through Colombia, the most dangerous country in the Western Hemisphere, to see the sights and visit Peter's relatives in Medellín and Bogotá. Finally we'd catch a connection to Quito, get our bikes out of customs, and continue south on six wheels. Colombia—and all its potential dangers—was our next stop. We stamped our documents, loaded our luggage onto the little conveyer belt, and boarded the plane straight into the mouth of the dragon.

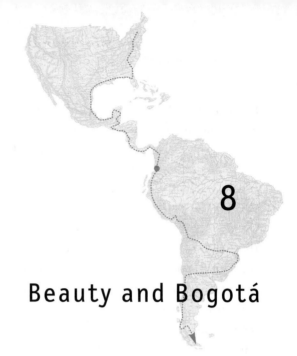

8

Beauty and Bogotá

➤ ARRIVING AT THE AIRPORT in Medellín was like arriving in any other airport—sort of. We collected our luggage and moved through immigration lines. While teens in fatigues and body armor checked our bags, their partners stood nearby with combat shotguns, pistols, and submachine guns at the ready. The message was clear: "Welcome to Colombia. Don't try anything stupid."

Colombia is a beautiful country cursed with more than its share of violence, both past and present. Little is reported in the United States of the horrors that occur there daily. Being therefore insulated from the news, I was shocked to learn that the hottest guerrilla fad was finding creative new uses for explosives, such as "dog bombs," or trained war dogs sent against the police with several kilos of explosives strapped to their backs in miniature saddlebags. The helpless police could only flee in terror or try to shoot the snarling, speeding missiles before they reached their location, where the explosive packs would be detonated remotely. There was also the collar bomb made of high explosive and PVC tubing, attached with silicone adhesive to the neck of Señora Elvira Cortés Gil, a farm owner who refused to be extorted for money by the FARC guerrilla organization. The collar exploded when the police attempted to remove it—Señora Gil was killed instantly and several officers were wounded.

Only partly aware of what the Colombian people have suffered and continue to suffer, I stepped outside the airport to meet Peter's family. His mother, Isabella, and stepfather, Alejandro, were there with his teenage sister and her boyfriend. After a brief and happy welcome, they took us to the family's ranch house in Rio Negro, a town just minutes outside of Medellín. Rio Negro is famous for its beauty, and infamous for being the birthplace of Pablo Escobar, the drug lord extraordinaire who waged war against the entire Colombian government—and nearly won. The family's farm became a place of luxury and tranquility for us during the next eight days. Isabella and Alejandro were consummate hosts, ensuring all our needs were attended to, often before we knew we had them. Like something from *Beauty and the Beast*, unseen hands made our beds after we rose and then turned them down before bedtime. Fresh glasses of water appeared on our nightstands in the evenings, and if you dropped a pair of socks they'd magically disappear, seemingly before they could even touch the ground, only to be later seen washed and dangling from the clothesline.

The food was outstanding. Hearty breakfasts included skillets of eggs with huge kernels of corn or ham and cheese mixed in; sides of sausage, cheese, fresh papaya, mango, and grapes; and blackberry, orange, and guayaba juices to accompany them. Peter would have none of the eggs, because when he was a child, his mother insisted they were good for him, and forced him into a lifelong dread of them. Scrambled, fried, poached, or boiled, he never met an egg he did not loathe. Home-baked breads came with every meal. Dinners consisted of traditional fare like a cream-based soup of chicken, potato, and avocado (grown there on the farm) and a shredded-beef chili topped with french fries, avocado, salsa, and white rice. Drinks were also plentiful; the bar in the rear of the farm was open all day and featured a stocked

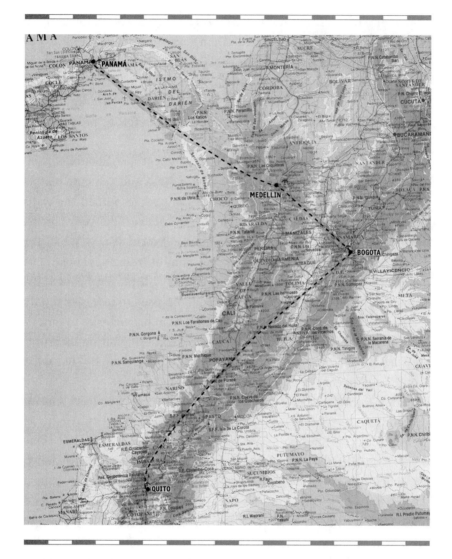

refrigerator of beer and several brands of the Colombian favorite, *aguardiente*.

The ranch house was set on a small plot of farmland, with overgrown fields for the lazy horses to graze (Isabella no longer jumped them). There was also an orchard of avocado trees and a field of bird-of-paradise flowers. The house itself was built in the old colonial style, with walls several feet thick made from concrete and manure. Next to central air, the fat whitewashed walls are unmatched for comfort in hot weather; the interior maintained a cave-like coolness at all times. The roof sported red tiles and the picture-frame windows were accented with red paint. Enormous trees and lush foliage provided the perfect secluding backdrop.

Indoors, the house was equally charming. Antiques abounded, and old tin signs from Coca-Cola, Colgate talcum, BSA and Triumph motor-cycles, Budweiser, and Orphan Boy smoking tobacco lined the walls of the living areas. There were model race cars and delivery trucks, old painted metal serving trays, and a pre–World War II Wurlitzer Model 800 jukebox that Alejandro had bought from a cathouse. The old jukebox was in amazing condition and still played beautifully. Being a bit of an adrenaline junkie, Alejandro used to race cars and fly ultralight aircraft. He had several trophies from his victories in car rallies during his youth, some of which were won using his mother's car. He'd tell his mother he was taking the car to go to church. "But what would've happened if you crashed it?" I asked him.

"You know, that possibility never once occurred to me," Alejandro said.

We took our time exploring the town and surrounding areas. One day we toured a place called La Quirama, the oldest hacienda in Medellín, which is now converted into a convention center. As we walked around one of the main buildings, Robert and I overheard what could only be described as a vigorous, quasi-violent lovemaking session, with multiple male and female voices coming from inside. We listened in disbelief; the boisterous sounds were surely unmistakable. Alejandro walked over and Robert commented that Colombia was culturally unique in so many ways. Alejandro laughingly explained that it was a group primal scream therapy session.

A few days later we visited a restaurant owned by an eccentric sculptor. He collected old glass to make artwork and decorations, like the triangle of green bottles assembled into a Christmas-tree collage against the wall, and the incredible stained-glass-style windows made from melted and hammered jars of different colors. Most of the multicolored pieces were packed up to the rafters to create a dazzling scattering of light in all directions. The backyard of the restaurant was replete with junk: huge helicopter rotors, thick anchor chains, engine blocks, airplane cockpits, ailerons, all kinds of windshields. The parts were mostly formed together into hulking, gangly sculptures from a Tim Burton nightmare, and what was not assembled was left standing alone in a prominent place to display its individual beauty, or to rot in peace.

The most memorable part of my time in Medellín was the evenings. They were spent drinking by the fire, exploding fireworks bought at the local underground factory (from the guy who'd blown off several of his own fingers), talking late with close friends of Peter and his family, and getting pestered by the crazy family retrievers. Isabella's three dogs, all females, were like plump, spoiled children. They chased us around, desperate for approval, affection, and any scrap of food they could snatch from our hands. Blondie, the eldest, had the best disposition; Sarah, the brown one, had a timid personality; and Carla, the youngest, was crazy jealous. I enjoyed giving lots of attention to Blondie and Sarah to make Carla wild with envy.

The evening conversations often centered on the political situation in Colombia. None of our hosts wanted to discuss Colombia's problems at first, but after we'd been there a few days they loosened up. One evening I met Diego, Peter's cousin, and his wife, Sofia. I noticed something strange about the 4x4 truck they'd arrived in. "Oh, it just looks that way because it's been bulletproofed," Diego told me casually. Indeed it had. A closer inspection revealed welded seams on the roof and side panels where metal panels were installed into the bodywork. Plate glass windows over an inch thick were placed all the way around the cabin. The tires had special bead locks so that they could be run flat if shot out. The thing looked like a designer tank. "It's a real art," Diego told me. "Bulletproofing usually costs as much as the car itself. For example, a sixty-thousand-dollar car will need sixty thousand dollars worth of bulletproofing. Sofia's father is the president of a bank, and we borrowed the car from him for the night. He was worried about us driving home too late, you know, because of the guerrilla roadblocks. The bulletproofing is no guarantee of safety, but at least it can buy you a little time."

Perhaps you've been wondering why three big strong motorcyclists opted to ship their bikes to Ecuador instead of riding them through Colombia. According to *Peterson's Guide to the World's Most Dangerous Places*, Colombia is the least safe country in the Western Hemisphere. More people die by bullets here than any other place in the Americas. There are several revolutionary organizations currently in operation, including the most notorious and powerful, the FARC, or Fuerzas Armadas Revolucionarias de Colombia. In the eight days I was there, twenty-five people were taken hostage on the roadways, thirty police officers were surprised and gunned down in the back of a truck, and a commuter flight (usually the safest form of travel between cities) was hijacked. Such national pastimes are not to be taken lightly.

The greatest danger for a foreigner is definitely getting caught in a roadside *pesca milagrosa*, a darkly humorous reference to the biblical story of Jesus' miraculous fishing that fed the hungry multitudes. The guerrillas set up these temporary roadblocks between cities to stop passing vehicles, taking anyone that could be worth a ransom, or just about anyone they feel like taking. Being invited to join the guerrillas of the FARC or any of the other radical organizations often results in an extended hike through the jungle, possibly for years, until something drastic happens. That could mean succumbing to malaria, headbutting a speeding bullet, or, if lucky, getting released when someone pays the exorbitant ransom placed on the hostage. For someone like me, it could've been bad—the United States has a strict policy of nonnegotiation with terrorists, so if I got caught, I was on my own. To drive through guerrilla-controlled territory on a motorcycle is like rolling the dice for your life every time you put on your helmet.

There was no question in my mind that it was unsafe to ship the bikes to Colombia and ride south from there. Every travel advisory and trip report warned of the dangers of traveling overland between cities. Robert was, at first, unconvinced of the danger, stating that many motorcyclists had ridden through unharmed. Peter viewed the situation completely differently. "Those are the ones you heard about," he said. "What about the ones that never made it back to do a trip report?"

The most convincing argument for avoiding motorcycling through Colombia was that Peter, having lived much of his life there, flatly refused to do it. No. No way. No argument. He told Robert in Panama: "If you want to go, I'll stay in Medellín with my family an extra week, then fly down to Quito to meet you. But there's not a chance in hell I'll ride through that country. When those guerrillas set up a roadblock they stop everyone, and if you look one inch above complete destitution," he held his thumb and forefinger an inch apart in front of him for effect, "you're going for the ecotour of the Colombian jungle."

But how could this be? There were no sounds of gunfire in the night. This wasn't a bombed-out shell of a town. How could there be any real danger in this place where the public seemed so peaceful and happy? In the daytime people enjoyed the sun, calmly bicycling in the park or walking about. I saw a couple in a cab, the taxi driver had his girlfriend on his lap—he appeared to be teaching her to drive and they were laughing together as they swerved down the road. "Don't be fooled by the way the people look," Peter said. "Living in Colombia instills a kind of madness. Every day, people are kidnapped, extorted, and killed. You never see them, but everyone knows someone who's been taken by the guerrillas. You become like something less than human—afraid for your life and the safety of your family on the one hand, and trying to live a normal life on the other. It's insane."

I ran my fingers across the cool, copper-colored metal of the armored SUV, admiring the artfully welded seams. What a piece of work. That thing made your average Volvo appear about as safe as a balsa-wood skateboard. I wondered what could inspire someone to feel that kind of protection was necessary. Anytime I naïvely asked such questions, Peter would launch into a scary story. Being a bank president, like Diego's father-in-law, can be a dangerous job. It simply didn't pay to take chances. Peter had certain friend, the son of a CEO in charge of a major corporation, who was taken for ransom when they were in school together. "He was kept blindfolded and handcuffed to a bed, beaten often, and psychologically tortured every day. He'd wake up and hear: 'Good morning, we'll most likely kill you today,' or sometimes they just shoved the barrels of their guns in his mouth and pistol-whipped him." After a few weeks of this they took him to a warehouse and tied him to a chair. He assumed that his time had come. Moments passed as he waited in breathless terror for the bullet that would take his life. Abruptly, his blindfold was removed and he discovered that his captors had left. His family had managed to cover his ransom, and the police had arrived to pick him up. "He's still not the same today," Peter said.

Partly spurred by my interest and partly by his reimmersion in the surroundings, Peter spewed forth grisly stories like a bloody fountain. We were eating frozen green mango *paletas* in the main square of Rio Negro when a small two-stroke motorcycle zipped past. Peter looked up sharply at the sound and then relaxed. Small 200cc bikes were the preferred vehicles of assassins when Peter was growing up. They're fast, maneuverable, and strong enough to carry two people—a driver and a gunman. Nowadays in Colombia it's illegal for two men to ride together on a motorcycle because of that.

"Every time I hear one of those high-pitched little motors, I clench up," Peter said. "I was leaving a drugstore, and it was near evening, but there was still enough light to see as I stepped onto the sidewalk. I'll never forget it—a nice 4x4 pulled up to the intersection in front of me, waiting for traffic to pass in order to make a U-turn. The driver was an attractive woman in her thirties, and in the passenger's seat sat an older lady holding a baby—she looked like a nanny or a grandmother. Then I heard the high-pitched whine of one of those little two-strokes." Robert and I were silent as Peter recounted his memory. "I watched as a bike with two men pulled up next to the 4x4 on the driver's side, and I remember the window had been cracked open just a little, maybe four inches. The driver of the bike pulled up really close to the vehicle, and the man on the back stood up on the footpegs, reached his right hand inside the window, and emptied all six rounds of a revolver into the driver." Peter paused as he spoke. "I'll never forget how he stood up on those pegs to stretch his body all the way to reach his hand inside. . . . The cabin filled with smoke, the woman slumped to the floor, and the gunman calmly pulled his hand out, sat back down, and tucked the gun away. Then the driver sped them off down the street."

Peter didn't seem to like to dwell on these things too much, but he couldn't help it. His happy reunion with his family was tainted by never-ending bad news. That evening Alejandro read an article for us regarding the latest miraculous fishing. On the road leading from Medellín to Manizales, a city about sixty-eight miles to the south, fifteen people were taken. Between Medellín and Bogotá another roadblock occurred; this one netted four hostages for the guerrillas. "They seem to be in need of money," Alejandro told me, "because the paramilitaries have been hitting them very hard lately."

The paramilitary groups operating in Colombia are the latest backlash against the guerrillas. They're supposedly funded by farmers, police, politicians, and other civilians frustrated by the government's inability to stop the terrorism that affects them daily. For many complicated reasons, the police and military often can't act quickly enough to defend or retaliate against the hit-and-run tactics employed by the guerrillas, and they certainly aren't authorized to fight the guerrillas with their own methods, such as ransoms and dog bombs. The paramilitaries, however, have no such limitations. They're well equipped, trained by mercenaries from Israel, the United Kingdom, and other countries, and hardened by battle and personal losses to the guerrillas. And they also operate with brutal vigilante procedures comparable to the guerrillas' own.

The guerrillas, threatened by their own violence redirected at them, were calling for peace talks with the government while I was there. They demanded that the Colombian government call off the paramilitaries, which had been hitting the families of their generals and other high-ranking officers, taking their children hostage, torturing and killing them. The guerrillas claimed the paramilitary group's actions were "not human." Most Colombians seemed to find this laughable—the devil crying foul play.

But apparently the paramilitaries can be a danger to the general populace. They travel to farms believed to be guerrilla sympathetic and mete swift justice on anyone they think is guilty of helping them. Meanwhile the guerrillas have coerced the people, often at gunpoint, to assist with money, lodging, medical attention, or whatever. So when the paramilitaries arrive to punish those that have helped the guerrillas, the landowners find themselves in a deadly Catch-22: either refuse the guerrillas and get a new pipe-bomb necklace, or assist them and face paramilitary wrath later on.

That night I looked out at the stars after everyone went to bed, and a soft breeze slipped through the humid countryside. The darkness seemed more pervasive than normal because it was so silent—no cars dared pass on the roads. Everyone was ensconced in the safety of their locked houses, which in reality were not very safe. All the parents had tucked their children into bed, but they couldn't reassure their young ones not to fear the monsters roaming the night because they know all too well that the monsters really do exist. That evening we'd raised our aguardiente to peace in Colombia, and shot off fireworks in the name of peace, the cracks of the miniature bombs ringing out in the evening sky. I went to sleep thinking how strange it was that people of such talent, ambition, life, and natural gifts as those of Colombia, a country of thirty-seven million, could be held captive in a nightmare of fear by an army of fifteen thousand men catching malaria in the jungles. The danger was surreal—implausible—in those beautiful surroundings. Truly there couldn't have been a more fitting juxtaposition to understand what it meant to live in Colombia: on the one hand we were surrounded by comfort and plenty on the farm, smiling and pretending not to notice the cold fog of death that loomed on the other hand. I could feel the madness creeping into me, starting to make sense—you may die tomorrow but why think about it? What good will that do? Enjoy yourself, relax . . . it probably won't happen to you.

The next afternoon we drove into Medellín, enjoying the winding mountain roads that took us from the height of the ranch down into the city. We descended, ratcheting through the switchbacks. What a great shame we couldn't safely motorcycle here; these were among the best roads I'd seen for the sport. We passed a bicycle track that Pablo Escobar had built for his personal use. Further down the road we saw a blown-out building, lying in disrepair for years, which also belonged to the former drug lord. We shopped in town; Robert needed new glasses and I needed a few pairs of socks.

Afterward we went to Isabella and Alejandro's other house, in the city, where Alejandro showed us his small yet truly incredible collection of pre-Colombian gold that he found while growing up. He was very fortunate to have unearthed such a stunning collection, right on the family farm, and it was an excellent primer for the wonders we were to see at the Colombian Gold Museum in Bogotá. His exquisite collection included several gold fertility frogs, multiple larger statues up to three inches high, and a small warrior's breastplate, the most brilliant of all the works. My personal favorite was a pen-sized hairpin depicting an ape masturbating.

Robert and I were restless. The visit was pleasant, but after almost a week had passed we felt the itch to move on, to see Bogotá quickly and get back to our bikes and the trip. Although we felt welcome to stay as long as we liked, our ass calluses were growing soft and the tarmac called out like a lover. Peter seemed hesitant to go. He was surrounded by the warmth of the family he didn't often visit and, under-standably, wasn't in any rush to leave. With some gentle reminding, he acknowledged the need to move on and we made flight plans for the next day.

The plans were not followed to the letter, which upset Robert a bit, as usual. However, it was nice to have him totally pissed just at Peter for a change. Peter tried to get his rim fixed, with limited suc-cess, and instead of taking our flight at 1:30 P.M., we flew out at 10 P.M. In the airport, Isabella seemed truly sorry to see us go, and she cried because Peter was leaving. She hugged each of us good-bye and she and Alejandro were kind enough to extend an open invitation for me to return whenever I wished.

After a quick plane hop to Bogotá we found Peter's father's apart-ment, which became our base for the next couple of days. In the morn-ing I found Robert and Peter breakfasting and reading the paper. The big local news was that the day before, May 7, a police convoy was stopped about 60 miles from Bogotá, and thirty police officers were gunned down by the guerrillas, mostly while still sitting in the back of the trucks they rode in. That was only an hour from us by car. We were happy we chose to fly.

Earlier, someone had told me a joke that had me thinking: God and his assistant were deciding what natural benefits each of the world's countries would receive. "This country will be a desert, that country will receive constant floods, that one will have volcanic eruptions." God said as his secretary dutifully took notes. "But Colombia," God reflected, "Colombia will get fruitful land, all varieties of wildlife, tall mountains, handsome people, gorgeous beaches, lush jungles, fantas-tic weather . . ."

"But God," the secretary said, "how can you give that country so much when all the other countries are going to be so awful?"

"Wait," God smiled, "until you see the politicians I'm going to give them."

Although it seems easy to blame the government for Colombia's woes—I did at first—apparently it's not so simple. The logical question for me was, "Why doesn't some strong person step forward to take control of the situation and crush the guerrillas, like Peru's President Fujimori did with the Shining Path?"

"It could totally backfire," Peter replied. "It could be another Argentina or Chile, where thousands of innocents suffer or die for the crimes of the guilty as every last guerrilla is tracked down and killed. No one wants to be the Colombian Pinochet."

We caught a cab and rode through pothole-riddled streets to the Museum of Gold. The museum was impressive in the quantity of gold artifacts it contained. The display methods were a bit disappointing, especially the "now you see it, now you don't" grand finale that took place in a small, sealed, circular room. They ushered us in, flipped the lights on briefly to illuminate the exhibit, and then herded us all back out again. My favorite part of the museum was the small dioramas representing the lives of the peaceful peoples that inhabited the area before the Spanish came. Tiny bronzed villagers worked together in the salt mines, tranquilly crafting clay pots and trading in the bustling market. You could practically hear them whistling while they worked. Surely such fancifully idyllic human societies must only be possible when viewed in miniature, with the softening filter of retrospect.

After the tour was over, Peter decided to go back to the apartment to check on the status of our bikes with Servi-Carga in Panama. Robert and I toured the famous Monserrat church overlooking all of Bogotá. Cool gondola ride, spectacular view.

Aside from the sight-seeing, the only worthwhile thing we did in Bogotá was party. Peter had his mind set on showing us why Colombians rank among the best revelers in the world. Assisting Peter in his mission was consummate-party-guy-turned-Harley-Davidson-distributor Andrés Camargo. Andrés was a friend of Peter's from back in their college days, and he was now somewhat of a celebrity since he owned the only Harley-Davidson dealership in the entire country. All of Colombia's wealthiest motorcycle enthusiasts knew him, as did most of the trendier Colombians who kept up with the latest happenings.

We met Andrés at his dealership in downtown Bogotá. He was of average height and build, with dark hair and a friendly countenance. His office sported many photos of beautiful women he had known, girlfriends, ex-girlfriends, and former employees. But he no longer employed his "Harley girls," the attractive female sales representatives that encouraged customers to buy motorcycles, sometimes too enthusiastically. "Yeah, I had to get rid of them," Andrés lamented, "they were really giving us a bad name." His office had another notable feature—a fireproof, externally lockable back door with an escape exit to the rear of the building. He kept a pistol stashed there just in case. He took other protective measures as well. Andrés rarely drove to work in the same car, instead alternating between two or three different vehicles, to make him harder to case. His shop had an armed guard out front twenty-four hours a day, and security cameras running all night. Of course, all doors and windows were hard-wired to a central security agency that could arrive within minutes of a break-in.

The shop itself looked like any other Harley shop, loaded with big, shiny motorcycles that were rarely ridden (that's just a little Harley joke). The walls featured custom-painted tanks, leather saddlebags, and other accessories. Andrés's dealership was comparable in quality to any I'd seen in the States—he had an immaculate repair shop in the rear, a wide variety of merchandise in the store, and dozens of bikes on the floor. "Most of the bikes don't belong to the shop," Andrés confessed. "My customers ask me to keep the bikes here for them because they're more secure. How many people can afford security cameras and armed guards for their garage?"

The moment had arrived. The sun had disappeared over the horizon and the much-vaunted Bogotá night life was starting. Andrés took us to one of the restaurant-cum-discos that were the latest Colombian fad. A typical night began around 9 P.M. The patrons would have some drinks and a nice meal, and as the evening progressed, the plates would be cleared, the music picked up, and suddenly everyone was dancing on the tables, chairs, and every available inch of floor space in a raucous display of gyrating Latin bodies. It's a stunning spectacle. These dancing restaurants had become so popular that only two "strictly dancing" clubs were still operating in Bogotá at the time.

The place was called San Angel's, and we were disappointed to find a long line outside. "Not to worry," said Andrés, and ushered us to the front of the line, where we were quickly let inside, after the bouncers frisked us for weapons, of course. We'd eaten pizza at Andrés's shop, so we just ordered drinks. I was feeling charitable so I splurged and bought a bottle of Jack Daniels. Apparently my experiences in David, Panama, had not sunk in deep enough. It's enough to say that the following morning I didn't go with Robert and Peter to see the Salt Cathedral as planned. Instead I spent the day reading, getting a haircut, e-mailing, enjoying the neighborhood, and of course, sleeping off the hangover. Fortunately I was rested up for the fantastic night I had ahead of me.

That night I saw the single best thing I was to see in Bogotá, and probably all of Colombia: a young woman by the name of Catalina Aristizabal. Andrés had told us he was taking us outside the city that evening, to a place famous for food, atmosphere, and entertainment. We were going to another restaurant-discothèque Andrés called Carne de Res. Andrés planned to pick up Catalina along the way. All we knew was that she was a friend of his; other than that he didn't say much about her. Peter, Robert, and I were in the truck, bounding along while Andrés drove. Peter and Robert sat in the back sharing a beer, and Andrés and I split one up front. We passed a mountain just outside of the city, with thousands of tiny lights burning a white fire across the hillside in the distance. The view was captivating. "What is that?" I said.

"Slums," Andrés said. "Lots of slums controlled by the Bolivian Mafia."

"The police avoid it." Peter added. "Even the military won't go there without a great show of force—tanks and helicopters."

"I bet you never heard anyone say this before, but those slums look beautiful," I said.

"Sure," Andrés said, taking the beer from my hand, "they do look pretty, at night. From here."

We pulled up in front of Catalina's house, and Andrés went to the door to get her. I scooted into the back with Robert and Peter—once again the rum riders were awkwardly squeezed together into an uncomfortable place—we were getting used to it. Catalina climbed into the front seat and greeted everyone hello, but the dark night didn't really reveal much about her, and she didn't talk much to us, either.

It was not until we were inside the restaurant that I was struck by this woman. Catalina was completely radiant, gorgeous, and utterly stunning. I can't remember what she wore that night because I only saw her as if she were unclothed, not in the slimy frat-boy way, but in a way that my mind envisioned her beauty as though it were criminal to hide it from my eyes—and my brain refused to acknowledge any barriers to it. For me alone her naked skin shimmered with an angelic glow. She was the single most beautiful creature I've ever met. In the truck earlier I'd asked Andrés about the girl he was bringing. He modestly brushed off her beauty as though she weren't an internationally recognized model. His macho Latino reply was "Oh, she's all right—but she has small breasts."

She was about 5′10″, thin, with long sandy hair and blond highlights. The cut of her face was as if sculpted, slightly asymmetrical, with a high forehead, raised cheekbones, lips like melted taffy, and a petulant, slightly upturned nose. Her thin body tapered up from the legs to the perfect sort of Latin backside that has inspired and maddened mankind with its rhythmic swing since we dropped out of the trees.

We ordered appetizers, four steaks, and iced aguardiente with lime juice—no small feat given the fact that Peter and I were speechless. Robert seemed unfazed. Peter, ever my willing (yet unable) co-conspirator, and I were like two little boys, exchanging awestruck glances and saying "Oh my God" over and over. It was ridiculous; we were afraid to meet her gaze.

The restaurant was set in a long building, with rows of heavy wooden tables filling the dining and dancing area. Lights hung low over the tables, and wonderful barbecue smells permeated the air. Music played, and everywhere happy, gorgeous people sat, talked, shouted, observed, or wandered by—I'd heard that Colombia had beautiful women, but I had had no idea. Waiters sped between tables taking orders and carrying menus. The atmosphere was a combination of old and new, kitsch and cutting edge. The walls teemed with ornamentation: masks, wands, colored paper, antique lanterns, murals, collages. Sculptures lay scattered on wood and stone floors: half-torsos from mannequins, wooden reliefs, stone monoliths. Even the bathroom was decorated. The toilet seats were hand painted with vines and flowers, and the walls held framed paintings. Each of the tables had a specific name, like Freud, Amor, or Adobe. The place oozed personality.

I was not distracted by the surroundings for long. Despite all attempts not to, I soon found myself staring at Catalina again. As we all talked I learned that not only was she a professional model, at only twenty years old, she was also the entertainment anchor for a news station in Bogotá. She was auditioned, not surprisingly, for her looks— but it was her poise, confidence, and intelligence that landed her the job of anchor. Although young, she seemed sophisticated, mature, and very womanly. Catalina's and Andrés's celebrity created a bit of a stir at the bar; our table got a lot of looks. Were they merely noticing the two famous residents out partying, or trying to guess who on earth were the three scruffy men with them at their table?

Then the most amazing thing happened. Catalina asked me if I wanted to dance. Sir, your table on cloud nine is ready. You bet your sweet ass I want to dance. Rhumbita, salsa, meringue, techno, polka, whatever. If I didn't know it, I'd have learned it on the spot or died trying. We stopped to have a drink with the others, then danced some more. After a few aguardientes she took me on a tour of the place. We found a quiet corner and talked. We discussed Western philosophy, Buddhism, the problems of Colombia.

So we talked and we danced, and I became one of Isabella's pathetic dogs, in need of attention and acceptance, but with no idea how to go about getting it. At one point, as we moved together on an elevated part of the dance floor, about even with the tables, I stepped near the edge and nearly lost my balance. She told me to be more careful, because it was dangerous. So I backed against the edge while facing her, hanging on by the balls of my feet and balancing there. "Life is dangerous," I said, as I started to fall backward. Her hand shot out, she grabbed me by the belt buckle, and she pulled me into the middle of the floor with her. Maybe I had had too much to drink, but how often do you get the chance to be grabbed like that by such a woman?

I normally don't like to dance to Latin music for too long, mostly because I'm not that good at it and I run out of steps fast. Plus it makes my hips hurt like a mo'fo. But still I danced, doing whatever she wanted. I was at her mercy, but she would never have learned that from me (until now, of course). We dropped Catalina off at her house and bid her goodnight. I gave her a hug and she kissed me on the cheek. She gave me her phone number and I gave her my e-mail. I knew she would never write me, and perhaps she knew I was never going to call. I can't say why I knew she wouldn't write me, but my reason for not calling her can best be explained by the old story of the dog that chases the car. The dog puts on a great show, but what would happen if it actually caught the car?

We went to sleep at 3 A.M. and were awake three hours later to pack and catch our flight at 10. We loaded all our stuff onto the plane, did the paperwork, sent some e-mails, changed our Colombian currency to Ecuadorian, and bought stickers. All through Latin America, Peter and Robert had been buying stickers of country flags to decorate their bikes. I tried my best to keep up, but after missing a few countries' stickers, I quit trying. We boarded our plane and watched one more country fade off into the depths of imperfect human vision.

And so ended my experience in Colombia. Who's to say it wasn't better without the bikes? If we'd had the motorcycles, we wouldn't have had time to explore Bogotá and Medellín, and to get to know everyone as we did. Hell, we may not have even made it out of there. Colombia is a country filled with pain and beauty, specializing in the best and worst of humanity. There were big lessons for all of us in there somewhere, and possibly answers to the greatest troubles of our violent nature. I didn't find the answers. All I knew was that it was time to find our bikes and keep riding.

9

How Peter and Robert Plunged into a Volcanic Crater

➤ WE JIGGLED IN OUR SEATS as the plane rocked, bobbed, and descended sharply. The wings suddenly caught lift again and lurched us upward. I watched the dinner-plate-sized view of the mountain city of Quito bumping before my eyes. Quito, the second highest capital in South America at 9,400 feet, is notorious for making travelers altitude sick shortly after landing. And if the altitude sickness didn't get me, the airsickness was going to. We swooped in down over the mountains and finally landed—hard—on a runway filled with military cargo planes.

At the tourist office there was a girl behind the counter, thin, pretty, with her hair pulled back in a bun. I asked about hotels and she made suggestions while Robert and Peter waited for the luggage. I asked her name, and she told me it was Carla. She asked why the three of us had helmets, and I explained our trip to her.

"So are you like a sailor then?" she said.

"No, I'm afraid I don't know what you mean."

"You know—sailors keep a different woman in every port."

"Oh," I laughed, hopefully without a trace of culpability. "Don't be ridiculous. Do I look like that sort of fellow?" Changing the subject, I asked her about clubs, nightlife, and the like. She listed a few places for me and made her recommendations.

"Do you ever go to any of these clubs?" I asked her.

"No, not usually, I have a lot of studying to do at the university."

"I see. Well," I said, "since it's unlikely we'll see each other out at any of them, we'd better make plans to go to one together." She laughed, agreed, and gave me her phone number.

We found a place to stay, the Howard Johnson's La Carolina, and even secured a discount. A triple cost us sixty-five dollars per night. The hotel was nice in the way that massive chain hotels can be; it was a relatively new building, and the managers were very proud of it. The place gave off a clean, industrial feel—like a hospital, or a prison. The hotel had modern technology like electronic keys with magnetic strips that consistently failed to function.

Upstairs, Peter began calling around for our bikes immediately. Since it was Sunday, the shipping offices were closed, so he quickly decided it was better to fulfill his religious obligations and headed straight for the bar downstairs.

Quito is a modern city with all the amenities: theaters, art museums, sports arenas, and lots of places to shop including the enormous mall next to our hotel. Quito had the best movie cinema I'd seen, with deep reclining seats and impeccable sound. We spent our days tracking the bikes and relaxing in the calmness of the Ecuadorian culture. People everywhere were smiling, strolling around sedately with guitars, and enjoying the passing of the days. I've never seen so many people carrying around guitars; every fifth pimply teenager had his ax in a gig bag strapped to his back.

Such tranquility was surprising given the recent economic scandals that were rocking the country. Two major banks had closed recently, having tidily "lost" all the money their customers were saving and investing. During our stay in Ecuador, Filanbank, another

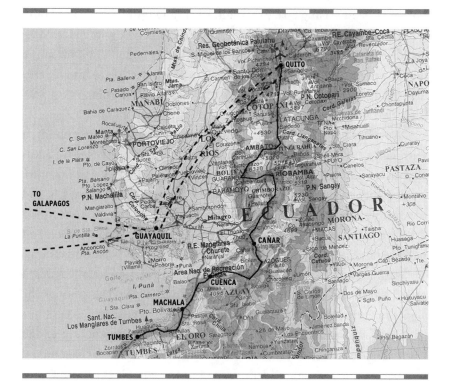

major savings and loan, shut down, again unable to account for the peoples' funds. A few days later the previous owners of the defunct Filanbank announced they were starting a new national beer company. Soon Ecuadorians everywhere were going to be able to pay money to drink their savings from a bottle. Ah, sweet Latin American corruption—it has haunted the path of every golden-eyed, half-starved, homicidal Spanish explorer as night chases the last faint specter of day.

One hundred and twenty dollars worth of phone bills revealed that our shipper, Servi-Carga, had not known that Girag, the airline they subcontracted to fly our motorcycles, no longer had permission to use the Ecuadorian military cargo planes for transport of cargo into Quito. Ecuador, presumably in an effort to fund some politician's vacation, had been leasing space on military cargo flights. They could only fly cargo out of Quito—specifically flowers. This was grim news. Who could tell how long we might be stranded in Ecuador? To lighten the mood I commented that the world might be a better place if more military planes were used to transport flowers. Another glimmering one-liner that went totally unappreciated by my companions. Savages.

We resorted to what came naturally—we wept like little children with empty cones and melting ice cream on our shoes. No, we actually just switched to tourist mode. As long as we had to wait in Quito, we decided, we should see all there was to see, and then if we still had to wait, we'd make a trip to the Galápagos Islands. For me, that would fulfill an interest I'd had since I first cracked open a biology book and became fascinated by Darwin and his innumerable damn finches.

Rather than hang out some more with my grumpy colleagues, I called Carla, the girl from the airport. She took me on a tour of the sights in Quito Viejo, the older part of town with most of the fabulous churches and stunning Baroque architecture. The churches, of which Quito apparently has six million, are entirely made of marble, and all nonmarble surfaces are gilded, draped with red velvet, littered with fresh flowers, splattered with murals, frescoes, and friezes, and adorned with the bloodiest collection of religious statues ever seen by Western eyes. Every image of Jesus had multiple lacerations and blood pouring from all orifices. To Ecuadorians, a saint isn't really a saint unless he or she sports a bleeding heart, head trauma, multiple bruises, contusions, and a sword sticking out of his or her back. The bloodier the better. Even the portly little cherubs looked as if, at the very least, they'd been smacked around and verbally berated.

The next morning Peter began the calling process all over again: back and forth to Panama and the Quito airport, Servi-Carga, our contractor, and Girag, the shipper.

Servi-Carga in Panama: "There is no flight."

Girag in Quito: "Yes, there is a military cargo plane coming in today."

Servi-Carga: "We retract previous denial of flight, there is a flight but it can't carry cargo."

Girag: "That's not true, there is cargo on that flight."

Servi-Carga: "OK, we can confirm cargo coming to Panama, but that flight can't carry cargo back to Quito."

Girag: "Yes it's true—No cargo coming from Panama because there's no permission to use military planes and no other planes are available. Would we like something shipped from Quito to Panama, flowers perhaps?"

Us: "No, for fuck's sake, we just want our rides."

Them: "Sorry. No permission, no cargo. Please wait until further notice. Thank you for wasting another $120 in phone calls, please bang phone on forehead, repeat as necessary."

We went shopping and purchased a flight from Quito to the Galápagos, via Guayaquil. Young, unwashed Euro travel bums lined the streets, hawking woven leather bracelets and little clay marijuana pipes with gnome faces and dragon heads carved in them. I bought gifts to send to my family back home and Robert bought some more dresses for his wife.

We had plans to go to the Galápagos the next morning, so I went to see a movie with Carla. Apparently Carla had had a somewhat sheltered upbringing. I thought her denial of attending bars and discos when we met was a demurely feigned innocence, an image some Latin women like to portray. But she was, in fact, as pure and sweet as refined Belizean sugar. She even confessed that for a long time she believed she was meant to be a nun. But now she knew she was pre-ordained to have a husband and children. Her eyes opened up wide and soulfully as she told me that last part. Caught off guard, I stammered something like "More popcorn?"

On the way back from the theater I got another scare. Carla and I shared a cab home, first to her place to drop her off, and then to my hotel. Just as we happened to be passing a very bad part of town the cab started having engine trouble. I'd heard of the dangers of using taxis in Quito, of drivers taking tourists to secluded areas where men would climb into the back seat and mug passengers with a gun or a knife. Everyone hears the warnings to avoid walking in certain areas, especially tourist favorites like Calle Morales, a pickpocket and razor-thief alley. (Razor thieves are sneaky, lazy fellows who'd rather not mug people the old-fashioned way, that is, to their faces. Instead they prefer to walk behind backpackers, slicing open the fabric of their bags, and then gathering up the trail of goodies as it spills out.) We'd also been advised not to walk up the path to Mt. Panecillo, where the "Big Virgin" statue stands guard over the city and blissfully waves at all the muggers lying in ambush along the tourist trail.

The time was now 11:30 P.M., the streets were poorly lit, and either our cab was having serious mechanical problems, or the driver was doing a great job faking it. The taxi lurched as the motor stuttered weakly. My blood pumped thickly as we slowed to a crawl up a dark hill. Our driver talked quickly into the radio, too fast for me to understand. I expected some men to come running out from behind a parked car and hop into the cab at any moment. Ever so suavely, I leaned past Carla and locked her door, then my door and the passenger door. The driver apologized to us, explaining that the car had problems. Then he asked me why I locked the doors. There were no street lamps anymore. Our single flickering headlight illuminated tiny stones and broken glass that slowly moved toward us on the road. Suddenly a set of headlights approached from the rear.

I'd already removed my Multi-Tool from the sheath I wore on my belt. During my trip I swear that Multi-Tool got more use than my left hand. It had screwdrivers, files, a saw, vise-grip pliers, and a mean-looking little blade that could snap open with the flick of the thumb. I was now armed, ready for anything, impending panic squeezing lines into my palm where I crushed the tool in a moist grip. I wasn't sure what I planned on doing with it—I thought if anyone tried to jump into the cab I might whip out the blade impressively, hold the driver's head by the hair, and rest the semiserrated edge on his neck while screaming "GO! GO!" in Spanish. Either that or I'd have hooked the can opener under his nose and pressed his face to the ceiling of the car, also while screaming at him to drive. Of course I could've used the old "snap the vise-grip pliers onto the bad guy's right testicle" gag. The beauty of a tool like that is I had options.

Fortunately nobody had to see what my actual response might've been. The car pulled up alongside us, and it proved to be just another harmless cab. Our driver stopped, and the other car's driver got out and opened his door for us. The cavalry had arrived just in time to save us from my delusions. The rest of the ride home was uneventful and disappointingly anticlimactic.

We were shocked to discover the following morning that Girag got the shipping permission granted and our bikes would be sent on the next available flight. Peter's persistence got the ball rolling, but I wondered if there was more to it than that. I'd been noticing for quite some time how people seemed to treat us differently from other travelers. We met fellow bikers all the time in the streets who admired and envied what we were trying to do. Even nonbikers gave us helping hands, and in the case of the shippers in Panama, I think the fact that we were stuck without our bikes motivated them to speed things up. Being motorcyclists separated us from the crowds of normal tourists, and we often received special treatment because of it.

Now we'd finally be able to get our bikes back on the road. We made arrangements to go to customs at the airport the following morning. We also sent home the gifts we'd purchased for our families. In an effort to help save expenses, I offered Robert some room for his purchases in the box I was sending home.

You know how they say no good deed goes unpunished? Well, sure enough, that little attempt at generosity would become another point of separation for Robert and me. In Miami a customs agent opened my package and stole five of the fifteen items I'd sent, and a pair of golden frog earrings that Robert had sent home to his wife.

An earlier attempt at helping Robert was becoming a nightmare as well. I offered my companions the opportunity to forward tires for their bikes to my uncle in Buenos Aires, so they could pick up some fresh rubber when we got there. Peter had a friend in Mendoza, Argentina, that he was shipping his tires to, but as cruel fate would have it, Robert agreed to take me up on my offer. The tires were forwarded from Panama and they arrived in Argentine customs.

Because of a screwup with the name I put on the package, the tires eventually became irretrievable. All my life I've known my uncle by his English nickname, Dick, so it never occurred to me to mail him anything with his full legal name, Ricardo. Because of this oversight, my uncle was unable to get the tires from customs in Argentina. The customs agents wouldn't accept his identification, which read "Ricardo," to retrieve a package that was clearly addressed to someone else. At least not without a serious bribe. Never mind that his last name, Carlstein, is probably the only one of its kind in all of Latin America. There was also the issue of the incredibly high importation taxes. Even if the tires could have been retrieved, they were going to charge him more than their original cost—between two to three hundred dollars—on top of the price that Robert had already paid to buy them and ship them. This would be the most expensive set of tires he'd ever thrown on a bike, if he could even get them at all. Plainly stated, Robert was frustrated and once again I found I was to blame.

That night we celebrated the return of our iron steeds by going out for sushi and dancing with Julia, the beautiful bartender that worked at our hotel. She was twenty-four years old, a little taller than the minimum height requirement for most roller coasters, and had a thick mane of black molasses hair. Peter and I had been wooing her for my benefit over the past few days, and after reviewing my options thus far in Ecuador, Peter candidly advised me: "Drop the nun, Devil-o, that's going nowhere. But Julia, on the other hand, now that woman is something else."

He was right, of course, she was something else, but little did we know how much of something else she was because we'd never seen her dance. At a club downtown, Julia showed us how a Latin woman dances, and moved by pity she tried to teach us to truly salsa, which proved nearly impossible. She'd simply developed beyond our level of coordination. Her abilities were so far advanced from the dyslexic hip gyrations of the white men from the north that she couldn't sufficiently lower the quality or speed of her movement for us to even crudely imitate her. We just weren't equipped properly. She was like a bee slumming around the lower parts of the hive with the wriggling larvae, trying to teach them to fly.

We dropped the lessons and settled into something a bit more familiar—drinking. As usual, Peter treated all of us to the first round. Peter bought more than his fair share of the alcohol on the trip, partly because he drank more than his fair share, and partly because his gregarious "party guy" code demanded it. Whenever we arrived somewhere, invariably he was the first to offer Robert and me a drink. His code was the chivalry of alcohol, the Bushido of booze.

Robert and I each bought another round, but Peter felt extra giving that night. He bought a few more for us, and at some time during the evening we achieved honorary master's degrees in drunken salsa. For a brief span of time we were no longer wriggling larvae, but agile bees, floating on effervescent gossamer wings created by the all-powerful forces of imagination and intoxication, of will and wine. I had to hand it to Robert, despite the language barrier, not to mention the age barrier, he always came out, relaxed in bars filled with people that were generally even younger than me, and as far as I could tell, enjoyed himself.

That evening I asked Julia to leave with me, and she agreed. Robert and Peter went back to the hotel. I often wondered how open-minded my companions' wives must've been to allow them to just ride off on this six-month journey. Had they been different men, they might've been the ones inviting Julia to leave.

Robert had been married to Sandy for over ten years. According to him, she was now used to his need to take motorcycle trips. They often took trips together. Robert told me: "I'd say to her, 'I want to go here for the weekend. Would you like to come?' and if her answer was

yes, we packed up our stuff and went together, and if no, I would go alone, and she'd stay home and do her own thing." For various reasons, one of them health related, Sandy chose not to take this Latin odyssey. Robert once eloquently described his relationship to his wife this way: "We understand each other. I can cook some things that she can't, and she can cook some things that I have no idea how to. And there are some things that we cook together."

Peter's marriage story seemed a little less rosy. He and his wife had been a couple since college, and they had decided to get married a few years before. Contrary to her current position, his wife was all for him taking this motorcycle adventure when he left. But now, his wife sent e-mails that clearly upset him, and when he called home he spent a lot of time consoling her. When Peter began the trip his marriage was unstable, with conflict over where the couple would live and what they'd do with their lives together. Peter was frustrated living in New Mexico, preferring to live near Miami, so that he could more readily fly to visit his family in Colombia. His wife wanted to continue her education and that meant staying somewhere out West. Peter was tired of his job, needed time to think, and when he learned of the opportunity for this trip was excited, yet reluctant, to leave. Peter said that she'd insisted he not miss the opportunity, and eventually, he agreed. They'd parted in a state of marital disequilibrium, and now she was having serious second thoughts. Unbeknownst to Robert and me, Peter was facing a daily conflict between fulfilling his commitment to accompany Robert for the duration, and fulfilling the commitment to his wife.

I awoke a little later than planned and rushed back to the Howard Johnson's, finding a message to "get my ass to the airport," which I did, around 11:30 A.M. Robert was displeased with my late arrival. He told me later that day that I needed to get my priorities straight. I didn't say so to him, but I was pretty sure that I had my priorities all figured out (let's see, go home with two hairy bikers after a night of drinking, or go home with an incredible Latin woman and arrive a little late for the motorcycle reunion—yeah, I'd say I got that one settled, thanks). Peter feigned annoyance with me for Robert's benefit—he had even taken care of all of the paperwork for my bike until I arrived. What a guy.

In every tier of power, there are those that have real authority, and those that beg, claw, and wrestle over the scraps of power those in authority drop off the table. In our trip we saw every variety of petty tyrant; they're as omnipresent as they are unoriginal. These days every guy with a hat or a badge tries to throw his limited weight around, and I'm certain that each successive dealing with one of them permanently saps a small portion of the goodness from the soul of a traveler. We encountered lots of these people in the airport customs offices. Before we could see our bikes, we had to fill out a small phone book of papers while hopping on one foot and smiling politely. Pretty standard. But then we were stopped by a guy withholding a stamp. I don't even remember what his reason was, but he flatly refused to approve our papers. We were at an impasse.

Fortunately Peter saved the day again. While socializing at the hotel bar, he'd met a couple of people who knew a couple of people, one of whom was a colonel that worked at the customs office. Peter's new friends gave him this colonel's name, and when Peter mentioned it, we were able to pay all the fees, get our papers stamped, and have our bikes pulled out of the warehouse with no trouble.

The warehouse was a huge, white, corrugated tin structure with men in coveralls and hard hats shuffling about. Armed with loaner hard hats, we were ushered inside to inspect our crated bikes. Aside from the faint smell of flowers, everything seemed in order. Employees in white hats supervised in perfect petty tyrant unison, while shippers, business people, and other hangers-on watched us with curiosity through the chain-link fence. Everyone positively fevered to see what we had under that crudely wrapped black plastic. Peter was lugging around his repaired front wheel all day, and people wanted to find out what it bolted onto. I'm sure the only reason these people noticed us at all was because they had nothing else to do while waiting around for some jerk with a stamp to hand back their papers. As soon as they saw we just had bikes, and everyone had a chance to ask how much they cost and how fast they went, we were pretty much ignored.

We rode out of there in triumph, all tyrants, stampers, and incompetent shippers behind us. How strange it was to be on the bike again. There was a greater feeling of danger now; South America was more remote and the potential for injury was greater in a large city of bad cab drivers. But this was a great day—we were back on our bikes.

The next morning we left for the Galápagos. We stored our bikes in the hotel garage and took off, just like that. The journey was incredible, and though I won't go into the details here, I encourage anyone even remotely interested in nature, biology, and Darwin to visit. Our return was a bit sad, because it's the kind of place that can alter your perception if you let it, and if you find little furry creatures that aren't afraid to stand two feet from you particularly entertaining, you'll never want to leave. We had to wait an extra day for Peter to come back, because he couldn't fly for twenty-four hours. After scuba diving in high-pressure water he was at risk of getting a nitrogen gas embolism in his blood from ascending too quickly to the altitudes that planes frequent.

While waiting for Peter's return, Robert and I went to the Banco Central de Ecuador Museo Nacional, which had a fine selection of pre-Colombian art and artifacts including an amazing array of musical rocks. The rocks were roughly the size and shape of newspapers folded in half, and they hung in a row of five. When rapped with a xylophone striker, they let out five distinct, clear notes. Amazing. What impressed me most was not that their creators had cut and formed the rocks for this purpose, or even that they were among the oldest musical instruments known, but that the archaeologists who found them were actually able to conclude what these rocks were used for. The museum also had lots of religious artwork: more bleeding saints and bitch-slapped cherubs.

The following day I lay sick in bed and watched old war movies between sprints to the bathroom. Robert and Peter decided to take a ride up to Mitad del Mundo, the landmark of the equator just north of Quito. They were to have a half-day excursion, but they didn't make it back until nearly dinnertime. They entered the room covered in dried sweat and road dirt. "How was the middle of the earth?" I asked.

"I don't want to talk about it." Robert said. Peter just looked at me, then fell flat on his back on the bed.

"What the hell happened to you two?"

"It's all his fault!" Robert laughed. He held his white leather gloves in one hand and shook them furiously in Peter's direction.

"How can it be my fault?" Peter said. "You were the one that chose to follow, I didn't make you come after me."

" 'Let's ride down the trail into this volcano,' he said, 'it doesn't look that steep,' he said, 'Come on, Santa, don't be a candy ass,' he said," Robert muttered to himself as Peter walked into the bathroom chuckling. Peter rushed back out a few seconds later.

"Christ, Devil-o, what did you kill in there?"

I later learned that Robert and Peter had found the landmark at the Mitad del Mundo, and after shooting the requisite equator photos, began looking for something else to do. They discovered a trail leading down into an old volcanic crater, which was overgrown with jungle plants and populated by a small number of Ecuadorians. Peter led the way, and they began working their bikes down the narrow path until they realized it was much steeper and more difficult to negotiate than it first appeared. Having come too far to turn back, they had to slowly walk the bikes down the trail one by one. They carefully descended, nearly sending the bikes crashing down the inside wall of the crater as they lost their footing several times. Eventually they reached the bottom, and since they didn't know the area, it looked as if they would have to get the bikes flown out by helicopter. Finally they found a road out, after meeting some interesting crater people. They bought sodas from an old woman who'd been born in the crater and supposedly never left it to see the outside world. They also met a ranger who hit them up for a bribe for "illegally entering" the crater. I never really wondered how one could illegally enter a crater, but if I had to pick someone that would be capable of such a feat, my choice would definitely have been Peter.

Finally it was time to get moving again. The sun was shining and the road south to Ambato was straight. A cop passed us on a trashed Moto Guzzi—the saddlebags and fairing were scratched and dented, and the rear tire flapped around dangerously. He flew by us at 75 MPH, apparently untroubled by the disrepair of his bike.

We were delayed because a bicycle race was in progress. Some roads were closed completely, and we had to wait at an intersection for about twenty minutes while traffic slowly passed the blockade for the racers. After clearing the bottleneck we rode quickly through expansive hills and forests of trees that looked like a cross between a palm and a birch. They had huge fat fronds and long strips of bark that peeled from the trunk like sheets of papyrus. Along the way we passed the barracks of the Ecuadorian Special Forces, and signs warned us not to take photos of the giant statue of a soldier in a special forces uniform.

Following a long gravel drive lined with trees, we pulled up in front of a regal white estate house, overlooked by Mt. Cotopaxi, the world's highest active volcano. At just under 20,000 feet, the volcano is an austere and menacing backdrop that is woven into the history of the incredible guest house we stayed in. Built in 1580, La Ciénega has been declared an historical monument by the Banco Central de Ecuador. The wonderful old mansion has been converted into a hotel, and has numerous rooms with antique furniture and paintings. The garden in back was filled with expansive agave plants, palms, and dozens of the off-white pitchers of calla lilies. Most impressive was the chapel, bearing a spectacular set of nine-foot-tall, hand-carved doors.

Over the centuries, La Ciénega has housed several important political figures in the history of Ecuador, including former presidents and heroes of the Ecuadorian revolution against the Spanish. While climbing nearby Mt. Pichincha to explore its crater, French explorer and scientist Charles-Marie de La Condamine witnessed the eruption of Mt. Cotopaxi on June 15, 1742. Intrigued, he stayed in La Ciénega on several occasions while observing the nearby volcano. Perhaps the most famous mind to visit La Ciénega was Baron Alexander von Humboldt. He visited the mansion while carrying out his study of Cotopaxi in 1802. Educated in the glow of the Berlin enlightenment, von Humboldt typified the Renaissance man. Zoology, sociology, botany, art, literature, cartography, and exploration were but a few of his talents and interests. Von Humboldt's trip to the Americas was the first of its kind for a Westerner, pursued solely for the purpose of research and lacking any political agenda. He hoped to find "proof of the working together of all the forces of nature as a whole." He performed countless investigations and explorations, charting unknown regions of the

Americas, cataloguing thousands of plants and animals, and even measuring the ocean current along the west coast of the Americas, now known as the Humboldt Current.

That night we huddled under our sheets in our freezing room, unable to sleep because our bodies shivered to keep warm. "You know, that woman we met in the crater yesterday," Peter said, "she must've been at least seventy-five years old, and she told me she was born in the crater, spent all her life there, and planned on dying there. She never set foot outside that freaking crater."

"Yeah," Robert added, "for a while there I thought we weren't going to leave it either."

The next day we rode through Ambato on our way to Mt. Chimborazo, the highest mountain in Ecuador. The steep hills seemed to sprout buildings in prolific tufts of concrete, clustered together like dozens of matchboxes shoved into sand. The structures all had tinted windows to protect the inhabitants from high-altitude solar radiation—from this distance the dark glass gave the impression that all the windows had been blown out and the buildings were gutted by explosions and fire.

The gravel pass we hoped to take was supposedly blocked by a recent avalanche. All attempts to persuade my companions to try the road anyway failed. They felt they'd seen enough adventure in the crater, so I dropped the issue. Besides, I knew I couldn't win any arguments with them that day since they were still grumpy over the coffee I spilled on them at breakfast.

Our alternate route on the Pan Am Highway was mostly paved and docile. On our steady ascent we passed smooth cultivated hills with rectangular plots of different crops, which decorated the land like a giant quilt with patches of forest green, aquamarine, canary yellow, lime green, and brown. We passed squalid buildings in tiny towns. Stacks of old tires lay in front of some of the houses, the word *Vulcanizadora* hand-painted on them. Squat Indian women plodded along between these dismal places, dressed in black and bright red clothes, sporting gray, brown, or black fedoras. They walked along the road hauling loads so large they would've been laughable, if the sight didn't fill one with pity over how hard their lives must be. Native women of all ages carried the loads of firewood, vicuña wool, or food like human pack mules. I noticed one in particular; she looked about forty years old (their hard lives seem to age them prematurely, making their true ages tough to gauge). She was carrying a huge load in a burlap bag on her back, a baby on her front, and was spinning wool in her hands as she walked—a model of efficiency.

"Come on, hurry up and take the photo," Peter said. He and Robert posed next to the bikes at a scenic roadside while wild vicuña wandered around behind them. The tufts of grass and scrub and the utter lack of trees due to the high elevation reminded me of some of the islands I saw in the Galápagos. I lined up the camera on its miniature tripod, and when I jogged back for the photo I found that Peter and Robert had placed old llama jaws and small stones in artful piles on my plastic saddlebags. Robert completed the sculpture with a big rock on my top case. They smiled strangely as they performed this ceremony, looking at me the whole time. Sometimes spending too much time alone on the roads can instill a kind of madness. Especially when those in question don't live too far from the crazy side of town in the first place.

We shortly found ourselves near the climbers' base camp of Chimborazo without a badge-toting tyrant in sight. Normally a fee had to be paid to enter, but since nobody was around, we just went the rest of the way to the top. There were no more plants at this altitude. There weren't even any lichens—only rocks, gravel, sand, and one huge, white-capped peak. For fun I tried cut in front of Peter at a switchback by skirting straight up the hill, but the sandy earth gave no purchase and spun out from underneath my back tire in a great ten-foot arc until I was buried up past my rims.

At the top of the hill we found the *refugio* where climbers camp and plan their ascent of the mountain. Like an act of the photographic gods, the thick fog and clouds gave way, allowing us thirty minutes for shooting the peak. The moon was clearly visible, parked above Chimborazo's dome in the daytime sky, and for many miles off in the distance clouds floated at eye level. We got our photos just in time. As we came off the mountain and walked back to the parking lot, we found hordes of teenage tourists from Guayaquil, students on a field trip, climbing all over our bikes. Nothing can take away the sense of accomplishment you get from riding some lonesome, difficult trail to a beautiful reward like Chimborazo more than having a busload of tourists pull up behind you. We rode back down to the main road, and since we were traveling downhill I took all the shortcuts, just for fun. I rode straight down the mountain over rocks, ruts, and single-track vicuña trails. Let's see a tour bus do that.

In a couple of days we were at the ruins of Inga Pirca, which were well preserved and an excellent preview for some of the great Incan sites we'd see in Peru. The Posada Inga Hotel provided us with refuge and dinner for the evening, as well as conversation by the fire. We met a group of tourists, two vacationing couples and their two guides. One of the guides was named Segundo, the Ecuadorian version of "Junior." Segundo told us of the strange names invented by some of the uneducated peoples that live along the coast. They wanted their kids to have grand titles, so they named them after things that impressed them, such as products like Coca-Cola or Alka-Selzer, or gave them impressive-sounding names they dreamed up themselves, such as "Semen of the Gods."

We made fast time over the next couple of days. In Cuenca, the third-largest city in Ecuador, we stopped to check out the main cathedral being prepared for a festival. Some soldiers had built a cross out of guns and ammo belts and balanced a camouflage helmet on top of the uppermost bayonet. I had to look away from the completely incongruous construction. Symbolism overload.

As we rode to Machala, we took a turn onto a road that petered out of pavement and became narrow dirt. Rough mountainous cliffs crept up in the distance, their tops covered with green forest, looking like moss on jagged bits of wood. Clouds painted shadows across the rough terrain and formed dark, shifting patterns. The pavement returned, and we sharply descended as we accelerated and raced between red cliffs that shot up more than thirty feet perpendicular from the road on either side, like bloodied walls. The merely passable road had now become a motorcyclist's dream, perfectly paved and civilized, wavy as the silhouette of a 1950s starlet, built for 80 MPH curve-burning. The dream ended with DANGER signs, and we were once again slowed up over more bad roads.

After stopping for a military checkpoint we continued to Machala, where we decided to attempt the border crossing to Peru. The timing would be tight, but we thought we could finish and find a hotel on the Peruvian side of the border before nightfall. We found a new wave of heat in the lowlands, and the vegetation reflected it. Deciduous forest gave way to tall grasses and banana trees, as the mountains were beaten back by the remarkably flat terrain. This seemed like an entirely different country. The sky looked as though a pane of clear glass divided the spotless blue top from the bottom, and on the bottom half, huge tufts of cotton were glued to, and dangling from, the imaginary glass.

At Immigration we were stuck behind a busload of tourists. Unlike other borders, the various stamp points were separated by kilometers instead of meters. We waited in line behind all the tourists, and as soon as we were cleared we rushed to beat the bus to the next stamp point.

Gonzalo Castro, a pudgy, mild-mannered guy about sixty years old, saved us hours of waiting by processing our paperwork personally. We were already on our way to Peru while people who'd been waiting in line ahead of us were still sitting in his office. That's how it went sometimes—occasionally we ran into people that just wanted to help us out, with no explanation or compensation required.

On the Peruvian side, money changers hounded me. I had the equivalent of about $100 in Ecuadorian sucres, and they offered the worst exchange rate I'd seen to date. They wanted one-fifth of my Ecuadorian currency to give me the rest in Peruvian. Finally, one offered me a reasonable rate for dollars, until I saw he was trying to give me a fake $100 bill. Feeling simultaneously insulted and amused, I explained to him that if he planned on fooling United States citizens he'd should make sure he knew what United States currency looked like, because we sure do. After that I just ignored them and made plans to change the money somewhere else later.

Finally we made it to the Peruvian customs office, where the young woman inside was efficient and professional. She told us we needed *tripticos*, or vehicle bonds, in order to pass. The triptico is one of several ways countries try to prevent vehicles brought into the country from being resold there. *Libreta, carnet de passage*, and triptico are all terms well-known among foreign motorists in Latin America. Each is some form of deposit put on the vehicle, varying from roughly $150 for a libreta in Venezuela to a sum equal or greater than the value of the vehicle for some carnets. Depending on where a vehicle is bought, it can be sold at a great profit in Latin America, especially if you can avoid the hefty import duties and taxes. Of course, to sell a vehicle without paying these fees is illegal. Governments in Latin America don't like anybody making a nice profit without them getting a cut, so that's why vehicle bonds exist. We'd opted early on not to bother with any of the vehicle bonds. They were a tremendous hassle, and most of the people we'd read about had never really needed them down here anyway. As we climbed back on our bikes and fired them up to leave, we asked the young lady if she thought we might have a problem in Peru without a triptico. "I hope not," she replied.

10

The Desecrator of Chan Chan

➤ WE RODE INTO THE PERUVIAN DESERT, past thick underbrush, irrigated lowlands, and mountainous dunes that seemed as though giant B-movie ants could come crawling from them any second. Mats of dead gray scrub covered everything. Any stationary objects with height—trees, fences, telephone poles, even sand dunes—had been grown over and suffocated by the plants in their struggle for access to light. The rainy season deluges that catalyzed their rapid growth now long gone, the dead plants were just one more hazy gray tone in the desert, as far as the squinted eye could see.

Down the sandy highway we rode, through beige towns over dusted asphalt, until we sprinted along the coast, paced by the ocean. Robert led, and Peter and I alternated our places behind him. In contrast to the dry desert air, a thick fog covered the ocean water. Soon we encountered the Hotel Punta Sal, with a mock Spanish galleon in its center. There was a pleasant beach, but the place was devoid of life save for the mosquitoes. During the night the hotel's power shut off, and when my ceiling fan stopped moving, the mosquitoes found easy purchase and left no patch of skin unbitten.

Getting bitten was more than just an annoyance. It could have ended my trip and possibly my life. Malaria is caused by the Plasmodium parasites that inhabit certain strains of mosquito. The parasite spends part of its life cycle in a human host, specifically in the liver and bloodstream, and part in the female mosquito. The symptoms of malaria in humans can easily be confused with other illnesses: nausea, fever, diarrhea, and headache. The disease causes near-fatal bouts that repeat cyclically and bring a victim closer to death with each relapse. If untreated, malaria will usually kill every host it infects, both human and mosquito. Fortunately there are treatments, but by far the best treatment is to never have gotten the illness at all.

I'd only brought a few malaria pills with me from the United States. There were two kinds available to me before I left: mefloquine, known for causing delusions and semipsychotic fantasies in some subjects, and chloroquine, which was less effective with certain strains of malaria, but had no loopy side effects. I'd repeatedly been told that both varieties were readily available in Central and South America, but this was not the case. In fact, mefloquine, the more effective of the two, was nowhere to be found. Before I left the United States I bought a small supply of the drug for nine dollars per pill, way too expensive. Believing the rumors that malaria pills grew on trees in Latin America seemed like a pretty good option at the time. My supply lasted through most of Central America, and I wasn't worried while we were in the mountains of Colombia and Ecuador because mosquitoes don't thrive in high altitudes. But now mosquitos were everywhere. I was unhappy at having inadequate protection in a place crawling with blood-sucking death-injectors. Flying home in a delirious fever with little protozoan orgies erupting in my liver didn't seem the ideal way to end the trip. This was not a problem for either Robert or Peter, because they both were able to get enough mefloquine pills pretty cheaply before they left.

The next morning I wanted to make good time to the next sizable town so I could buy my pills. Unfortunately, we encountered a cus-

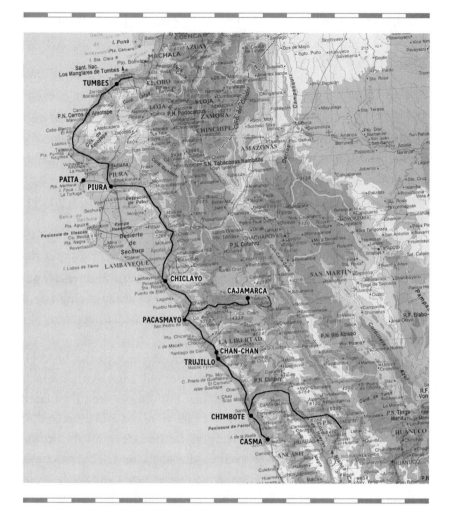

toms checkpoint six miles down the road. A man that looked like a burly professional wrestler in green fatigues came out to greet us. He said we didn't have the proper documentation for the bikes, and despite all our protests he sent us over 100 miles back to the border to get them. Robert was not happy. Even Peter wasn't joking. The customs lady was shocked and embarrassed when we came back, because she forgot to give us the temporary importation stickers we needed.

She apologized awkwardly until we left. One hundred miles back to the checkpoint, the beefy customs official waved us through, and we were finally, legally, on our way.

We'd blown half the day and done 270 miles of riding but had only netted an hour further south. In Piura we stayed at the Rio Verde Hotel, one of the nicer places we'd seen, with a pretty garden and deer running around the grounds. We ate grilled lobster and crab cakes for dinner, and Robert treated us to a bottle of wine. I wrote another e-mail update and looked for malaria pills until late in the evening. There was a hospital in town claiming to have them, but the hospital pharmacy wouldn't open until morning.

Was I finally going to find the pills? The following morning we started about ninety minutes later than planned because I went to the hospital to find out. Finding the place was a nightmare and when I got back Peter was really annoyed. He accused me of always being late. I told him to fuck off because I needed the pills, which, much to our mutual aggravation, I still hadn't found.

We rode past miles of shrubs that looked like gigantic broccoli heads toward Paita, a port town five centuries old. Apparently it hasn't changed much in that time. The colonial buildings were dilapidated and blowing apart in the wind. The boats were old and clustered to the shore like grimy soap scum clinging to the side of a tub. On the way to Chiclayo we stopped to see the ruins of Tucume. The structures were built from weak mud bricks, which were pitted and washed out from erosion and the attacks of tomb raiders looking for valuables.

Upon leaving the ruins I met three travelers in a massive tourist vehicle, which was as big as a dump truck with three-foot-tall wheels. The beast had the capacity to hold fifteen people, but all the tourists were conspicuously absent. There was a driver, a guide, and Philip, the only tourist. The drivers explained that the truck was brand-new; the cab and frame had just arrived in Quito, where the trailer was added. Now that it was assembled they were taking it on a test run to La Paz, where they hoped to pick up more passengers—their plan was to continue south to the millennium party in Ushuaia, Argentina. "See you there," I replied.

Chiclayo wasn't far. We approached a ruined bridge up ahead, and we were forced to ford the wide, shallow stream that had overflowed the detour. Several vehicles were parked in the middle of the rushing water, and their owners scrubbed them and threw buckets of soapy water over the hoods. The long main road led us to the nicest hotel in town, the Gran Hotel Chiclayo, which doubled as a casino, and we burned some cash there over the next two nights, especially Peter, who in an outbreak of electronic poker fever kept pounding the buttons and shouting "Double it, double it!"

One of Chiclayo's greatest attractions is the famous Lord of Sipan exhibit, centered on what is believed to be an ancient Mochica ruler buried near the present-day town of Sipan, in the valley of Lambeyeque. The Moche were an advanced pre-Incan culture, and the burial of their former ruler is seventeen centuries old. When the dig began in 1987, the impressive collection of gold and silver treasures seemed comparable in quality and quantity to some of the burials of the great pharaohs of Egypt. How the Lord of Sipan escaped the *huaqueros* and looters that have ravaged nearly every other burial site in Peru is unknown. The museum had stunning displays of artifacts, including gold, pottery, and beaded jewelry.

The Lord of Sipan was known far and wide in his day; his tomb held Chilean lapis lazuli and seashells from the coast of Ecuador. Nearby were more than one thousand pottery jars filled with tributes. Apparently it was good to be king, but not so good to be a close associate, since several of his people were buried with him to keep him company in death, including a few women, a small boy, and two dogs. A warrior and a standard-bearer also went with him, one on each side of his coffin for protection. To ensure that his guards didn't lose heart and run away from whatever dangers the master faced in the afterlife, they were interred with their feet removed. All of his companions were presumed to have been buried alive.

Next we moved on to the ruins where the Señor de Sipan was found. Desolate tent concessions sold soda and crackers near the parking lot, and the vendors' shoeless children wandered between us repeating "I'll watch your bike, I'll watch your bike." The kids said this phrase over and over for minutes on end in a maddening Gregorian monotone. Their persistence paid off, but not exactly how they'd have liked. Peter finally gave the job to guard his bike to the only one who wasn't annoying us, a young girl quietly watching all the commotion. He was hoping they'd learn from the example and not be so aggravating, but this act only renewed their vigor and they pressured Robert and me even harder. I became deaf, and when they saw Robert replace a pen into his map case the chant became: "A pen for school, a pen for school."

The site was impressive, with a reconstruction of the burial contents, right down to hundreds of fake clay jars. As we were leaving, the enormous white tourist tank I saw earlier pulled up behind us, with Philip the lonely tourist and his two guides. We greeted them on our way out and headed back to the hotel for a day of Zenless motorcycle maintenance.

The following morning we visited Cajamarca, the town that witnessed the final push that felled one of South America's greatest cultures—the Inca. The tale of the collapse of the Inca is a fascinating account of the power of religion and the lure of gold—a story of bravery, greed, treachery, and a bad interpreter. The story has many versions, depending on who tells it. Here's some of what I uncovered, most of it taken from Garcilaso's *History of the Inca*.

After several years of failed landings on the western shores of South America, Francisco Pizarro, one of a triumvirate of ambitious old Spanish farts, decided to attempt the conquest of an entire continent with a few hundred soldiers, a few dozen horses, and a boatload of rusty weapons. His first efforts at landing on shore earned him hails of arrows, resulting in multiple casualties. One of his two cohorts, Diego de Almagro, who later becomes Pizarro's bitterest enemy, lost an eye to an Indian arrow. Pizarro himself was struck seven times but still lived.

They landed at Tumbez, and Pizarro fought battles on the continent against extreme numbers. He took the small island of Puna, and there found a translator who the Spanish called Felipe. Felipe's knowledge of the Spaniards' language was terribly lacking (he'd only just met them), as was his ability to speak other dialects commonly used on the mainland. Pizarro's party took Felipe with them and continued the conquest.

Unbeknownst to the conquistadors, the Incan empire was ripe for overthrow. There were internal jealousies between the two current Incan rulers, both sons of the late Huaina Capac, the last great Inca. Huascar, the rightful Inca, ruled the south from Cuzco, until the day the northern armies of Atahualpa, his half-brother, defeated him and took him prisoner.

Enter the Spanish. The Inca were no fools, and were aware that the Spanish ships had been patrolling the waters offshore during the reign of Huaina Capac. Huaina believed that the ships held the *Viracocha*, a race of semidivine beings whose coming would bring about the end of the empire. Pizarro's greatest asset, of which he was unaware, was the strength of the Incas' religious and political systems, and the faith they placed in their leaders. Huaina told his people that the Incan reign would end with him. And when an Inca spoke, the people believed.

The Spaniards were no fools either. They realized the intimidating effect they had on the Indian peoples and made every effort to capitalize on it. Furthermore, they saw that the Incan empire was completely dependent on its ruler to function. If they removed the head, they reasoned, the body would quickly collapse.

In their typically bold style, the Spanish agreed to meet with Atahualpa and his contingent of five thousand personal bodyguards in the mountain citadel of Cajamarca. Diplomacy was probably not their true intention, as evidenced by the fact that they hid members of their party in ambush around the area. Regardless, any attempts at peaceful negotiation were made impossible by the incompetence of their translator, Felipe. The Dominican chaplain to the expedition, Friar Francisco de Valverde, approached Atahualpa and attempted to explain how a faraway Spanish king had a sovereign claim over everything and everyone that the Spanish happened upon, including Atahualpa, his wealth, and all his subjects. If that line of reasoning wasn't hard enough for the Inca to follow, Felipe the lousy translator misinterpreted everything.

One can imagine the argument that ensued, but one can hardly imagine how 160 conquistadors rushed from their hiding places to defeat five thousand armed Incan warriors. Supposedly Atahualpa gave orders that none were to strike out against the Spaniards. When an Inca commanded, the people obeyed. That, perhaps, is the only reasonable explanation for how such small numbers were not completely overwhelmed by the Incan forces. Most of Atahualpa's guard fled for their lives, and others shielded his litter with their bodies and were cut down in turn as the Spanish cleaved their way to the Incan leader.

In Cajamarca we entered the small building where the captured Atahualpa offered the Spaniards his famous ransom. In the very room we stood, Atahualpa pleaded for mercy, and then drew a line above his head, high on the wall of his stone cell. In exchange for his life, he said, he'd fill the room once with gold and twice with silver. I traced my fingertips along the rough wall; it felt cool and moist. I wondered if Atahualpa noticed how cold the stones were.

The Spanish waited impatiently for Atahualpa to fulfill his promise, partly disbelieving what he offered was even possible. Meanwhile, fearing Huascar might regain his freedom and reclaim the throne, Atahualpa ordered his men in Sausa, by word of mouth, to kill his Inca brother.

Atahualpa actually didn't survive to realize his bid for freedom. Just before he filled the room a second time with silver, the Spanish convicted him in what amounted to a mock trial for the death of Huascar and for plotting a revolt against the Spanish. The trial's official

interpreter was none other than our boy Felipe, who by now had fallen for one of Atahualpa's many wives and was eager for a chance to get rid of his royal competition. Felipe supposedly fabricated a story of Atahualpa's revolt plans in an effort to rapidly make his new lover a widow. Atahualpa was found guilty and advised to convert to Christianity by a few of the Spanish who had befriended him. In a humiliating ceremony he revoked for all time his former way of life, and was then hanged by the neck until dead. He suffered less than most, since any pagan Inca that dared cross the Spanish was usually burned alive, such as the guard that watched over Huascar and eventually killed him. So ended the lives of the last heirs to the Incan throne, and so ended the Inca empire.

While in Cajamarca we stayed at the most unique and rustic hotel I've ever seen. La Hacienda San Vincente, as it was called, was an entire building made from roughly hewn wood and stucco walls painted rose and peach. All the furniture was formed from varnished tree limbs, with knots, bends, bark, and all. Huge supporting trunks jutted out of the walls, and instead of being cleaved off and planed to match the surfaces, their gnarled ends were left polished and thrusting out in all directions. Lampshades were stick frames wrapped in horsehide. Rocks poked out from wall panels, apparently placed there solely for aesthetics. Pieces of logs and stones were selected for their shape and texture and displayed in random corners, becoming works of art. A single room cost just ten dollars, greasy dinner included, so we all got some privacy for a change with separate rooms.

Robert and I were up and packed before breakfast, and when I came downstairs I noticed a group of teenagers outside. They had obviously been celebrating all night and were still drinking beer straight from the pitchers. Peter wasn't up so I knocked on his door, reminding him we had to leave. "Fuck that!" Peter croaked painfully through the door. "I was partying late. Leave without me." It seemed Peter had been kept up by the noise of the festivities and decided it was better to share their beer and guitar by the fire, rather than to lie in bed sleepless.

I slipped a piece of paper with the name of a hotel in Trujillo under Peter's door before Robert and I rode off alone towards Cajabamba. We bounced along a very poor dirt track covered in washboards. Nothing is more annoying to ride. The constant bumping of a washboard-covered road restricts your speed and beats the crap out of both rider and vehicle, and as your brain gets throttled you lose the ability to calculate how many essential bolts may be vibrating off your motorcycle. By 9:30 A.M. Robert and I had had enough of riding in second gear. We didn't feel like putting up with two more days of that, so we turned back and took a more direct route to Trujillo.

This road was spectacular. We curved and wound along the twisted path that a river had carved down the mountain. The road spun along a cliff side, occasionally twisting under menacing rock overhangs that blocked the sun. Near Pacsmayo we stopped for lunch at a roadside restaurant. The parking lot was full of cars covered with sponsorship stickers, some sporting special exhausts, four-point harnesses, competition suspensions, and who knew what else. An amateur road rally was in progress. For the first time on our trip we didn't look out of place carrying helmets—inside we asked for service and the restaurant owner told us to wait until we'd finished the race. We explained that we were just motorcyclists passing through, and he apologized and brought us plates of duck, rice, and fried potatoes right away.

A portly woman walked up to our table from the crowd and introduced herself. She said she came from Trujillo for the race, which was being held in memory of her brother, an amateur racer that had passed away a couple of years before. She also invited us to enter the rally if we wanted. Robert and I looked at each other, eyebrows raised. "We could leave the Givi bags in a corner here and come back and pick them up when we're done," I said. Robert shrugged his shoulders as if to say, "I'm game." We thought better of it, politely declined, and continued on our way.

The sun was brilliant, and I saw some little kids sitting on the side of the road playing in the smoldering embers of a fire. They were squatting in the blackened dirt, doing God knows what as the smoke curled around their heads. The road became rough and unpaved, winding down a hill, sawing its way back and forth along the mountain. There was a straighter path that didn't look too bad and I decided to take the shortcut. I rode straight down the hill, bouncing and rocking the bike, occasionally putting a foot down for balance. I gained a lead on Robert, and I also passed a lumbering bus, the only other vehicle on the road. I found such occasional wild shortcuts a nice off-road diversion from the typical day's riding.

About forty feet down the hill, I felt the right side of the bike abruptly shift in weight. The mounting bracket for my saddlebag had come loose, and my heavy saddlebag was suddenly dangling from just a single mounting point. I pulled over to inspect the damage as the big bus passed, and Robert soon came up behind me.

There were six mounting points on that Givi system—three on each side of the bike. On the KLR 650, one of the mounting points actually uses the turn signal housing for support. The second mounting arm on my racks had broken some time ago, and with that added stress the nut holding the turn signal had finally come loose. The mount then bounced free, cut the turn signal wires, and the entire signal housing was severed from the bike and fell off. And that's why my saddlebag had suddenly started dragging along on the ground. No problem, I thought, I can just pick up the fallen signal, throw it back on, splice the severed wires, and we'll be on our way. I'd deal with the second mounting point later.

Robert went looking for my turn signal while I inspected the bike. He came back a few minutes later, slowly dismounted, and solemnly handed me one of his big white gloves. They had long gauntlets and looked just like something a pirate would wear. Inside his glove was my turn signal, or what remained of it, after the bus had ridden over it. The part was utterly demolished, just plastic shards and a metal stump. All that open road and the signal had to fall directly under the path of the bus.

I temporarily rigged the thing as best I could and we hit the open desert again. We zipped along the sandy roads and passed a couple of guys riding two-up on a 600cc sport bike. A few moments later they passed us right back at high speed. These guys liked to play. I took one look at Robert over my shoulder and he seemed to know what I was thinking. In a statement for dual-sport riders everywhere, we blew past that sport bike on the straight desert road and didn't let up until they quit trying to catch us.

The outer limits of Trujillo were two long miles of depressing shacks and mud brick houses with corrugated tin doors. Some huts were just four sticks shoved into the ground as corners, and plastic tarps stretched between them for walls. People actually lived there.

For a change I was leading into town, and I dutifully took Robert the wrong way down a one-way street. A motorcycle cop pulled us over. He was a pudgy little man with a helmet brim low over his eyes and black aviator sunglasses. I knew right away he wanted a bribe; the stink of corruption oozed from this person. He pretended that we had done something very, very bad, and I pretended not to understand as much Spanish as I do. I talked and talked, wasting time and trying to be only partially comprehensible, while he continually tried to explain to me that we went the wrong way down a one-way street. "Yes," I said obliviously, "we came one way all the way from Cajamarca!"

"No, no, no," he said, pointing. "You two drove your motorcycles this way. It goes that way."

"Oh, I see," I pulled out a map and pointed to it. "You mean we should've come this way from Cajamarca?" He looked at me like I was mentally retarded. Suddenly there was lot of honking and noise; a bus had stopped at an odd angle down the road. The cop, sensing a crime (or potential bribe) was in progress, hopped on his bike, warned us to stay where we were, and sped off down the road the way we'd come—the wrong way down the one-way street.

Robert looked at me for an explanation. "I think he told us to stay here, but he might have meant that we are free to go," I said. "But if we are free to go, we'd better hurry." Robert caught my drift, and we sped off toward the Hotel Peregrino, our meeting point with Peter.

The following morning found us just north of Trujillo at the ruins of Chan Chan, the greatest city of the ancient Moche culture and the world's largest complex of adobe structures. But since I never read the guidebooks I had to learn that the hard way. We visited the interior of the site and then followed some roads that led behind the main complex; Robert and Peter wanted to have a further look around.

While chasing the tire tracks around the site, we drove up onto a little ridge for a better look. Peter rode his bike up onto a still higher ridge, and I waited behind Robert. "Aren't you going to follow Peter?" I asked Robert, and he replied something that I didn't quite hear (probably because I always rode with earplugs) but I took as a "no." He pointed to the ground as he spoke, and I thought he was saying something about his front tire and that he didn't want to go up there. Shame on you Santa, I thought, afraid of a little off-roading. So I followed Peter, we rode over the little hill surrounding some small irrigated fields, which we circled, and then we rode up over another ridge and went to catch up with Robert, who'd already exited the other way.

Robert seemed pissed. Great, now what? I thought. Peter followed Robert but I wanted some alone time, so I rode off in another direction, came around some trails to the highway, and met up with them there. "Have you done enough damage?" Robert asked me. I didn't understand what he was getting at, so I ignored him, which was becoming the only method of dealing with him when he got this way. We headed for the town of Huacachuco, famous for the supposedly traditional all-reed fishing boats, which are now actually made of reeds wrapped around very nontraditional Styrofoam. We stopped for lunch, and the occasional group stress we experienced, never too far away from our party, was now manifesting itself like an evil spirit.

"I can't believe you guys were ignorant enough to ride on the ruins," Robert said, eyes flaring. Peter passively nodded his head in agreement. I looked up at Robert from my seafood and rice, a crusty, buttered roll in my hand and confusion on my face. What the hell was he complaining about now? Seemingly reading my mind, he said, "I told you that you shouldn't have ridden off the trail because it crossed part of the ruins." I realized that he'd been pointing at the ground, not at his bike, and that he must've been saying we shouldn't ride off the trail because it crossed part of the ruins. Since I hadn't actually heard him I assumed he was wimping out over getting dirty, and I roared off without asking him to repeat himself. The grassy hills around the irrigated fields were actually crumbled, overgrown, ancient adobe walls. Peter and I had ridden over them twice.

Just when I thought I was done pulling rookie jackass maneuvers, I was back at it again. But since I had no idea of the vastness of the ruins, I couldn't have known that the area we explored was part of the site. After all, the land was being irrigated and prepared for crops, as if privately owned. Who plants crops on top of ancient ruins? What had started out as a normal day suddenly got a lot worse. I've always hated people who come to a ruin or ancient temple and scribble their names or moronic statements across some clean, well-preserved wall, forever proclaiming their ignorance and disrespect. And to think I might have done more damage with my bike than those idiots with penknives could ever have done! I consoled myself later that at least the only part I might have damaged was the walls I rode over at first with Peter, because every other place I rode had tracks laid down before me. Even those walls we scaled were not really walls, but had become hills, long since covered with dead grass and sand. They could not have suffered too much from the passing of two bikes. Or so I hoped. Regardless, for the next few weeks Peter admonishingly referred to me as "the desecrator of Chan Chan."

The next day we visited the famous Casinelli Museum, a diverse collection of ancient Mohica and Chimu pottery, one of the best in Peru, and surely one of the few museums of its caliber run from the basement of a gas station. There were earthen jars and pottery in shapes anthropomorphic, architectural, mythological, vegetable, animal, divine, and instrumental. Deformities and sicknesses were represented: harelips, dwarfism, hyperthyroidism, as well as maimed and injured people. Skeleton figurines were everywhere, dancing, sitting, and engaging in sex, some with other skeletons and some with figurines of living people. An amazing variety of sexual positions were represented. Every aspect of these ancient peoples' lives was recorded in their pottery, including (based on their disproportionate endowments) their considerable fantasies. Archaeologists believe that perhaps the pottery acted as a visual form of record keeping.

Our tour guide in the museum was a portly older man. He was squat and bore a white five o'clock shadow, a pair of chins, and huge horn-rimmed glasses yellow with age. His gray hair was slick and he smelled of mothballs. Our guide had some interesting farfetched theories. He believed nearly every aspect of world culture was represented in this pottery, created before Jesus was born, and that the people had imagined and represented all the races of the world, including figures that looked Asian, Caucasian, and Negroid. Then, as his coup de grâce, he showed us one that looked like the typical bug-eyed, bald-domed alien and claimed that the ancient peoples may have come into contact with extraterrestrials as well. That's about the time that I wandered off to check out the pottery alone.

That afternoon I looked for a shop to fix my broken saddlebag rack, and found a small auto repair garage around the corner from the hotel that could do it. The shop was just three walls and a sliding door, with a giant pit in the floor over which the cars stood while mechanics worked underneath. I parked next to the pit, and Jorge, the owner, in a Hawaiian shirt stained with grease and dust, tackled my problem. His pregnant wife Rose Marie and his twelve-year-old son assisted. I noticed that his son had a stumped index finger, perhaps a result of helping out around the dangerous shop. In the back two skinny older men and a pudgy matron stuffed wads of padding into the seat of VW beetle.

On the wall over the messy desk was a beer poster of a blond girl turned three-quarters from the camera, her ample backside absurdly covered with the tiniest of tiny blue bikinis. These sorts of posters are all over Peru, and they seem far more risqué than posters you'd find in the United States. It's not just the poses, which are quite suggestive and lewd, that made the posters so overtly sexual, but something indefinable in the culture of Peru in specific, and Latin America in general. Sometimes the posters shocked me, because they could be found in the most incongruous places, like a pin-up calendar in a church restroom.

We removed the mounting racks and discussed the work to be done. They planned to repair the broken middle mounting point and reinforce it by welding a washer there. The reinforcing process was to be done on the other side as well. They started with the right side, and as Jorge welded the pieces, Rose Marie pulled the flowers from a nearby vase and used the water inside to quench the metal. Then they repeated this on the other side and spray-painted their work while the metal was still hot, so the paint would dry faster. They were efficient and friendly, joking and asking me about the trip. The kid suggested that if I met a nice Peruvian woman, I might never leave Peru. They all laughed. I said if he introduced me to the girl in the poster, I'd definitely stick around. They laughed harder.

They charged me ten soles for the work, about three dollars, and the family waved me off as I slipped into traffic. I left my bike in a parking garage a couple blocks from the hotel. As I walked back through the town, a horde of Peruvian taxi drivers swooped down on me, honking and offering me their services. Desperate not to miss a fare, they honk at everyone—all the time—making every Peruvian city a twenty-four-hour cacophony of beeping cabs.

After a tension-filled dinner with the guys, I decided to go to a club, alone. Captain Passive-Aggressive was still sore about the ruins, and no amount of Peter's jocularity improved the situation. Our togetherness had reached a record low. A cab driver told me about a club called La Luna Rota. He insisted that it was the only place that would have any life that early in the week. He was wrong; it too was completely dead. Inside, I had a drink and met the two bartenders, Sergio and Miguel. They asked me about my travels, especially about women from other countries, and they insulted each other playfully as a way of entertaining themselves, and me. Miguel said Sergio sniffed too much cocaine and Sergio said Miguel liked to wear women's clothes. After the bar closed, they were going to a better place, one they referred to as "the nightclub," or El Rey, and they invited me to come along.

Peru was a land of many firsts for me, and not all were pleasant. El Rey turned out to be a strip club, the first I'd ever been to. Our cab dropped us off. The chubby bouncer outside the club was playing cards with a taxi driver across the hood of his car. They didn't look up as we walked past. Inside, the bar was dominated by a huge stage with three poles in a triangular pattern near the front. The darkness was split by colored disco lights. The stage was about four feet high, faced the bar, and was surrounded by tables. Couches lined the walls.

Miguel's brother was inside, sitting on a couch with a woman named Mariel, whose leathery face looked worn from insincere smiles. She sported a white bikini with a see-through white mesh skirt over it. Mariel had tremendously large breasts and overly tan skin. The cost was nine dollars each to get in, and much to the embarrassment of my companions they could not afford to enter. They lamented how poor they were, but if I wanted to go in they would dutifully wait outside for me. "Nonsense!" I replied with admirable gringo magnanimity, "I'll pay." They smiled, flattered and pleased with my generosity, but still they refused. Finally, after an acceptable amount of convincing and protestations to overcome their discomfort, we all went inside.

We sat down and Mariel the melanin wonder asked me to buy her a drink. Being naïve about strip clubs, I said sure, and she clapped twice to get the waiter. She ordered a whiskey on the rocks and the waiter brought it right away, along with the three beers that were complimentary with our cover charge. My beer was foaming a bit more than the others, and I was suddenly wondered if they'd slipped a drug into my drink in order to knock me out and rob me. Paranoid? Maybe. But better safe than dead, I say.

There was nobody dancing onstage, so Mariel talked to me, despite my best efforts to avoid conversation. Seeing that I wasn't really inter-ested, she asked me for another drink, and I was a bit curious about that since she still hadn't touched her first. I said "Excuse me," and I got up to go to the bathroom. My companions followed right behind, and excitedly tried to explain the customs of the club. Since I'd bought a drink for a dancer (which costs more than a normal drink, usually about five dollars), Sergio told me, I was allowed certain privileges. Half the cost of the drink went to the house, and the rest went to the dancer. What did I receive from the deal? The woman's company for fifteen to twenty minutes, Miguel explained, and the right to touch breasts, caress thighs, and even kiss the girl. "That's not really my style," I told my companions. I tried to explain that I generally went for girls who liked me for me, and not for my wallet. Besides, I found the woman repulsive. Sure, on a purely scientific level I may have been willing to examine her leathery brown balloons just to see what, in fact, they were really made of. But—and I hate to seem rude here—it seemed to me that Mariel should've been offering to pay me instead.

My reply was met with confused looks. Obviously I didn't under-stand what they meant. They tried again. Buy a drink, have a grope and a peck. A woman you can fondle is a woman you can fondle, they reasoned, and the mathematics needn't go beyond that fact. They strove harder to instruct me in the ways of Peruvian strip clubs. I strove harder to instruct them in the ways of the moralizing gringo. Back inside, two chubby girls were dancing on stage naked. They danced well, but not very enthusiastically. The whole atmosphere was decidedly more depressing than arousing.

We sat down and had some more drinks. So far that night I'd spent $2 on the cab, $27 on the cover, $20 on drinks, and $2.50 on cigarettes for one of the dancers. My new friends had long since overcome their embarrassment at accepting my generosity. At this point they expected it.

I decided it was time for me to leave. Sergio and Miguel were right behind me because—in their embarrassed way—they couldn't pay for their own cab home. The bouncer folded up his cards and the taxi driver took us all where we needed to go. The trip only cost me one dollar, but by then I was really tired of being treated like a bankroll with a funny accent. I went home and slept.

The warm sun woke me up and I felt good. The unpleasantness of the prior evening was forgotten. I realized that I'd been on the road for over two months. Right then, accountants somewhere were counting other people's money. Pharmacists were filling prescriptions, builders were laying foundations, and children were shining shoes. I was riding a motorcycle to the tip of South America, and on that sunny day all other cares were put aside because there was something so indescribably right with the world. The other guys wanted to tour some ruins, but I'd had enough of ruins, and of them, for a while. I slept in. By noon they still hadn't left and again asked me to go, but still I declined. I squandered the day around town, ate in dark local places with truckers and farmers, and e-mailed home from an Internet café. When Peter and Robert returned, Robert and I got a chance to discuss the Chan Chan incident and finally put it somewhat behind us. As I was learning with Robert, however, disputes never really went away. You could eventually bury the hatchet after an argument, but as soon as another disagreement arrived, you'd find Robert glaring at you with an armload of rotting, exhumed hatchets.

The view along the highway south from Trujillo was plain and sandy. Or mostly just plain sandy: sand with shards of rock, sand with scrub, sand with ramshackle houses blooming pathetically by the roadside. We were on our way to Chimbote, a town who's name roughly translates into English as "This place reeks so foully of burnt, rotten fish flesh that I'd sooner commit suicide than live here." And if that's not the precise translation, it should be.

As the dunes skirted by, some bikers approached us from the front, waving as they passed. Peter and Robert liked ancient culture, which I was learning to appreciate, but I also liked modern culture, especially bikers that travel the world. Blood of my blood. My companions didn't seem as interested in meeting new people as I was, but once introduced they were always sociable. I pulled over and the other bikers slowed and parked next to me. They were two Germans named Elrich and Jeannette riding an older, slightly modified BMW and a tricked-out Honda. Elrich rode the Beemer with a thirteen-gallon tank and water bottles strapped everywhere, and Jeannette was on a red NX 650 with a gorgeous, handmade, seven-gallon aluminum tank. The Honda was a little worn; the damaged tank-mounting bracket and cracked magneto cover had been patched with an instant-setting metal compound.

Peter and Robert followed suit, pulling up next to us, and as we all got acquainted, three more motorcycle headlights appeared from the north. They were three riders on Japanese dual-sports and they stopped next to us and dismounted.

The first two riders I met from the new group were Leonel and Oscar, a pair of Colombian brothers in their mid-twenties. Alvaro, their third party member, appeared to be in his mid-forties. He had a distinguished amount of gray hair and a warm face lined from many years of laughter. Alvaro was a friend of Oscar's and seemed to be the leader of their trio. The bikers rode on two Transalps and a Kawasaki KLR 650, model C. Oscar's KLR C differed from my model A in many superficial ways, but was basically the same bike with a smaller tank and seat, and a different fairing and body panels. The bike was designed more for off-road use than mine, and I often caught Oscar enviously admiring my larger tank and more comfortable saddle.

After we'd all met, exchanged e-mails, and clicked photos for posterity, Robert led Peter and me south to Chimbote. The Germans continued north, and the Colombians followed in our direction at a little more leisurely pace. Jeannette had mentioned the foul smell that permeated the air in Chimbote, but I didn't pay much attention until it hit me. Sure enough, just as we passed a rock sculpture that looked like a giant hand holding an invisible serving tray, her words, and the horrendous smell, hit me like two colliding planets.

A smell is one of the hardest things to describe. But the evil odor spewed daily from Chimbote's fuming fishmeal plants is so foul that it deserves an attempt. One summer I worked at a salmon-processing plant in Bethel, Alaska. I mostly worked on the butcher line, which consisted of various stages to separate all the usable parts of the fish from the refuse. Some useless parts, such as the guts, could be washed into the river where they were rapidly degraded or eaten by scavengers. The heads, being a bit more durable, had to be chopped down and liquefied into a clumpy, cartilaginous ooze before they could be flushed into the water. This was done with a device called a grinder.

My fate was to arrive in a year of low salmon, and being industrious by nature, I told my foreman I was looking for extra work, even though we had no fish. Perhaps because the foreman liked me (or maybe because he didn't) he hired me wash the grinder. A friend of mine was hired to assist me and we began our work. We were the envy of all the other nonworking employees—we were going to get paid.

As you can imagine, the inside of the grinder had not been washed in some time. We removed the exterior cover panels and began to disassemble the heinous contraption, only to discover that a gray-magenta paste lined almost everything, and larger chunks of fish head were stuck in various odd corners and crannies. The whole mess had curdled black and hardened in the more inaccessible places. Then the smell literally knocked me to the ground. Like nothing I'd ever experienced—the odor was of ancient decay and miserable eternal fish hells wound up into tiny little bundles bursting with flavor. I covered my nose, mouth, and eyes as if Death itself was in the air, and I damned my industriousness with all my soul as I retched on the floor. Like a trauma victim, I've unconsciously blacked out the actual cleaning of the grinder from my memory, so I can't tell you how long it took or how much I got paid for it. I can tell you, however, that I have never once been industrious since that day.

Now, if you can imagine that foul fish paste reeking from the grinder, imagine scooping several handfuls of that muck into a frying pan and burning it until black smoke spews forth. That would be the smell that is pumped out of dozens of industrial chimneys every day in Chimbote. The town's very water and air smell of fish. As do the walls of the buildings. Food smells like fish, whether cooked or fresh, and you can't smell your soap or shampoo in the shower, unless it happens to be fish-scented. Every single thing that enters that town becomes corrupted with the stench.

We didn't have any plans to meet with the three Colombians in Chimbote, but they ended up staying in the same hotel. They were going to walk around town, so we waved to them as we rode out to nearby Casma, another archaeological ruin with a subpar museum. There was a small stone wall covered with images of severed heads and limbs. Peter admired the wall as we walked, and commented that it was most likely used "to keep the bastards out and stop them from humping your wife."

"Do you think that happened a lot? Do you think it's happening right now with your wife?" I said. Out of boredom I was goading him a little. He calmly replied that it was a risk. "What a horrible thought," I said.

"You thought it," Peter said as we walked. "It's like anything else. You could get hit by a bus, you could get mugged and killed, or someone could be humping your wife. You hope it doesn't happen, but it could happen. It's a risk." That struck me as a very lonely outlook. To think that marriage and love are business transactions—risks and investments made with emotional currency—and you hope your business partner isn't cheating you blind.

Further up the hill Peter turned to Robert and said, "Santa Claus, you have lost all credibility. First you take us to Puerto Pizarro, which sucked, then you brought us to Fish Hell Central, and now the crappy Casma ruins."

"I never promised you anything," Robert said.

"You promised us great ruins and nice places, not shitholes that smell like dead fish asses," Peter replied.

"Puerto Pizarro is where he landed—that's all I said. The only thing you get at a landing site is a footprint—like on the moon—it's only got footprints."

Back in Fish Hell Central we ate dinner with the Colombian motorcyclists. Their plan was to ride from their hometown, north of Bogotá, all the way to Santiago, Chile, along the Pan-American Highway. I asked them if they were worried about the guerrilla roadblocks, and Alvaro confessed he was scared the whole way through Colombia. In Santiago they planned on catching a flight back home and sending their bikes home later by plane. We all hit it off pretty well, and Peter suggested they take a little off-road journey with us, saying that with only a day or two more riding added to their trip plans, they would see much more. They agreed and our group now totaled six.

We awoke to the dead fish reek, forced down some food, packed our stuff, and left by 8 A.M. We rode on some ugly all-dirt roads along the Rio Santa, and the two KLRs were in the lead. I pushed the bike hard, playfully trying to stay ahead of Oscar, even though I was fully loaded with more than one hundred pounds of gear, my delicate laptop, and my extra body weight over his. Suddenly a rock flew up under my left foot and cracked my shifter. I stopped and took off my jacket and helmet to inspect the damage. A fissure ran halfway through the part, preventing me from changing gears and threatening to split the shifter in two. The rest of the guys appeared, and we were suddenly assaulted by a mass of tiny flying insects. The bugs flew up in our faces and into our ears, grabbing hunks of skin and tearing them off as they flew away. Robert was simultaneously bitten in several places; little spots of blood on his cheeks marked the attacks.

We quickly put our gear back on to avoid being polka-dotted by the strange insects. Peter volunteered to ride with me back to the last village to get my shifter welded. Robert suggested I put the bike in second gear for the entire ride, since I'd be unable to shift and second would offer the best compromise of top speed and low-end power. With Robert and Leonel giving me a shove to get started, Peter and I backtracked forty miles to find a welder.

The welder we found was on the side of the road in a greasy hut with mangy dogs and cats roaming out front. A crowd gathered to witness the spectacle we provided, and Peter bantered amicably with everyone that wanted to speak with us. The welder was a wiry older man with considerable skill. He welded the fissure and then hammered the shifter in the middle to fit it in place, tailored to my foot. After he was done the part felt better than new. He charged me ninety cents for the work.

We raced to catch the others. Tired of the rough path we'd already taken twice, Peter and I followed an elevated service road that wound along the manmade river of a hydroelectric plant. The concrete stream was on one side of the road and a cliff was on the other, and we rode close to falling into one or other. The path led down from the water's edge back to the main road, which was a disaster. Huge ruts were carved in the dried mud, and in some places, a fine white dust filled the ruts, sometimes as deep as a foot. The dust concealed rocks as big as shoeboxes, perfect for turning a front tire and slamming one into the ground under a mushroom cloud of white powder. Thankfully I didn't hit any of them, but we later heard that Alvaro wiped out in one.

Before we reached Yuramarca, a big orange dump truck blocked the road as workmen carved granite out of the cliff on the roadside. One of the workers took his pickax and cut the dirt off the berm, widening a trail for us to squeeze past. We hauled ass through more horribly rocky roads, fording streams and crossing mountain passes with 1,700-foot granite walls. Peter taught me a little geology, his major in college, while pointing out an igneous volcanic intrusion that had thrust itself up into the softer earth. The inverted funnel formed by the ancient lava was now visible in the split mountain wall.

Further along the bad roads Peter's bag mounting broke again. That had been happening with predictable regularity. This time it broke just above the last repair. He groaned in frustration, lashed it with his tie-downs, and we continued.

The quality of the scenery increased with the altitude, and the more exposed the mountains became, the prettier they seemed. The rock was sometimes striped with enormous natural swatches of yellow, red, and black.

As we passed next to a huge chasm, a man dangled over the abyss in a *garocha*, a little cart with pulleys, dragging himself hand over hand along the cable running from a roadside tower to the cliff on the opposite side of the river valley. The garocha is an updated Incan gondola used to cross between peaks at high elevations. Modern versions are made with metal cables and cages, as opposed to the ropes and wood the Inca used, but the purpose is still the same: to get something quickly from one mountain to another without having to climb there on foot. The Inca used this technology effectively in their defense against the Spanish—when retreating, they'd cut the garocha lines after they'd safely crossed. To continue the pursuit, the Spanish then had to either build some kind of bridge, or start climbing.

The river below had carved out the rocks, and it followed us along the road, promising a refreshing, cool grave if we fell off the side. Not to mention the multiple fractures, ruptured organs, severed limbs, concussions, contusions, and all manner of hemorrhages to be experienced before splattering to a merciful death below. Sobering.

So what did we decide to do? Peter "Satan" Maria suggested we get into one of those garochas and pull ourselves over the river for "action shots." I went first, climbing the little concrete tower with the rebar ladder rungs, the lower two of which were broken, as if someone was trying to prevent people from using the thing. I inspected the garocha for safety, and the cable seemed strong and the pulleys functional and oiled, so it appeared to have been used regularly. The basket itself was made of metal tubing and mesh. The rig was more than a little beat-up; the one side was smashed, as if it had once fallen into the valley and been salvaged, and the bent corner had been repaired—not with wire, screws, or even rope, but with a simple strip of cotton cloth—the same soft material one might use to make a baby's diaper. I expressed my reservations and Peter taunted me to stop being a coward and go out there so he could take the photos.

I pulled myself out with my leather gloves, and the wire cage bounced in the wind like a dangling cat toy. "Good, Danger Boy, this will make a great shot!" Peter exclaimed. I was damn high. Over the blustery heights it occurred to me that this must've been exactly how Peter and Robert ended up in that volcanic crater back in Ecuador. Finally I pulled my way back and it was his turn. He had no reservations as he headed out and I snapped photos of him from a nearby hill. While over the middle of the chasm, the impressive height struck him and Peter suddenly freaked out. "Andrés, hurry up, you dingbat! Get down from that rock and get me out of here—I'm scared!"

Further along we passed through half a dozen tunnels in the rock mountainside. Some were very long and curved, and most were too narrow to fit two cars side by side. The cave interior was unlit, and it was impossible to see if anyone was coming the other way, since people in Latin America often drive without headlights, even in the dark. The only thing to do was beep the whole time and hope that oncoming drivers would hear us or see our headlights and stop. We continued up some open roads, passing makeshift stone hovels that were home to coal miners while they worked nearby. A hydroelectric plant stood high up in the peaks where men tore tunnels into the sheer rock to tap the mountain water's potential energy.

Eventually we all met up again and went to our new home in town, the Chamanna Hotel Restaurant. The rustic hostel was run by a German couple who seemed nice, if odd. I really liked the place until the following day, when I noticed the imprisoned monkey they kept in a tiny cage made from a window frame and chicken wire. The poor beast had obviously lost its mind. Sometimes it rocked back and forth, staring at us pitifully with huge black eyes, just sitting there masturbating. More often it was spastic, hopping around the cage while it chirped, screamed in a high voice, whined, grunted, and jerked off madly with one hand, all the while looking balefully at those who passed.

The morning found us up at six, wakened by the very loud sounds of scratching and thumping coming from our roof near the door. The sounds were far too loud to be a rat. Each of us sat quietly, listening. The noise was intense—it sounded like it might've been a bear. Or a sasquach. "Devil-o," Peter whispered, "why don't you go open that door and see what it is?"

"You've got the super watch," I said, "you go."

"It's the monkey," Peter said, "he's coming to do you."

Even Robert was put off by the loud noise. Nobody wanted to step outside and see what it was. Unfortunately I had to relieve myself. Badly. I'm sure that wasn't the first time in history that a full bladder has created artificial courage. I dressed and carefully opened the door.

Outside was blissful silence. There was no trace of the noisy monster. I took a few more steps out and closed the door behind me. The mystery of what caused that racket was never resolved. I passed where we had drunk the night before, and the tables were set for breakfast, complete with juices and fruit cocktails, all ready to go. Apparently the German couple had been up before dawn preparing our morning repast. I have to admit it was awesome: fresh bread, blackberry preserves, liver paté, cheeses, honey, coffee, excellent hot chocolate, eggs. They even made hot dogs for Peter the egg-hater. Also, to their credit, they were the first place I'd seen with decent napkins. Every other restaurant in Peru uses small rectangles of something like waxed tissue paper.

Unlike most Germans, our hosts seemed mechanically inept and apparently did not know that water and electricity don't mix. The poorly constructed showers operated (barely) with an electrical heating element, so I had a quick shower that leaked icy mountain water from the broken element. Every time I tried to adjust it, I got a sharp jolt of electricity.

We all got into our gear, stripped the bikes of all extraneous weight for hard riding, and took off up the mountains to Lake Paron. Once on the dirt, the two Kawasakis were out in front. Misled by a little brat on the side of the road, I went the wrong way, and then played catch-up to Oscar the rest of the time as we raced up the rocky switchbacks. The road was extremely rough and we were riding hard, having a blast. The crystalline waters of the lake at the top seemed unreal. The double peaks of Huandoy North reflected off ice-cold water that was bluer than the sky on its clearest day.

"What would you like for lunch?," the anemic German man who ran the hotel said. Robert and I were enjoying some cold beers after the ride to the lake. I looked up at him from my drink and his face smiled back at me humorlessly, a notepad and pencil artfully poised in his hands. "We have chicken or steak; either comes with green beans and rice."

"Do you have anything else instead of green beans?" I asked.

"Yes . . ." he paused, as though he were about to reveal something very important. "RED BEANS!" he shouted and burst out laughing like a man who, finding himself hopelessly lost in the wilderness, decides to go completely insane.

"OK," I started to say, assuming he meant kidney beans.

"No, no, I was just kidding," he said, still giggling. "We also have broccoli."

As we ate, Robert and I discussed the sad state of the imprisoned, sexually frustrated monkey. I suggested a jailbreak and relocation. We could drop him off in a jungle area at the first opportunity, I offered. Robert patiently pointed out the obvious, that the jungles were on the other side of the Andes, the side without all the sparse altiplano that we'd been seeing for weeks. Good point. So much for Operation Monkey Rescue.

That evening I went to a mechanic shop to take another look at my forks, which had begun clicking again. Every time I braked, the noise was there, but it was more an annoyance than a danger. Still, I wanted to address the problem. The place I found allowed me to use their tools, and seven little kids that had been playing on the street offered to help. Mostly they just asked me questions, some of the best I'd heard. "Do you know the American Gladiators?" "Do you know Ricky Martin?" "Do you ride like this guy?" (One of the boys was pointing at my sticker of the flying Aerostich motorcyclist, a man holding the handlebars of his bike while sailing horizontally over the seat, stiff as a board.) A girl asked me if I knew Valeria Masa, the Argentine supermodel (she may have noticed a bit of an Argentine accent when I spoke Spanish).

"Sure," I said while wrenching on the triple tree. "She's my girl-friend." Mostly they laughed and didn't believe me, but a few raised their eyebrows and said "Really?" "But you are much nicer than she is," I told the girl, and she smiled wide-eyed up at me.

It was getting dark and I couldn't make the clicking stop, so I gave little Valeria some change and asked her and a pudgy boy to run to the store and buy me a bottle of water and some Chiclets. The young girl and boy in charge took great pride in bringing me back my purchases and the exact change. I took a photo with my pit crew and passed out gum. They waved and chased me down the street as I rode away.

By 7:30 A.M. we were up and electrocuting ourselves in the shower. Breakfast was predictably good. What I really hated most about these Germans was how they could do most everything so right (except the showers, of course) and do something so obviously cruel to the monkey, seemingly without realizing it. I just couldn't get past the idea of that poor little bastard, sad and scared, wanking himself to death.

The Colombians decided to take a pass on joining us for a ride up into the mountains to see the ruins of Chavin, preferring instead to continue their trip to Lima, then Santiago, Chile. We wished them good-bye and set out in our separate directions. We took a long, tough road up to a national park, which then wound through the park and continued over the mountains past the ruins of Chavin. The one-lane path climbed up to a cerulean lake fed by icy mountain runoff. Hiking tourists hoofed it up, and none of them waved as I passed. Probably conserving energy. Supposedly we turned through forty-eight switchbacks on the way to the peak. I passed more hikers that looked wretched and exhausted. One woman wore purple running tights and an enormous backpack with camping gear. She grimaced the whole time, her face a mask of pain. Her pudgy climbing partner had paused to put sunscreen on his nose—he was hunched over, supporting himself by resting a hand on one knee.

At the time, I couldn't imagine why anyone would want to climb all that way. I certainly felt fortunate to be riding a motorcycle, instead of pounding out those miles on foot. As I would soon find out, fortunes can be altered at a moment's notice.

11

Zen and the Art of the Inelastic Collision

➤ I LED AS WE RODE through the incredible Huascarán National Park, Peru, on our way to the ruins at Chavin. Peter and Robert were behind me somewhere, out of sight around some mountainous curve. Twenty-thousand-foot peaks, covered in snow, thrust out of the ground all around us. The sun pierced through my shield and sunglasses, and the road was a single lane of dirt and loose rocks. The path wound up through the mountains, above the frigid waters of a lake that reflected the flickering sunlight on the mountain walls as if from an enormous chandelier. The sides of the trail plunged thousands of feet to the valley below.

A feeling of serenity and calm overtook me as I motored through of one of the most pristine and peaceful places I'd ever seen. At over ten thousand feet, the dirt was as bright as brown can be, and canary-yellow wildflowers popped sporadically into view along the mountainside.

I was taking mental snapshots of the scenery as I rounded a corner, and with freeze-frame slowness, a clean, bright blue truck appeared in my path. I was dumbstruck. The truck was coming at me very fast and there was no time think. No turning. No stopping. No avoiding. My mind instantly processed my options. I didn't rationalize my decision at the time, but I somehow knew I was going too fast to swerve on the loose dirt. I could instinctively sense that I would just slide and fall over, and possibly end up underneath the truck. I remember thinking, "Wow, I'm going to hit this truck, and all I can do is watch." Reflexively, I grabbed a fistful of brakes and skidded toward the truck head-on. The truck's driver was also braking hard. I felt the front end of my bike crunch against the grille just before I bounced off the truck's hood and hit the ground on my side.

A truck. Oh shit. Wham. Just like that, the ordeal was over. Right before my front tire collided with the truck's bumper, I sensed in my gut that I was going to be fine. That sensation removed all fear, and I was free to relax and experience the moment clearly. I was pure sensation as I moved in the thrall of forces beyond my control. I suddenly felt tranquility and deep understanding. Zen Buddhists call a moment like that *satori*, a brief time without thought, yet with complete understanding, clarity, and focus—a feeling of infinite space. The front tire hit, the forks bent, and my bike pivoted forward on the axle of its front wheel, smashing the fairing and headlight against the grille. I slid forward and my helmet and shoulder smacked against the hood. I recall a flash of the look on the faces of the two guys in the cab. Their mouths were open, eyes as big as fried eggs. I also noticed upon my very close visual inspection of the truck that it was not as clean as it first appeared.

I hit the ground and felt nothing wrong with my body—I was fine. My next thought was for my bike and how badly it might be damaged. Suddenly there were hands touching me—a small man was trying to pick me up and make sure I was OK, but I felt as if he was patting me down for my wallet. He then tried to lift my bike and I became angry. Hey asshole. First you guys drive fast like idiots in the middle of the goddamned road, then you crash against my bike, and now you want to mess with it on top of that? I pushed him away and told him not to

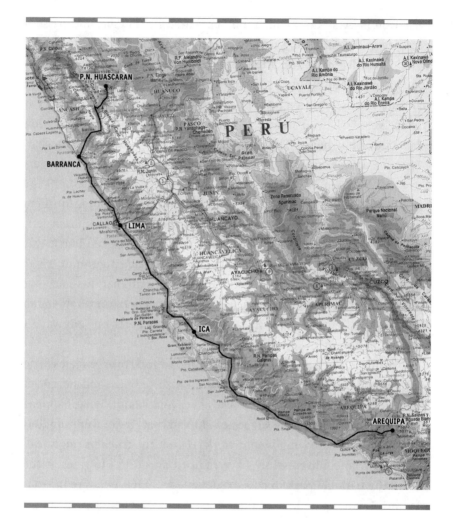

touch it. Still disoriented, I hefted the bike and set it on the side of the road on the kickstand.

I checked myself out: I could walk, I felt no pain, and my head was relatively clear. I was pretty sure I wasn't in shock. I was a little shaken but things were cool with me. The fairing on the bike was warped; the front light smashed; the handlebars slightly bent; and the forks were bent back, shortening the rake of the bike. A bus I passed earlier on my way up the mountain appeared behind me, and passengers began disembarking to gawk at the accident. They stared at me while I wandered around attending to the KLR. Meanwhile the guys that hit me were building up the story of the wreck for everyone, painting themselves in a favorable light until they began to believe it themselves. "Oh, you should not go so fast," they advised me, "you came out of nowhere." Their voices were slightly scolding, paternal. "This is a dangerous road, many cars." Fuckers. I know it's a dangerous road. You two morons are on it.

Robert and Peter showed up, and it took several minutes for them to fully digest that I'd been in an accident. The busload of tourists left, and it was just us and them. Soon after, though, it seemed like it was just me and them—the two truckers explained the situation to Peter in Spanish, and in my excited state I didn't catch all that was said, but by the end, Peter and the two menaces were negotiating how much I had to pay for the accident! Whose side was Peter on, anyway? I couldn't believe it.

I really felt betrayed. Peter wanted me to fork over some cash so we could get moving again. I asked Robert for advice, and he said it depended on who was at fault. "If it's everyone's fault, what happens if you just drive away?" he suggested. I liked that line of thinking, but Peter didn't think leaving would work. He felt the truckers might call the cops, who could possibly have radioed ahead to the gates at the exit to the national park to have us detained. He felt we were in trouble until I paid up and we could leave. Against my better judgment, I relented and negotiated to pay 180 soles. That was only about $50, but it was $50 more than I wanted to pay to these creeps who were just as responsible for the accident as I was. We were both in the same place at the same time. We were both driving too fast.

The real reason I had to pay for everyone's repairs was that I was the one wealthy enough to be on vacation. I gave them the cash. But I also said, "Look, I'll pay this only because my friend asked me to, but what you demand of me is not just." Then this little bastard has the balls to say, "Hey, we're all friends here, and I am just happy you are not hurt." Yeah, but not happy enough not to ask for money. He tried to shake my hand and I blew him off. First these guys wreck my bike, then they rob me, and now they want me to pretend I'm their pal and shake hands. Unbelievable.

Why wasn't I paying more attention? Now I have to find a place that can fix the bike. Why didn't Peter and Robert stick up for me more? It felt like they immediately believed the other guys' story and assumed I was at fault. All these things went through my head as I rode a bike with bent forks the rest of the way to Chavin. At the very least, the bike gained a name. It had survived the accident and suffered minimal damage. It was one tough bike—a badass, if you will. I rode the Badass to Chavin with Robert behind me in case of trouble, and Peter leading the way up front.

That night I drank and ate 'til the point of bursting. I was drowning my sorrows and trying to smother them for good measure. The next day Peter and Robert went to see the ruins at Chavin, but I skipped them and continued alone. My plan was to get to Lima by Sunday night and begin looking at my repair options Monday morning. The crappy dirt roads were loaded with more careening buses and trucks. Twice I was run off the road by oncoming buses, driving exactly like that truck I hit. But now I wasn't taking any chances and rode much more cautiously, expecting an oncoming vehicle in every turn. The roads were so bad that streams ran down the middle of them, filling two-foot-deep ruts with water and hidden rocks the size of volleyballs. The KLR took all the bumps with grace, and as Robert predicted it might, the bike seemed to handle better at low speeds with my newly shortened rake.

Mercifully, the road became paved and I found the bike was still dignified and controllable at highway speed. I felt secure enough to occasionally push it to 70 MPH. Farmers along the road dried black and red chilies in big square shapes—spicy checkerboards hardening in the sun. I stopped for a lunch before I finally hit the Pan-American and cruised quickly along the coast.

As I rode, I reflected on my experience in the crash. It seemed that the moment of enlightenment is just that. A moment. I always expected such an event would change me in some enormously significant way, and that I would automatically do everything in my life better after that point. But no, I was still just as petty, selfish, childish, and all the other bad things that I was before. Apparently, like so many things in life, and like life itself, enlightenment is fleeting. Grace has to be earned, I guess. Hopefully I'll encounter such moments of understanding again, but preferably they'll occur under less dangerous circumstances.

Just outside Barranca I came over a low hill and passed a white Toyota Corolla in a reduced-speed lane. Two policemen waved me over frantically from the side of the road, evidently to ticket me for speeding. I pulled over, removed my helmet, and waited. They seemed to be up to something, talking for a while before coming over. They wore open-faced motorcycle helmets and leather jackets—bike cops. The fat one told me the fine was 280 soles, about $95. Apparently someone had pulled a Tyson on him; a meaty chunk of his ear was missing. The other cop was skinny and tall. I apologized for speeding and told them I couldn't afford to pay that much right then, and I'd need to go to a city for cash. They didn't do or say anything for a few moments—they seemed to be stalling. Finally the fat one began acting as though he were about to start writing my ticket, but suddenly stopped and said, "Don't you know it's bad to use excessive velocity? What if there had been a small child in the road?" I agreed and apologized, and as I waited, he still wasn't filling out the form. What were these guys waiting for?

A white car blew past at about twice the speed limit—much faster than I was going. They watched it pass, and I eyed them both inquisitively. The tall one commented: "Oh, that's the one we got before, we need to give him another ticket." Then they turned their attention back to me.

I asked if there was a way to work this out. I suggested I take the ticket and send a certified check from the next city to the magistrate, but they frowned on this. I also offered to leave a portion of the fine with them, which they seemed relieved to hear. Apparently it was the solution they were waiting for, but they eyed me doubtfully when I told them I didn't have that much in cash. I reached into my front pocket where I kept some of my money and tried to count out twenty or thirty soles with my fingers, without making it obvious that I had many more bills in there. I actually had close to 500 soles on my body, a credit card, and $500 stashed in various places on my bike. Instead of the three tens I wanted to get from my pocket, I pulled out fifties, for a total of 150 soles. Damn. I was tired and nauseated by these corrupt police and I just wanted to go. With true exasperation in my voice, I told them I had no more for them.

The skinny guy doubted this and wanted to search me! I reached into my back pocket and pulled out my dummy wallet. Finally this old leather wallet I'd been carrying filled with voided credit cards, expired IDs, and a few small bills was going to serve a purpose. I opened up the billfold and thrust it into his face. "See?" I said. "Sixteen dollars." The fat one took the money out of my wallet, thought twice about it, and handed me back two dollars.

"You might need to pay a couple of tolls on the way into Lima," he said magnanimously.

While they did manage to get a little more than half of what they wanted for the ticket, I was glad they didn't get all of it. Peter and Robert were stopped the next day at the same speed trap. They were each taken for a little more than half of what I paid, because right away Peter noticed that the fine of 280 soles listed in the cop's ticket book was for payment ten days late or later. If paid on time, the fine was only supposed to be 140 soles. From there Peter was able to talk them down a bit further.

I later learned that Leonel, Oscar, and Alvaro, our Colombian buddies, were also caught in the cops' trap, but they were the most successful. The Peruvian cops tried dealing with all three at once, intimidating and pressuring them as they did me, but the Colombians just calmly admitted their error, apologized for speeding, and asked for their tickets, which they said they'd gladly pay immediately at the courthouse.

Frustrated, the corrupt cops pulled Alvaro aside, since he looked the oldest and most responsible, and tried to subtly make him understand that they wanted the cash to go to them, and not to the municipality. Alvaro played dumb for a while, repeatedly offering to legally pay the ticket until they practically told him to cough up some cash. "Oh, you want a bribe?" Alvaro said as he reached into his pocket. "OK, you can have five dollars." The cops didn't like that at all. In their mind it was three bikes, three fines, 280 soles each. Alvaro told them to take the five dollars or write them the ticket, but make it quick because he didn't have all day. The cops finally relented and took his offer.

"Pure greed," Alvaro explained to me later. "Once a corrupt official has shown that he wants a bribe, it's up to the person paying to set the price. I knew they wanted that money very badly—I could tell they'd rather take five than nothing."

Night began to settle as the lights of Lima appeared. I entered the city slowly; my damaged headlight pointed straight up and slightly to the right, making it useless for illuminating anything but the billboards on the side of the road. Buses were everywhere and pedestrians seemed oblivious to traffic, walking into the middle of the street as confidently as if it were a sidewalk. I'd never ridden in a huge Latin American city like Lima in the dark, and as I quickly learned, it can be chaotic. After getting several sets of directions, hopping a short concrete divider to get my exit, and (unknowingly) riding on an expressway that is off-limits to motorcycles, I found my way to Miraflores, the nicer part of town.

Once inside the city I met two bike cops on Harleys that showed me to my hotel. Robert and Peter had agreed to meet me there the following day, but the place was overpriced. I ate dinner down the street and walked around the main plaza afterward. That night I sent several e-mails, including one to Elena, the beguiling Irish-Spanish girl I met in Guatemala. We'd been communicating regularly, and it started to look as though she'd be meeting me in Argentina after all.

At 7:30 A.M. the hotel attendant woke me to say the motorcycle had to be removed from the parking lot. I got up, retrieved my bike, and rode down the street for breakfast. As I mulled over a newspaper, I noticed a couple of bikers checking out my KLR. I stood and walked toward them to inquire about any bike shops in town, and the small-world theory was proven again when closer inspection revealed it was none other than Leonel and Oscar! They seemed happy to see me, and I was happy to see them. They said they were staying in the apartment of a friend of Alvaro's who had given them full run of the place while in Lima. I told them all about the accident, and Alvaro showed up a few moments later.

"You'll never guess what happened to us," Leonel said. "We met these girls, and we told them we were going to Cuzco by plane to see the sights and to visit Machu Picchu. They said they wanted to come with us."

"That sounds like fun," I said.

"Yeah, sure, but they want us to pay for everything, their flights and all their expenses, and they each wanted to come home with an additional two hundred dollars cash in their pockets. They planned to tell their parents they were asked to be extras in a movie over the weekend and got paid for it."

"Hmm. Sounds like they've been in that movie before," I said. "What did you do?"

"We told them to get lost. Everyone knows extras don't get paid that much in Peru."

We teamed up to find some bike shops. Although I had contact information for all the major Kawasaki dealers in each country, the dealership for Peru was under new ownership so I couldn't find them. The location was so new that it wasn't even listed in the phone book.

We encountered a Yamaha dealership that was friendly and well organized. The sales rep recommended a local repair shop, so lacking any other options I went to check it out.

The entrance to Mavilla Hermanos's shop was hidden in an alley, but we found it and I pulled my bike inside. The facility was large, impeccably clean, and well equipped. The head mechanic seemed knowledgeable, describing in detail the process they'd use to straighten my forks. A smaller bike was being repaired in the same way, so he showed us how they carefully set the tubes right with a hydraulic press. The mechanics were evasive about how much it was going to cost; I couldn't get an estimate out of anyone. "Don't worry about it," the boss said, "we'll take care of you." Whatever that meant. I left explicit instructions to wait for my OK to begin the work, and that they were only to repair the forks, and nothing else, since I could probably get spare parts from the Kawasaki shop, if I ever found it.

The four of us made it back to my hotel just as Peter and Robert were arriving. It was like a high school reunion—a little stiff but altogether jovial and tinged with sentimentality. We moved to a cheaper hotel, and after Robert and Peter parked their bikes for the night we climbed on the backs of the Colombians' motorcycles and headed to the grocery store for dinner.

Everyone seemed to be trying to get their cut in Lima, from taxi drivers to four-year-old beggars to prostitutes. As we strolled downtown after dinner that night, a young girl walked up and poked me in the stomach, asking for money. I declined and she then tried to trip me! I asked her what her problem was and she just laughed as she walked away. Alvaro told me to watch out for her kind, "street rats," he called them, packs of young teens and preteens, male and female, who attack en masse and can be very formidable and vicious, taking everything down to your shoes, and maybe stabbing you or leaving you blind in the process.

On a cobblestone pedestrian street lined with bars, waiters practically begged us to patronize their establishments. The open-air patios were all connected, and you could see what everyone was doing up and down the street. Men wandered among the tables, selling serenades accompanied by guitar while others hawked flowers.

There was also a woman trying to scam tourists for change. Using an unimaginative yet often successful ploy, she carried around a fake United States twenty-dollar bill and asked tourists to break it for smaller dollar denominations. I could tell by her behavior—like the simple fact that she completely ignored all the waiters, in other words, those people most likely to have change for her—that she wasn't legitimate. I was surprised the bars allowed her, and others like her, to prey on their clientele. Perhaps she gave the waiters a cut if she was successful. After all, she's only hitting up tourists—they wouldn't be around long enough to complain when they figured out what happened.

Peter and Robert had passed the Kawasaki dealer on the way into town. Using their directions, I took a cab there the following morning. I presented myself at the office with my sponsorship letters of introduction, and the general manager was very kind and supportive. He directed me to Julio César Márquez, the sales manager, a twenty-eight-year-old man with long black hair. Julio helped me search for parts over the next few days and introduced me to Carlos, a great mechanic, who made it his personal crusade to do whatever he could to get my bike back up to speed. We three hopped into a pickup and went over to Mavilla Hermanos to see the KLR.

We found the bike disassembled and the forks in the process of being straightened. The scars from the bend were still visible, but by moving the fork positions in the triple tree, the Mavilla mechanics had ensured the weakened spots wouldn't be subjected to further bending. Despite my happiness over the progress, I was annoyed that they'd neglected to wait for my approval to begin work. I asked the manager why they did that, but he seemed to think I was complimenting him for taking the initiative. "Oh, no problem," he said, "we're just doing our best."

Seeing he didn't understand me, I plainly told him to leave all the other damaged parts of the bike as they were, and to just finish repairing the forks. He just nodded and smiled. When I again asked him for an estimate, he gave me a cryptic response and quickly wandered off. This turn of events worried me, but Carlos and Julio thought the work looked pretty good, so I was encouraged.

The next day, while waiting for the bike to be finished, I checked out the museum of the Spanish Inquisition. I took a fascinating tour, and even the Inquisition building itself was remarkable, with a handmade ceiling built of over thirty thousand carved pieces of cedar, and not a single nail.

Taking a cab over to Mavilla Hermanos to check on the bike, I found it was miraculously back together. Not only were the forks repaired, but the light was fixed (they soldered all the internal wires for strength and glued on a new headlight glass from a car), the Plexiglas light guard was replaced, and the entire bike was covered in motor oil, then polished to shine. I didn't know what to say. They had directly disobeyed my orders, again, and now I was pissed; yet here was the bike, albeit greasy, completely back together. The mechanics had even put oil on my brake discs, which I didn't realize until I was doing 50 MPH down the road and discovered that my brakes weren't stopping me! This overzealous mechanic nearly cost me my life and I cursed him righteously for about ten minutes. I've met many riders who won't allow anyone to work on their motorcycles except them. Robert was particularly careful about who touched his ride, and if anyone ever did, he usually watched them the whole time. After this experience I understood why. If it hadn't been for luck I could've died because of some thoughtless shop employee. Two full days passed before all the oil had completely burned off and my brakes worked properly. Never again would I trust the mechanical condition of my bike (and therefore my life) to just anyone.

The next morning I checked the bike's valve clearance and cleaned the air filter. I did some more sightseeing and at the end of the day I decided to send e-mails at a cyber café. On the way to the café I was approached by a thin woman, in her mid-thirties, with jeans and a Nike running jacket and sneakers. She stopped in front of me. "Do you have the time?"

"Sorry, I don't wear a watch." I smiled as I pulled up my sleeve to demonstrate while I kept walking. She turned around and followed me.

"About what time, roughly?" she asked. I told her it was around nine, and she said, "Where are you from?" I stopped and told her. "Thank you for speaking good Spanish." I said that I really didn't, but I appreciated her compliment. Her hair was black, curly, and had sprinkles of dust in it as if she'd just walked through an attic. She gave off a creepy vibe. I really just wanted to check my e-mail and she could sense me leaning that way—we were just outside the café doors. "You work at the Internet café?" she asked.

"No, just visiting it."

"Oh, ha ha. Well, nice meeting you." She put out her hand to shake. I thanked her and shook her hand. She kept shaking my hand. The normal time frame in which someone would let go of a stranger's hand passed, and I started to try to pull my hand away. Her eyes, I noticed, looked as though the fire that was supposed to be in them had burned out. She held my hand firmly and said: "Why don't you come to my apartment?"

"Uh, no thanks," I said. I tried to remove my hand from her strong grip and she pulled closer.

"You don't want sucky-sucky, fucky-fucky? Three dollars." She mumbled into her other hand, in English, as she made a fellatio motion. I almost choked on my chewing gum. I didn't know which was more incredible: the fact that she wanted only three dollars, or the fact that she actually said "sucky-sucky, fucky-fucky."

Half-laughing from shock, I forcibly removed my hand from hers, and suddenly felt very bad for her. Not wanting to hurt her with a harsh rejection, I said something like: "I'm sorry, I thank you for your offer, but I'm engaged and I'm a very faithful man." Come on, everybody has feelings.

"Oh, I see." she said. "I'm sorry. Sorry. Excuse me." She stuck out her hand again. "Good-bye." I don't know why I did it. I put my hand back in hers, reflexively—a Pavlovian handshake. She tried to pull me toward her apartment. I planted my feet and stopped her motion entirely, jerking her to a halt. I removed my hand roughly. "No, gracias," I said, and I walked into the Internet café.

Who would have sex for that price? The extremely low offer may have been an incentive to get an otherwise unwilling fellow to follow her to someplace where her pimp or boyfriend could roll the bargain john with a baseball bat. Or maybe she was an addict in need of a fix. When I met all the guys for dinner and told them my story, without pause Alvaro said, "Oh, you could've talked her down to two."

The next day Robert and Peter left for a trip to the mountains. I decided to stay with the Colombians and party in Lima for a couple of days. We all planned to meet up again in the town of Ica, to the south. Alvaro, Leonel, and Oscar were outrageous and fun-loving, and I couldn't pass up the opportunity to get to know them better. Besides, after the accident I needed to release some tension, and the Colombians were the perfect guides to Peruvian nightlife. We spent two nights hanging out in Barranco, a part of Lima known for its clubs.

I met a young woman named Zulma on that first night out—she had been dancing with a group of girls and my Colombian pals sidled up to them. She was small and friendly and we had a nice time dancing and talking, so I took her number. Two days later she invited me to see a cockfight. Although I'd never gone to one, nor really ever wanted to, now that I had the chance I was curious to see what it's all about.

The small stadium was surrounded by beer banners and filled with people. We found an elevated place to stand on one side of the ring. The ring was about twenty-four feet square, surrounded by an iron fence, and had a dirt floor. We arrived in time to see the three final matches. The handlers for the first match brought out their birds, which they held tightly in their arms as an official tied small spurs to the back of each animal's right leg. The spurs, which were about the size of small woman's finger, were meant to augment the cock's lethality when strapped to the rear claw—which the birds normally use as their main weapon. This made for a bloodier, and therefore more entertaining, fight. After the referee checked and approved the animals, the handlers took them back to their respective sides.

The cocks were simply referred to as "left" and "right" based on what side of the ring they started in. In the first match, the cock on the left was a big puffy reddish-orange thing, and the one on the right was all black with an iridescent, midnight-blue sheen to his feathers. The handlers carried the birds around the ring, so the spectators could see them and place their bets. Next the birds were brought near each other to see what each thought of his opponent. Naturally, they passionately disliked one another, and no sooner were the birds in range than they started pecking at each other's eyes and necks. Both came back with no more than a beakful of feathers and a boiling rage. Another round of betting followed, and the fight was ready to begin.

The birds were placed on the ground and the spectators cheered them on. The cocks wandered around at first, disoriented. When they recognized each other's presence, both immediately slipped into a glorious furor and leapt wildly forward. The cocks attacked with utter savagery—even the handlers were sometimes afraid to reach in and break up the bouts, lest they catch a blade in the forearm.

The birds became a black and tangerine swirl, whirling and twisting while they beat at each other with their wings. They moved and changed direction about the other in midair so fast that it appeared they were trying to take flight while tied together with a string. People shouted and cheered the chaos; my heartbeat picked up as I watched. Soon Big Red showed his superiority, coming down on his rival with a deadly stab. The black bird stumbled back with a gaping two-inch-long puncture wound just above its right wing. It was mouthing angry hisses and spitting blood. The referee separated the birds, and the handlers carefully picked them up.

The official then placed a small board about three feet square between the two birds as a blind. Each combatant was held down just inches from the other so that, when the board was removed, they saw each other and were completely overcome by surprise. Immediately they charged with renewed fury. Again the red bird struck first, this time landing and sticking his wicked spike solidly in the other's back. Big Red lost his balance and fell over flapping as his spur slowly pulled out. The black bird shuffled about lamely in the dirt, trying to strike at his enemy, but he didn't realize he was already dead. As soon as Red regained his balance he jumped up and down on the black bird, pecking violently at his head and pulling bloodied feathers and skin from his neck. By the time the referee broke up the fight, the black bird was in sad shape: his wings were bent in different directions, his feathers lay matted with blood, and his mouth was spread wide open at the end of his twisted, featherless neck.

I'd seen enough, but out of courtesy to Zulma I stayed until the final match. Big Red had two more fights that night and became the winner. The owners of the second- and third-place birds were visibly upset; their trophies seemed small consolation for the death of their champions. I realized I wasn't a big fan of cockfighting. I also wasn't a big fan of Zulma. We went out for burgers, and she started to make comparisons between United States culture and the ground beef we were eating. Then, at the culmination of our date, she went on a tirade about men in general and ex-boyfriends in particular as we strolled around town. I hailed a cab, opened the door for her, and then paid the driver in advance. I wished her a good evening and closed the door, and the cab sped off into the night.

The next day Alvaro, Leonel, Oscar, and I left for Ica early to meet up with Robert and Peter. The Colombians were supposed to part with us there and continue south on comfortably paved roads, but somehow I convinced them to tag along a little further.

In Ica we met Robert and Peter as planned and there was much rejoicing. Too much. We got ourselves the requisite rum and began to get drunk with a bottle of cola and plastic cups in the plaza. In our drunkenness we crammed our faces together in front of a passport photo camera and got some blurry pictures with half our heads cut off. We then considered hiring some of the three-wheeled, 250cc moto-taxis to run races with us in the back. That idea was vetoed by one of us who insisted we do something even better.

My intention is not to point fingers or damage his reputation, but I would be lying if I didn't point out that it was our very own Peter, the former safety inspector, that thought up and pushed the brilliant idea that we go riding in the sand dunes outside of town—right then. Don't get me wrong, I'm not casting blame; I am just documenting the ever present catalyst for bad decision making in our group. In this regard, Peter's potential for mischief was unsurpassed. It's as though, instead of having the cliché little angel and devil debating over each shoulder to represent the two halves of his conscience, Peter was born with two devils that always saw eye-to-eye. Obviously, I hold myself completely to blame for riding drunk. I was well aware of the dangers. Each morning I choose my path when I wake, and nobody forces me to walk it. The same could be said for the five other men, all otherwise intelligent and fully grown, that decided to ride drunk as well. At least we wore all our protective riding gear—which some will call a pathetic rationalization at best, but there is something that must be understood about being in Latin America.

In the States you can't ride a skateboard without some authority looking over your shoulder to make sure you are not hurting yourself or someone else. In Latin America, you can strap a rocket to your skateboard like Wile E. Coyote and go flying down the middle of the highway and nobody will care (except, possibly, for a cop that wants a bribe). That freedom is intoxicating and easily exploited to inappropriate levels. Especially when you're already intoxicated. The motto that night was, "You only live once, but not necessarily for very long."

So we went spinning our tires in the dunes and a few Colombians spun over in the sand. We took photos, documenting the night and our naked butts as we mooned the camera. At one point, when all the Japanese bikes were pushing red lines in the dark near 90 MPH, a certain unnamed black-robed rider (who's been accused of looking like a fat, generous elf famous for speed) blew past us, doing at least 110 MPH.

We all made it back safely that night, but I don't know if we deserved to. I think more than one of us vowed never to do something that stupid again. Robert's fate was sealed; after that day there was no moral high ground. He'd been debased and pulled down to the level Peter and I frequented, and now he couldn't go back.

Our next stop was Nazca, the home of the famously enigmatic Nazca Lines. They are supposedly ancient sets of lines drawn with stones all over the sandy ground in and around Nazca, in the shapes of monkeys, hummingbirds, spiders, and other figures. To be properly appreciated they must be seen from above, so the question seems to be, why were they created? The ancient people that made them had no flying machines that we know of, so what was the purpose if they couldn't even view the things? We rented seats in a single-engine plane to fly over Nazca and see the lines, but I found them disappointing, especially the so-called astronaut, which looked as if Maria Reiche, the best known proponent and student of the lines, had climbed out on the side of the hill and chipped it into the rock herself.

While in Nazca I did some work on the bike. Using a vise and a hex wrench I reworked the mounting bracket for the headlight, which was still bent from the crash. The bracket wasn't pretty to look at by the time I was done, but at least the headlight now pointed at the road.

We visited an ancient cemetery near Nazca. Decomposed bodies of men, women, and children, wrapped in cloths torn open by tomb raiders, lay disheveled and disturbed in open pits that used to be their graves. "Hey, look, there is still some beef jerky on that one," Peter quipped. He was in rare form these days and his joking was getting more and more out of hand. He pulled up a human femur sticking out from the sand and poked me with it, all the while laughing his ridiculous hyena howl. I could hardly believe this guy was my same species. Times like that I would've killed to be traveling alone.

The next morning we were packed, showered, fed, and ready to leave by 7:15 A.M., which is no small feat for six motorcyclists. Robert was frustrated by the complications of organizing such a large group, and he wanted everyone up and ready to go on time. That day he got his wish. Six motors revved and warmed up in the hotel parking lot as the sun boldly beat down on us. I suddenly felt a great swelling of emotion; a feeling of anticipation and fear in my chest. The day was a blank slate that could mark my death or my greatest triumph. That moment, that unknown, that excitement, was what this trip was all about for me. I wouldn't trade that feeling for anything.

The ride was idyllic—beautifully paved roads, little traffic, great weather. We rode on cliffs overlooking the beach, down into valleys, up into hills, across deserts, and through tunnels in mountains. Santa gave lessons in peg-scraping to our Colombian friends, and at one point Peter led an excursion off into the sand for some dune riding. Later on the ride, I happened to be out in front on the blacktop when some road workers signaled me to pull over. I'd just ridden through a tunnel in the mountain and came around the corner on a cliff overlooking the ocean twenty-five feet below. I followed their directions and pulled off the road. Just as I stopped, a thunderous BOOM sounded, making the air in my lungs reverberate. This was a serious obstacle in progress, whatever it was, so I got off the bike to wait.

As it turned out, road workers were making controlled explosions with dynamite to remove parts of the cliff wall above the highway, presumably to prevent rocks from avalanching onto the road at some later time. Peter and Alvaro talked to the foreman to try to get us through there if possible. The boss promised to let us pass after they detonated the next charge.

We all watched, afraid to blink or we'd miss it. The moment came, the rocks and dust shot out from the wall, and a split second later the devastating BOOM hit again. The sound was significantly louder the second time, since I'd removed my helmet and earplugs. In a few short minutes they cleared the path and we were on our way to Arequipa, in the south of Peru.

We entered Arequipa and got a personal escort from a motorcycle cop to our hotel. How cool is that?, I thought. We looked like a parade coming into town. He even stopped traffic and occasionally flashed his police lights to make way for our entourage. He rode a big 1,100cc Kawasaki, and seemed like a really nice guy. Then, and I don't know why it surprised me, we realized he wanted a tip. I loved how he delicately referred to it as "gas money."

After our stay in Arequipa it was finally time to say good-bye to the Colombians. With much regret, they left and continued on their journey south. We all took photos and traded e-mails. I felt like it was the end of summer camp. Even our normally stoic Robert seemed pretty shaken up. Maybe it was my imagination, but I thought I saw a single salty tear run down that rough Canadian cheek to moisten his frosty beard. Yeah, right.

Actually the breakup wasn't that clean. All the other guys had gone ahead, except for Leonel and I, who stayed around for one last night of partying in Arequipa. Oscar and Alvaro took off for Santiago. Robert and Peter went ahead to Colca Canyon—they needed to be there early the next day if they hoped to see the canyon's famous condors, which (with a complete lack of consideration for night owls like me) are most active around 6 A.M. I'd have to ride alone to catch up to them, but I didn't really care. I liked the freedom of being with people that ran a less-structured trip, and I wanted to enjoy their company for as long as possible. Besides, Arequipa is a fun town, it was Saturday night, and Leonel and I had a double date with two girls we met the night before.

That afternoon I used my free time to change the bike's chain. The original wasn't completely worn, but I was tired of carrying the heavy spare I picked up in Lima. I'd come a long way from the time when I was inept at motorcycle maintenance. I still had a lot to learn, but at least I wasn't a beginner anymore. The feeling of empowerment I got from performing a new maintenance task myself was liberating, but such freedom does exact a price. In my inexperience, I squashed some O-rings and overcompressed the chain's master link, and had to use my only spare to replace it.

Leonel and I partied until early the next morning. We spent a night out with two young ladies that included dinner and a movie and ended up in a sophomoric game of truth or dare (well, the Spanish version anyway) back at our hotel. Leonel and I finally fell asleep around 5 A.M. We were up and ready to go just two hours later, but neither of us were in shape for the day's ride.

12

Beware of Falling Tourists

➤ I WISHED LEONEL A GOOD TRIP, then hit the road to Chimbay at 7:15 A.M., after only two hours' sleep. Leonel was headed to Santiago, Chile to catch up to Oscar and Alvaro, and I was trying to catch up to Robert and Peter, who I expected were still admiring the condors in Colca Canyon. I rode like hell to Chimbay, thinking I might overtake them as they started their day's ride. If I could find them my ride would be easier—I could stop worrying about directions on the unmarked roads and just follow Robert on autopilot, as usual. That would've been nice since I was wiped out from the previous night's festivities.

Instead I had to resort to using a map, after all this time. I'd been doing well without them, but this area was so desolate that I suspected I'd need the reference, so luckily I picked up a map of southern Peru in Arequipa before I left. Not far from town, a lady in a passing van pulled over and told me they'd be coming my way—she'd stayed at their hotel and met them both and, according to her, they'd be along any minute. While I waited on the side of the road, I tightened and oiled my new chain. After half an hour I was tired of waiting and rode closer to the canyon, only to meet another passing minivan that stopped with news that they were not, in fact, ever going to pass. They had already left. The first lady had given me inaccurate information, and they were by now long gone.

I continued on to Tuti and the roads sucked. I was exhausted and dehydrated, and now, frustrated at being further delayed by bad information, I stopped for lunch and then continued on the ever climbing roads, higher and higher into the Peruvian altiplano. An hour after lunch I stopped and drank a liter of water and napped for thirty minutes on a big concrete block off the side of the road. Altitude sickness was attacking me for the first time, and I suspected my dehydrated state was the cause. I continued on and found that getting fuel in the middle of nowhere was risky and expensive. The orange-brown gas came from one-gallon jugs, and a couple coffee filters I brought along just for this purpose removed the orange metallic chunks that floated in it.

About seven or eight hours into the ride I began making errors in judgment. Robert repeatedly told me that mistakes come most often when you're in a hurry. Perhaps that's why he did everything with such determined slowness. For some reason, I decided I needed to reach Cuzco that night and that's what I was going to do no matter what. I could've easily found a hotel, but I wanted to get to Cuzco. Unfortunately, that city was still very far away, and I picked a bad time to get ambitious. The roads were some of the worst we'd seen, and huge trucks and buses charged around like giant angry bulls, kicking up stones and gravel everywhere.

The fun was just beginning. The roads went from really crappy to super crappy, and the KLR and I took a serious beating. My only consolation was that Robert and Peter were probably slowed a little by the rough roads and that might give me a chance to catch up to them. The hard seat on Peter's bike was notorious for leaving his butt welted. As I rode along and suffered, I couldn't help but smile at the image of Peter complaining loudly to Robert about his swollen ass as they road along.

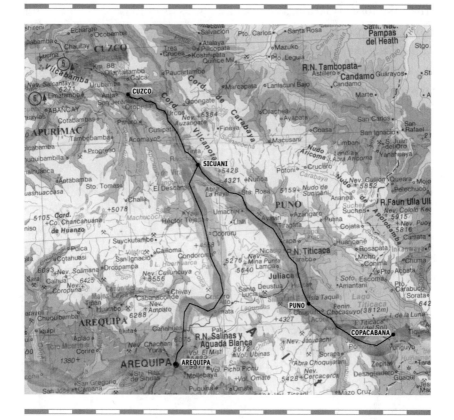

I was stuck behind a slow-moving truck with unusually large wheels—from up close they seemed to reach my shoulders. The road was narrow, and deep mounds of the odious Peruvian dust had settled in furrows on either side from passing vehicles. As I accelerated to pass on the left side of the truck, the dust began to give way from under my front wheel and the bike veered, heading toward a ten-foot embankment. I bore right to counter the new direction I was taking, and the bike set itself into a fishtail I couldn't control. On my left was the embankment waiting to break my arm. On my right were the four-and-a-half-foot-tall spinning trailer tires, waiting to do something worse. I struggled helplessly as the bike high-sided me. That is, when the bike loses traction, the tail end slides around, and then regains enough traction to catapult the flailing rider sideways into the air, usually in the original direction of travel. In mid-flail I realized that if I landed under that truck wheel, my pelvis would be crushed like balsa wood, and I'd be stranded out here to bleed. And, if that truck tire crushed me underneath it and I started to lose blood from my wounds, I could easily die before any help could be summoned to get me to a hospital. As I flew through the air I was acutely aware that there was nothing I could do about it now.

I landed hard near the truck's wheel, but unbelievably it rolled past me harmlessly. The wind was knocked out of me and my arm was bruised below the elbow when I landed. The sleeve of my riding jacket was torn, and I scratched the bike up pretty badly. Plus I made an ass of myself in front of three kids on two bicycles. Crashing is always more painful in front of an audience. Other than my embarrassment and the bruise on my arm, I was fine.

I kept moving, and not long after my first fall the dust-covered ruts in the road got the best of me again. I was only doing about 10 MPH, but as I came around a hairpin switchback, I hit a large rock hidden under a pool of fine dust. The rock turned my front tire and despite my slow speed I went down hard. In fact, I hit the ground so hard that a pointy stone punched a dime-sized hole clean through my right saddlebag, which is saying a lot because those plastic bags are nearly indestructible. The force of the crash also wrenched the bag off the mounting bracket. That spill really knocked the wind out of me, but I didn't have time to brood. A bus was coming and I had to scramble to get out of the way. I moved the bike to the roadside, mutely watched the bus thunder past, and then sat down with my head in my hands. I almost felt like giving up. This was easily the worst ride of the trip. After the dust settled, I collected myself and the bike back together and continued at a steady pace, vowing that as soon as I got where I was going, I would just go to sleep, and things would look better in the morning.

The morning was still a long way off. The late afternoon sun was slowly falling, and still I rode. I crossed a bridge made of logs and planks and covered with peat and stones—every time a vehicle passed, parts of the structure vibrated free and dropped into the abyss below. I dodged more buses and trucks, clambering along the ever dusty, rocky Peruvian roads. As dusk settled I realized that my headlight wasn't working. Since my heated handgrips were also out, I concluded that it was my main fuse, which was stashed inconveniently underneath my seat. (On other bikes that may not be a big deal, but on a KLR removing the seat involves a few minutes of screw and bolt loosening to get at it.) Too tired and frustrated to stop and replace it, I just switched on my turn signal and kept riding in the dark. I figured at least oncoming drivers would see me.

As I rode into the city of Sicuani, night jelled on the skyline. At this point I was cold, tired, hungry, frustrated, and sore from my falls. The only thing driving me was the knowledge that if I made it to Cuzco that night, this hell ride would be over and I wouldn't have to continue it the following day. All I had going for me was that the road from Sicuani to Cuzco was paved, and it would only take about two more hours to get there.

After gassing up and changing the fuse, I rode into the high beams of countless other drivers and froze my ass off in the night wind. The air currents blew bitterly, but I didn't want to stop and dig my electric vest out of the bags. There was all that unpacking and repacking, and the thought of removing my coat to put on the vest was appalling in this cold. I also didn't want to lose time by eating, so I went hungry. Once stopped, I was afraid I wouldn't be able to get going again.

The vest was really what I needed; with each moment my temperature was dropping and I was unwittingly losing my motor skills, reaction time, and ability to make quick decisions. This is commonly known as the beginning of hypothermia. It didn't help that I'd been riding for twelve hours, hadn't eaten for eight, and only slept six hours in the last two days.

Near 8:30 P.M. my exhaustion was extreme. As I crawled through a traffic jam in some small town, celebrating crowds paraded the streets. I could actually feel my blood pumping coolly in my neck. As if in a bizarre dream, drunken faces laughed near me as I passed, empty bottles sailed overhead, and bonfires blazed. People lay in vomit in the gutters, or stumbled along the pavement around me, patting me on the back as I picked my way between the meandering masses—I was just one more freakish spectacle that seemed completely appropriate to them in their reveling. I cleared the howling crowds and rode on.

Mercifully, the lights of Cuzco appeared. The time was near 9:30 P.M.; after fourteen hours and 370 miles of shit roads I wanted nothing more than to find a hole to crawl into. I visited the so-called "tourist police" in town to find a hotel; they were supposedly good at helping travelers with such information. A couple of the officers inside found me an inexpensive place nearby and offered to keep the bike locked up in the police building, which sounded fine until one of them chuckled and said that after all their help I'd be compelled to let him take my bike for a ride in the morning. Ha, dream on, you giant testicle. I laughed and said, "Sure, Sure. I just need to go get some dinner first." I rode out of there and found a hotel and parking on my own. Fucking Peruvian cops.

A Swiss couple I met suggested a certain youth hostel—a real rat's nest. At that hour it was my best and only option. Removing my mangled boots, which were all flapping soles and torn laces after the day's crashing, I climbed under the covers at 11 P.M. and did the world's greatest impersonation of a corpse until they kicked me out at 10 the next morning.

Welcome to sunny Cuzco, the former seat of power and spirituality of the Inca empire. The city is still blessed in certain areas with remnants of Incan architecture—many of the walls and even some entire buildings are made from Incan stonework. The stones are carved from solid granite, each block individually shaped to fit precisely into its intended spot. Each block is unique, though they're generally rectangular in shape. Many have more than four sides, and some have projections sticking out to help the stone fit exactly next to the individual blocks around it. The work is so meticulous that the blocks fit perfectly flush (a piece of paper couldn't be slid into the cracks) and mortar was unneeded. The incredibly tough structures have survived earthquakes, time, and erosion. The only thing that hurt them was the arrival of the Spaniards; the conquistadors destroyed many of the better examples of Incan architecture. However, the construction methods of the Inca were so effective that the remaining Incan stonework (much of which had been incorporated into the foundations of some of later Spanish buildings) never failed to outlast the later colonial structures built over them.

It's not known exactly how the Inca worked with this incredibly tough stone, because they had no material harder than granite, such as a diamond-tipped saws or drills. How the Inca managed to cut the rough stone is a mystery, but supposedly once it had been cut to the general shape needed, they smoothed the rocks by rubbing them with sand, water, and blocks of wood. The sheer man-years of work to sand even a single block this way is staggering to contemplate. Everything in Incan country was made from these stones, and the Inca ran a truly massive empire. Three-fourths of the population must have been stone sanders.

Cuzco was in celebration that morning, as it was every July. Brightly dressed men and women danced around the plaza. The stones of the ancient city streets and sidewalks, long ago worn smooth from shoe soles, now reverberated the thumping of the dancers' feet. The palatial cathedral dominated the plaza and cast a refreshing shade on the crowds watching from its steps. Spectators wandered everywhere. Locals and tourists gathered to watch alongside each other. Apparently partying was a way of life here, since Cuzqueños, as the residents are called, have daily celebrations almost straight through from May to August, a three-month blur of parades, dancing, and public drinking.

I stood above the crowd in the balcony of a cyber café, where I had just sent an e-mail to the guys to try to find them. The café had an excellent view of the dancers below. The women wore bright red wraps and white hats, and the men carried small wooden hoes and had alpaca wool caps with earflaps in amalgams of colors that would make an art teacher retch. Despite the discontinuity of their appearance, all together, the parade was astoundingly beautiful. The men and women moved separately, performing different dance steps that coincided with the same music. The women and men crossed paths, spinning, stopping, and bending down in time, then coming up all together with a loud "hey!"

"Devil-o!" I heard a voice call out. Peter smiled up at me from the curb.

He had found me quite by accident, and together we went back to their hotel, where I signed in and we gave our bikes some much-needed maintenance. Despite the warmth of the days, the temperature dropped rapidly in the evenings at this altitude. Our room was absolutely frigid that night; even a brief walk across the room sent shivers of cold pain up through bare feet. "Robert," I said, addressing him as he left the bathroom, "Peter is shivering under his blankets and he wanted you to heat him up." Robert looked at me for a moment, and then lay down on the bed behind Peter and threw a big paw over his chest. Peter's face was blank. Robert then tossed his meaty leg over Peter's hip, pinning Peter to the bed in a big Canadian bear hug. We burst out laughing and Peter squirmed underneath Robert to knock him from the bed. We were back together again, just the three of us, and despite all our earlier problems there was a giddy happiness to this moment.

After dinner that evening I went to the Norton Rat motorcycle bar, our new headquarters. Peter and Robert showed up with the tickets they'd just bought for the Inti Raymi celebration, which we were all very excited about coming up in just a couple of days. Inti Raymi, or the Festival of the Sun, occurs only once a year, and is of great significance to the Peruvian Indians and all people of Incan descent. The celebration was hundreds of years old, one of the few links to the past that the Spanish were unable to obliterate. We felt very fortunate to be in Cuzco in time to see the spectacle, essentially a parade made up of people representing the various Incan rulers and subjects from across the ancient empire. They move en masse from the Temple of the Sun to the main plaza and then up to the ruins of Sacsayhuamán. We were told that the festivities end there with the sacrifice of a llama on the faux stone stage built for the show.

The next day I had my riding jacket repaired for three dollars, and the soles of my boots replaced for six. To stop the damn fork-clicking noise once and for all I also bought a meaty 27 mm wrench to torque the head nut on the bike. I also finally found the Holy Grail of malaria pills, Larium, that had been eluding me since I began the trip. After all the headaches and searching, I discovered the branch office of the South American Explorers Club in Cuzco had some. As a side bonus, I was able to buy them with my leftover Equadorian currency. Pleased with such a productive day, I adjourned to Norton Rat's and continued my notes. I was pretty far behind, and since taking trip notes was something I did almost religiously, it felt good to catch up. My companions showed up and we began a philosophical debate about justice. I live for such discussions, and I don't even mind it being two against one, which was often the case with these guys. Their position seemed to be that if someone murders someone, they should be killed—no mercy. I argued that killing does no good, since it doesn't return the victim to life, and therefore only makes the society or person that executes the murderer their moral equal.

Peter insisted on the necessity of removing dangerous elements from society. Peter owned four guns (one of them an AK-47), and Robert said he owned six. "You aren't one of those antigun nuts, are you, Devil-o?" Peter asked. "Have you ever shot a gun?"

"Sure," I said, even though I didn't really see how the question related. "A few times."

"That's good," he said. "Then at least you weren't completely brainwashed."

The next morning was the beginning of Inti Raymi. We followed the parades and the crowds from the Temple of the Sun to the main plaza, up the rocky path to the ruins of the fortress at Sacsayhuamán. For the main event, the royalty (played by select members of the community), were carried into the stage area on gilded litters. Dancers representing military processions and visitors from all corners of the Incan empire recognized and honored the event with their traditional local dances.

Robert and I waited with cool beers in hand and hot breath in our throats as they carried the bound llama onto the stage. He was a big one, black and white, and he struggled mightily for freedom. Although Peter didn't seem to mind the idea of taking human lives, he couldn't stomach the thought of watching an animal killed and had already left. Robert and I weren't sure what to make of this either, but we were worried for nothing because the llama wasn't really sacrificed anyway.

Six people held the hairy creature down while a priest went through the motions of removing the living heart, and then triumphantly held up a heart and part of what appeared to be an extremely long aorta, or a piece of intestine. Even to the intoxicated observer, this was obviously faked. The organ pieces that the priest displayed were blood free, and Robert said he'd noticed them sitting in a bowl earlier by the sacrificial table. They were probably picked up from the butcher store that very day. Plus the llama was still kicking and wrenching its neck as they stuffed it into a secret door under the stage. Ironically, despite my feelings on killing humans, there was a murky little part of me that was disappointed the sacrifice didn't take place. The chance to go back in time and see something of a culture so foreign to mine, especially one that no longer exists as it did, was very enticing, even if it happened to be gruesome. And as long as they ate the animal and used its wool, how was that any different from any other butchering happening in slaughterhouses all over the world every day?

The day after Inti Raymi we took a train up to Machu Picchu. The train bumped its way up the tracks, ratcheting forward and backward to scale the steep mountain walls on the way up to the ruins. This was the last major tourist stop we had planned in Peru. We would've taken the bikes, but there were no marked roads all the way there, and we were hesitant to try to follow the train tracks (for good reason—the trains happened to be using them). Furthermore, we found out later that Aguas Calientes, the tourist town that lies below the ruins, does not allow motorcycles. One more place I could never live.

We casually wandered the vendor's stalls that lined the main street and browsed the handmade wares. This was something Robert particularly enjoyed, and he often stopped to negotiate with vendors. I was just there for the walk, and Peter followed at a distance, obviously bored. Robert began a discussion with a merchant regarding a certain tapestry. He wanted to know if he could get one custom-made, similar to the one displayed, with just a slight variation in color. I tried to explain what he wanted to the vendor, and Peter walked over, hands behind his back and neck craned forward, listening with pretend earnestness.

"He would like this same pattern," I explained in Spanish as I pointed at the fabrics, "but with these colors."

"Yes," Peter added with a solemn look, also in Spanish, "the gentleman also wants it cut into the shape of a hooded cape, something that can flow elegantly in the wind behind him while he rides on his motorcycle."

The vendors looked a little confused, and I'm sure I did too, because none of us knew what the hell Peter was talking about. One of them had enough composure to say, "Yes, I think we can come up with something like that . . . what cape length would the gentleman require?"

Robert watched us, waiting to see what the results of the inquiry would bring, and when I finally realized what Peter was saying, I burst out laughing. Peter joined in, practically falling on top of the merchants as he was stricken with pealing laughter, apparently wrestling with the image of a big, bearded Robert riding his black BMW with a colorful llama cape flowing majestically behind him. I explained the joke to Robert. He was not amused.

Robert stormed off and wouldn't talk to Peter the rest of the night. For a while he didn't talk to me either, probably because he suspected I was an accomplice. He felt Peter's joke belittled the vendors and their craft, and made us all look bad. I guess he was right, but Peter didn't see it that way. Like most everything else, he found it hysterical. As far as the vendors were concerned, they simply shook their heads at the silliness of it and probably wrote us off as drunks.

Aside from the fact that motorcycles were illegal, Machu Picchu was incredibly cool. We spent two days visiting the ancient, well-preserved structures that were packed together amidst the jungle mess on top of a vertigo-inducing precipice. Several tall peaks stood nearby, covered with fat mats of vegetation, as was the mountain upon which the ruins lay. Peru's government employs many workers whose sole job is to continually hack away at the ever encroaching vegetation that threatens to bury every last trace of Incan handiwork under a heavy green carpet, as it did once before, after the Inca finally abandoned it.

Above Machu Picchu is a path leading to Huayna Picchu, a mountain overlooking the ruins. A staircase formed with jagged, crudely hewn steps leads up to the top, and handrails of white rope and green-painted steel cables are anchored into the cliff for safety. Other climbers coming down encouraged me on my way up. "Ten minutes more," they said. "It's worth it." I scaled the peak in about thirty minutes despite the severe cold I was coming down with. I'd picked it up while necking with a charming Canadian tourist I met before the Inti Raymi celebration, and to the fury of Peter and Robert, I'd passed it along to them.

The view was fantastic, the day brilliant. Rough grass, rampant super ferns, and climbing vines were sprawling reminders that this place was still wild. I rested at the apex, looking down at the Machu

Picchu ruins set on top of these scattered, green-colored monoliths beneath cream-swirled clouds. Agricultural terraces were stacked in angular, thrusting projections, running up the sides of the hills in incongruous patterns, yet still in harmony with the jutting forest outcrops on these mountains. Down in the valley, the river pulled like a string of thick sapphires through the brush and rock.

Without a doubt, I was in the right place at just the right moment. Here once more that sense of calm harmony I craved. Machu Picchu, as a whole, screams that sensation. This place proves that once, long before any of us existed, some group of humans had done something incredibly right. No, it's not just the buildings—there are excellent examples of Incan stonework in many other places. The feeling also comes from the location, the way the structures lie, and how the massive stones force shadows from the sun, at angles just so. And the added wonder is the sense that it's on the verge of disappearing, because the jungle is constantly creeping in, jealously reclaiming the rocks. This place has a holy feeling, like a temple, and as I walked between the buildings I felt I was privileged to be among them, but that I was somehow profaning them at the same time. These ruins aren't magical, because no work of human hands is magic. What they are is something indefinably *right*—a physical proof of some small glimmer of divinity in the human soul.

Speaking of existence, there is something laughable about our presence on this planet. Like opposite sides of the same coin, our divinity is coupled with our banality. We seem incapable of making anything of great value without later corrupting it. The government of Peru has decided it's a good idea to build a casino up there next to the ruins. At that time, the construction of a suspended gondola to ferry high rollers to the top was just beginning. Soon visitors would be able to enjoy the view of these ancient structures bathed in the neon lights of the casino strip. Yes, the ruins as they stood were indeed in danger of disappearing, but the creeping jungle wasn't the problem.

We were taking in this soon-to-be-debased place when Peter had an unpleasant experience. He was examining one of the clever Incan staircases built into the walls of some of the farming terraces. The "stairs" are really just oblong stones that stick out perpendicular to the wall, stacked in an ascending pattern for climbing. The design wastes no space and won't interfere with crop growth, but also has no handrail. When the compact steps are viewed while directly facing the wall, they're all but invisible.

Peter decided to climb down the staircase to take a closer look. Nothing strange about that, but the surreal is best camouflaged in the midst of the ordinary. A rather large tourist, whom I'd overheard speaking French earlier, came along and attempted to follow him down. The Frenchman had a VHS camera bag in one hand, a big bottle of water in the other, and an expensive 35 mm with an enormous telephoto lens wrapped around his neck. Robert and I happened to be looking in their direction, and we watched in helpless silence as the tourist lost his footing, right leg flailing, and went crashing toward Peter, back first, arms splayed out pathetically in an effort to protect the items he carried. He was at least ten feet from the next terrace when he slipped. Surprisingly, the man uttered no sound as he fell, and for a moment I was unable to speak as well. I could only watch in horror as this fat person plunged silently toward Peter. The impact quickly followed and a loud crunch came from Peter's spine. Both men hit the ground and quickly jumped up again, the Frenchman dazed, muttering and fumbling for his camera equipment, and Peter spurting curses and cradling the back of his neck in both hands. "You big-balled idiot! Son of a whore! Moron!" Of course, the swearing sounded cooler in Peter's Medellín Spanish.

Both men were OK, but Peter was sore for days. If he'd been hit a little differently his neck could've been snapped in half. And Peter may have actually saved that Frenchman's life—the ground was covered with sharp stones that could've split his head with the combined force of gravity and his wine-and-cheese obesity. The event seemed so bizarre because of its sudden danger. One minute we were calmly enjoying a marvel of the ancient world, the next Peter was nearly killed by a tumbling tourist.

We took a train back the following day, and decided it was time to leave Cuzco for Puno, on the shore of Lake Titicaca. The only way there was to retrace part of the roads we'd already been on, but that was fine because the road was nicely paved and the day was a treasure. Peter and Robert had gone ahead of me, and I was taking my time enjoying the trip. The route was infinitely nicer on this warm day than on the freezing night in which I'd arrived. However, nearly everything that could've appeared on the road in front of me did: dogs; cows; sheep; goats; little children and their half-inflated balls; crusted, white-haired grandmothers bent in half with huge bundles of sticks; drunks; boulders; fat birds. Even a great yellow earthmover suddenly backed out onto the road. By the end of all this, I wouldn't have been surprised if a chunk of an airplane cabin dropped from the sky in front of me.

I knew Puno was a strange place the minute I rode into town and saw a row of guys sitting in front of sewing machines on the roadside, just waiting. They sat around expectantly as if the magical sewing fairy was going to fly down from the mountains at any moment with baskets of cloth for them to work into dresses, pants, and frilly cravats under the glittering, sunny sky. What a strange sight they made. But that's not what people go to Puno to see. People go there to see the famous Floating Islands.

Puno is located on the shores of Lake Titicaca, renowned not only as the world's highest navigable lake, but also the lake most frequently the butt of prepubescent jokes. It is home to the so-called Floating Islands, large, semianchored floating docks made of dried yellow reeds, where people live. As the reeds under the water decay and cease to keep an island afloat, the natives add more dried reeds to the top of the island, and so the cycle supports itself. Centuries ago the inhabitants developed this unusual way of life, but now the islands seem to offer more benefits as a tourist trap than an actual place to live. The islands are somewhat stationary, because they're tethered to rock formations near the surface. But they do fluctuate with the elevation of the water. At different times of the year they'll do little more than rest on top of said rocks, and during rainier times they bounce and sway gently on the swollen lake.

At the Puno docks our boat lay among an inch-thick film of algae that looked just like shorn golf course grass. Our chubby captain offered a three-hour tour aboard a boat with a car motor; the rudder was made of rebar and sheet metal. As we pulled out of the dock, the thick green mat of algae parted and closed back around us, giving the impression that the boat sailed across a manicured green on the twelfth hole. The first couple of islands we visited were unremarkable. They didn't float very well, they smelled like sewage, and they looked worse. The Indians on the islands were selling the same tourist crap found on shore, only more expensive. Kids everywhere begged for money. The islands were small and the huts there were pitiful mounds of sheet metal, woven reed walls, and cloth doors that snapped in the stiff breeze. A few piles of human excrement dotted the crushed reed ground.

Back on our boat, Peter noticed an island off the beaten waterway and asked the pilot to take us there, but he waffled. The boatmen who bring tourists to the various islands probably receive some kind of kickback from the sales the islanders make. Perhaps the captains only take tourists to islands where their families live. But somehow, Peter convinced him and we puttered over.

Peter's island was different, appearing much more orderly and well maintained, even from one hundred feet away. The reed surface was soft; as we jumped onto shore the whole thing gave like a sponge, like walking on a stiff gel that sank past our ankles with each step but wouldn't break through. This island was immaculate and the huts were all made entirely of the dried grasses. It was much more attractive.

Woven reed boats were docked nearby, their bows curved up and worked into the heads of giant llamas and sea monsters, complete with dead dried fish in their mouths. Peter found a man who operated one, and we hired him to take us to shore in his charming reed craft. We hopped on board and our new captain made sail (even his sail was made of woven reed and, amazingly, it was only held in place with a thin stick and some twine). Our new guide said it takes about one month to make a reed boat, and each one lasts for about a year. I floated into a nap listening to the captain speak as we drifted our way silently to shore on the back of the fibrous sea monster.

After forty days in Peru, it was time to move on. Robert had accomplished his goal of seeing all he could in this country that had always interested him, so now the plan was to enter Bolivia. The scenery along the road was pretty as we moved along, and in the far distance the shimmering white-tipped Andes slowly clambered across the expansive waters. One town we passed along the way had giant red rock formations like the arched, spiky backs of stegosaurs. We took a break for lunch, which was odd because these days, Robert and Peter never seemed to want to. Perhaps the illness we got in Cuzco was keeping their appetites down.

Near the border the road became earthen and rocky. The Peruvian border officials were courteous and efficient. Bang—in and out. The Bolivian officials were friendly but disorganized. While getting the border check, the chubby cop in the Bolivian police office asked me for a bribe: "A donation to buy candles for the Virgin." He smiled and pointed over his shoulder at a statue of Mary.

"Oh, sure. Damn. I'm out of change, let me go ask my friends for some." I was used to all this by now. He must've known I wouldn't be back.

We went to Copacabana, a grungy tourist town that was, at times, surprisingly pretty. The town is situated on the shore of Lake Titicaca, so we decided to check out the supposed birthplace of the Inca, the nearby Islands of the Sun and the Moon. The tour was to leave in the morning; the evening found us at a bar run by a German fellow and his Bolivian girlfriend. We played chess and passed the hours, finally arriving back at our hotel so late we had to bang on the door to wake someone to let us in. In the morning we overslept and rushed to catch the boat to the islands. After all the rush, the tour was disappointing. Based on the low quality of the ruins, I found it hard to believe that any Inca had ever been there.

The next day Peter's rear tire started us late on the road to La Paz. The tubeless-style tire had seen better days—the inside looked like a quilt, it had so many rubber patches. While squatting to remove the rear wheel and find the new leak, Peter chatted up the *vulcanizador.* "You must be careful along the roads to La Paz," the man told him. "The farmers are protesting the government." Being a talkative guy, Peter was always getting these kinds of useful tidbits, but we never knew whether to take them at face value or not. Supposedly there were roadblocks set up all the way from Copacabana to La Paz. Rumor mongers exist everywhere, and you can't spend your whole life running from every potential problem. We decided to try our luck anyway. The worst-case scenario, we thought, would be that we'd have to turn back.

In the end Peter's tire was unfixable. He resorted to using my spare rear inner tube to make his shredded tire hold air. We thanked the repairman for his help and set out to see what the road had in store for us.

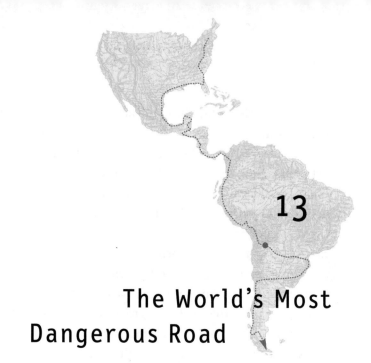

13

The World's Most Dangerous Road

➤ As predicted by Peter's informant, the road to La Paz did get exciting. We enjoyed the beautiful curving views as we slid along the shores of the lake, noticing that in a few places some rocks had been laid on the asphalt in an effort to slow traffic—most of them had been kicked aside. Those were just small indicators of the big trouble to come.

From Copacabana we rode to the narrowest part of Lake Titicaca, where we hired a ferry to take us across to the town of Tiquina. The ferry was just a huge, flat raft, like a small barge, powered by an outboard motor. Our ferryman was expert in the extreme. He instructed us to back the bikes onto the rickety float and guided us surely across the water, pointing our front tires toward the docking area on the other side. With perfect timing he shut off the motor, calmly walked up to the fore of his craft, and secured the rope to the dock before the ferry even touched it. As the boat's momentum closed the gap, our captain cinched us tight to the dock, and we came to rest without even a small bump. He made docking his massive raft look as easy as slipping an electrical plug into a socket. We fired up the bikes and rode straight off.

I've noticed that the there seems to be an inverse relationship between canine intelligence and latitude. In other words, the further south one travels, the dumber the dogs become. Bolivia's dogs proved to be the stupidest I'd seen. Instead of running into the street after us, Bolivian dogs just sat on the roadside or even on the road itself and waited for us to come to them. I almost hit two.

We cruised along on good pavement until we came upon a little town called Janko Amaya, where we encountered a crowd of farmers and fishermen in the road. The group seemed to be led by two men— both lean, one tall, and the other shorter and more grizzled. The crowd blocked our path and a couple of the men flagged us down. The lead-

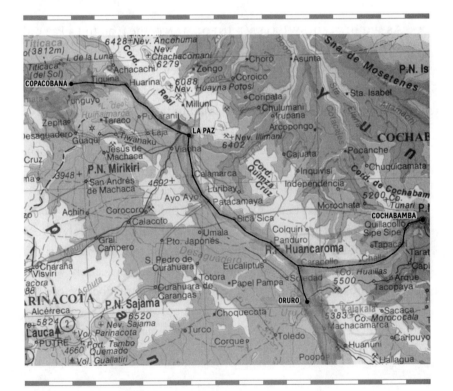

ers approached, and we asked them what was happening. They said a peaceful demonstration was in progress against many of the problems in the government. We asked how long the blockade was to last, and if they would allow us to pass.

They told us they planned to stand there every day until their issues were addressed. Foremost was that in two days the government planned to privatize the school system, and these people would now have to pay to educate their children. That seemed to be what catalyzed the revolt. "If we can barely afford to eat, how are we to pay for school?" they said. "And if we can't go to school, how are we to improve our station in life?" Following that reasoning was a string of related problems, none of them good.

They said government corruption was strangling the people. Much of the aid that the United States and other countries sent to help them never trickled down to those it was intended for. The money vanished at higher levels, and government officials just got richer. They were requesting the removal of these new school laws, among others, and asking for increased economic freedoms for the lower classes. That, they said, is the reason these roads were now shut down with dozens of roadblocks between here and La Paz, and also the reason why, regretfully, we would not be allowed to continue.

We listened quietly through all this. When the leaders finished speaking, Peter began to probe if they would let us by—I could tell he planned to offer an economic contribution to the cause, provided they'd let us pass. Sensing where he was going, I quickly interrupted. This could've been a bad trend starting here, one that—on a purely ethical level—reinforced the corruption in the system. On a more practical level, we could've blown a lot of cash trying to buy our way through every blockade we encountered on the way to La Paz.

Peter looked at me with annoyance as I addressed the leaders. I hoped my idea would work, otherwise he'd never let me live it down. I tried to sound professional and humble. I told them I was writing about our motorcycle trip, and that if I included them in the tale, maybe someone who could do more for them may one day read about their problems. Although I said I didn't think it would do much, if they wanted my help I'd gladly give it. All we asked for was permission to continue our journey.

They went for it. I quickly pulled out my pen and paper and started taking notes. Peter made a show of translating any finer points I missed as the men spoke, and I scribbled furiously. They didn't want to give their names or have any photos taken, for fear of recrimination, but they did want to give a quote.

The taller of the two men, who'd been doing most of the talking, thought a minute before saying: "Tell your friends and associates that hunger does not wait. We must be heard because there is no equality when only the poor have to live by the law." The men in the back nodded approvingly. I told them we respected their cause and the peaceful manner in which they organized their protest. They thanked us, told us we were free to continue, and we wished them luck in their efforts.

The rest of the ride was filled with similar encounters. We were halted at six or eight different roadblocks, but a couple of them we avoided by taking side roads. Things looked hairy for a minute when we stopped in front of a group of adrenaline-pumped teenage students. There were about fifty of them, all edgier than self-loathing Oxy-10 users at a Marilyn Manson concert. They weren't very receptive to our offer and things looked bad for us until their teacher showed up.

A few other vehicles were on the road, but we were the only ones getting past the roadblocks. Sometimes we had to talk our way through, and sometimes we didn't say a word and they let us pass anyway. The fact that we were foreigners on highly maneuverable vehicles was a big help.

Some stretches of road were littered with rocks, sticks, and broken glass that must've been placed there by every available hand, because the obstacles often stretched for kilometers at a time. Weaving and braking, we made our way slowly through the mess. Between the roadblocks and debris strewn on the road, we covered sixty miles at an average of 15 MPH. Riot police and military police were sometimes camped near the protesters, dispassionately watching the events unfold, but ready to act if any violence broke out.

Just a few miles from our destination we saw a big group of cops in riot gear and trucks approaching. They were clearing the rubble from the pavement and seemed ready for trouble. They questioned us and then let us pass. I wanted to warn the protesters somehow, to protect them. Theirs was a peaceful fight and the show of police force could only serve to incite violence. Peter advised us to be careful with people we were to meet now. "Wherever those cops have been, the protesters are probably going to be pissed off."

We made it through without further incident. Cars lined up near a tollbooth, heading the direction from which we'd just come. A few people stopped us to ask about the road, hoping our arrival was an indication that the route was now clear so they too could pass. We assured them that there was probably no way a car would get through.

As we took a circular road into the giant bowl La Paz sits in, the sun painted a glossy sheen on the city. Technically not the capital, La Paz is the world's highest pseudo-capital, set in a canyon at 1,650 feet. Sucre is the actual capital, but La Paz is where the Congress meets and most governmental functions occur. In the midst of Bolivia's economic stagnation, La Paz seemed as modern, successful, and interesting as any major city in the Americas. There were digital surround sound theaters, twenty-four-hour Internet cafés, and the comfort of McDonald's, refreshing and homey in its revolting sort of way.

We made a few day trips, to the ruins of Tiahuanaco and the town of Coroico. On the route to Tiahuanaco we saw more brainless dogs lying by the side of the highway. Peter theorized that these dogs eked out their existence by waiting for, and feeding off, road kill. Engaging but implausible. These dogs seemed too domesticated, and as I learned later, they actually stayed by the thoroughfares because drivers fed them as they passed. The roads in this part of Bolivia are dangerous, so truckers and travelers believe that if they appease the "dog gods" by feeding their mortal brothers that line the roads, they will have safe journeys. So the drivers throw out a few crackers or part of an unfinished sandwich to the dogs in exchange for secure passage. The trade contradicts the obvious—many dogs wandering the roads pose a hazard to motorists (especially motorcyclists). Encouraging more dogs to hang around to partake of all the free food creates more potential for accidents. That's why I was so surprised when Peter and Robert jumped on the stupidity wagon and bought some bread rolls to throw to the dog gods.

On the way out of the Tiahuanaco ruins Peter and Robert stopped, conferred a moment, and then started off. "So what's going on now?" I said. "Or do you guys mind telling me?" They paused and turned to look at me.

"We wanted to check out some sacred rocks located on the other side of town," Peter said. Robert described them a bit for me.

"OK," I said, and followed. Robert wanted to ride behind for a change, so Peter led and I followed him in second place. I was a few hundred meters behind when he suddenly stopped, turned around, and went riding down into a ditch. I slowed down and realized that he was actually chasing a little shepherd boy. Peter was up on the pegs and bounding along after him; apparently the kid threw a rock at him. Peter was deservedly upset—he spurted out curses with a rage to make a convict wet his pants. The rock was as big as a baseball and had missed Peter's face shield by inches. He was doing over 70 MPH when he passed, and if that rock had hit him he surely would've been sent home horizontally, in refrigerated storage. First a falling Frenchman and now this. Obviously Peter, more than any of us, needed to keep his eyes open for flying objects.

Back in La Paz my companions stopped to confer at a red light near our hotel. Then they turned toward the hotel garage and pulled in. We parked and covered the bikes. "I'm really hungry," Peter said. When to eat was yet another bone of contention in the group; I was usually the only one hungry around midday. Actually, I was pretty much hungry all the time. The other two were fine with just two meals daily. "I'm surprised Devil-o didn't have an attack of hypoglycemia and freak out because we didn't eat lunch," Peter added.

"I thought you guys wanted to go see the rocks on the opposite side of town." I said.

"We thought it might be too much of a hassle to get over there with all the rush-hour traffic."

"I wish you guys would tell me when you come to these decisions," I said.

"Why, Devil-o?" Peter said with a smile. "Do you feel . . ."

"I feel left out when you guys make decisions without me," I tersely cut him off. "You've been doing it a lot lately and I'd appreciate it if you'd include me in the plans. OK?"

"Sure. No problem." Peter said. They both looked a little surprised at my outburst.

The following day we made our way to Coroico. The little town was of no interest, except for the fact that the only way there is along the World's Most Dangerous Road. That name, in part, comes from the road's contribution to Bolivia's worst mass transit disaster ever, in which over one hundred people died in a single crash. Carlos Pizarrino-Inti was driving an overloaded *collectivo* truck that plunged off the narrow dirt path and fell thousands of feet to the jungle floor below. There were no survivors. That accident happened back when the Coroico road was bidirectional. Regulations for traffic have since been changed to make the road less dangerous. The road is now one-way to Coroico for part of the day, and then one-way back to La Paz (the opposite direction) for the rest of the day. Don't be deceived—the road is still profoundly unsafe.

First of all, it's very narrow and fraught with bad drivers. Big trucks and buses careen around the corners, never concerned that a car could be broken down or stopped in their path around the next blind curve. There are no guardrails on the roadside as it weaves along

sheer cliff walls. The road is almost entirely dirt and dried clay, which is incredibly slick when wet (only slightly less slippery than an oil patch). Several waterfalls cascade onto the road off the mountain, and wherever they hit, the dirt washed away to reveal slick rocks and the scary clay mud. Even if you try to be safe and drive in the very center, you're still only two meters and a stifled scream away from the longest (and last) thirty seconds of your life. The road is built on a high precipice, and a glance down offers a vertigo-inducing view limited only by the green rainforest flora and the finite capabilities of human vision. I can't imagine how unsafe it must've been when the road was bidirectional.

We registered our names with the police at a checkpoint (if we didn't make it back to sign out they would begin the search for our bodies), and paid 5.50 bolivianos each to use the road. "Be very careful," the cop said.

For me that road was, in a word, unfun. I instantly decided how to handle it; I took my time. Every last bit of it. I paid complete attention to the road—100 percent. All my concentration was focused on not falling off the side of the road, not getting pushed around by the jerks in the SUVs, and not stumbling over the mud ridge formed between the tire tracks in the trail's center. Did I mention I was also very focused on not falling over the side?

The aforementioned SUV drivers didn't help matters much. I've had some experience with dangerous driving situations. New York cabbies are notoriously belligerent, and drivers from Massachusetts, collectively known as Massholes, are famous in the Northeast for their lack of courtesy and poor driving ability. Drivers on the World's Most Dangerous Road all greedily vied for room, and made the worst Massholes I've known look like gentle nuns driving musical ice cream trucks. Each of those vehicle operators considered himself significantly more important than anyone else on the road—especially motorcyclists.

I made lots of passing room for any of the maniacs that got near me. When stuck behind a large vehicle, I waited patiently until it pulled over a bit to let me pass. Generally it was always safer to pass on the inside, or the wall side, of the road. Once I tried to pass on the outside, but as I scanned ahead at my chosen line, I noticed a narrow trench running perpendicular to the road—it was formed by runoff from a small stream trickling down the cliff. The end of the stream bottomed out sharply near the edge, leaving a foot-and-a-half gap that would surely have tripped me up and sent me tumbling off the side if I tried to get ahead of the truck. I let off the throttle and squeezed the brakes, veering back into traffic. I always passed on the inside after that. And I always passed slowly, waving and tooting my horn in a friendly fashion at every vehicle. You need a lot of friends on a road like that one.

I soon came upon Peter, who was stopped, taking an action photo of me riding under a waterfall. "Pretty cool, eh, Devil-o?" Peter said.

"Yeah, real cool. A bus is coming. We should get moving."

"You seem scared," Peter said, laughing. "Well, you probably should be since you didn't leave any sacrifices for the dog gods."

Across the valley, parts of the jungle walls had moistened and slid down in great scarred strips, leaving jagged lines of red and brown a kilometer long in the green. A great effort was needed not to look over the side—the sheer profundity upset my equilibrium and threatened to suck me down into its beckoning depths. Perhaps my overconcentration was getting to me, but the heat became oppressive. I removed my coat's liner and waited near a small vendor's hut. Peter and Robert finally caught up. Peter had taken a spill over one of the wet clay ruts in the road, but he was fine.

We survived the trip, ate lunch, and turned right back around to go to La Paz when the road reversed direction at 5 P.M. It was like the start of a Grand Prix. Cars lined up in order and people testily revved their motors. Young boys wandered around selling oranges and, out of boredom, whipped rocks at chickens with homemade slingshots.

We skirted up to the front of the line and stopped. There we fielded questions, as we often had to when wearing our gear in public. "How much does your motorcycle cost?" one of the kids asked me.

"Fifty thousand oranges," I said.

He counted ten out of his bag and offered them up. "Can I pay the rest later?"

Even though we were near the front, we weren't first. A couple of the SUV drivers insisted on trying to race us. Trying to compete with off-road motorcycles on a road like that is pure insanity. That's the kind of thing our bikes were designed for, and Peter dogged the 4x4s, riding their bumpers and beeping, trying to get past. The drivers obviously felt their machismo threatened and struggled to stay out in front. One Toyota had a man driving, a woman in the front seat, and what looked like a white-haired mother-in-law behind. The truck was flying. He nearly drove his family off a cliff, doing 45 MPH on curves that should have been taken at 30 MPH on a dry dirt road, let alone the slick, dangerous mess we were on.

We, on the other hand, weren't taking the road at unsafe speeds. We braked and took the corners calmly. But by virtue of a motorcycle's more rapid acceleration and our semi-knobby tires, we could make much better time than any other vehicle on that road. Finally the driver pulled over and let us past, but then he desperately tried to ride our asses to show he could hang. His stupidity risked the lives of everyone involved. Once out in front, we disappeared and made him look foolish.

The following morning, back in La Paz, we walked to the twenty-four-hour Internet café we'd been frequenting for an early breakfast. We were all still hacking away with the Cuzco cough. Robert looked like he felt the worst of it, but by the way Peter complained you'd think I'd given him ebola. And Peter made sure to remind me every day that I was to blame for his suffering.

As we ate, we noticed a large man, probably over 260 lbs, with black hair and a graying beard, seated nearby with another man who looked like a lackey or chauffeur. They must've been drinking all night; their suits were crumpled and the assistant was just an enormous bloodshot eyeball. The fat man was fall-down-into-traffic, drown-in-your-own-vomit, get-disowned-from-your-family-style drunk. He wavered between boisterous slurred chatter and head-bobbing drowsiness. We tried not to stare. Just as we were finishing our meals, they decided it was time to go. The fat man stood, took two steps forward, three back, two to one side, leaned on a chair and table, and then, finally, accepted the support of his driver. Other patrons watched, and waiters and a barman stood around nervously, unsure if they should rush forward to help or pretend to be busy with other things.

Then the drunk man noticed us and approached, talking to himself for a moment and then sitting his bulk down next to Peter. He tried to communicate, but I couldn't understand him. I asked him to repeat himself. He smiled a drunk's smile, rolled his eyes theatrically, and tried again. As he slurred I was sure he felt himself the most noble and charming of hosts, welcoming the foreigners to his country. "Excuse me?" I said. "I don't understand." He finally gave up on me, exasperated.

He seemed to like Robert, though, because he stood up and balanced himself on Robert's chair, shaking burly hands with him. He ignored Peter entirely because Peter chose to be ignored. Peter employed a skill I'd never seen him use, a technique that's the exact opposite of his normal extroverted charisma. He now seemed to have utterly disappeared, shrunken back into his seat.

The fat man leaned in over Robert's chair and put his arm around Robert's shoulder, buddy-buddy-like, and brushed the back of his hand along Robert's furry cheek carelessly, as one might do to a very familiar person, like a son or a lover. Did he actually just do what I think he did?, I thought. This was too surreal for breakfast and I had to double-check the instant replay in my head. Yep, I saw what I thought I saw—he just felt up Santa's face. Peter was stunned, his quivering coffee cup tickling his lower lip. Robert was an oak, rooted in his chair, beady eyes straight ahead, as wide as they could go. I saw muscles I'd never seen on Robert begin to flex, growing and pulsating under his shirt. He suddenly looked very powerful, and very dangerous. Waiters' mouths hung open in shock; there was silence as everyone stared. I thought the drunk would lean in to kiss Robert on the cheek, and that Robert would explode upward and decorate the man with purple welts.

Suddenly the fat man stood upright and began to lean away, as if preparing to leave. Everyone released a secret breath. He said a few more smelly words at us, glanced at me disapprovingly, and said something like, "I don't like your presence."

"That's not important to me," I replied, as he stumbled down the stairs with his toady at his elbow. He stopped and locked eyes with me. Everyone grabbed another breath. A tense second passed before he brushed off his assistant's arm and stubbornly forced his steps out the door.

We paid our check and left. Shoe-shiners walked the street around us carrying the wooden boxes of their trade. They wore all kinds of hats: wool hats with earflaps, baseball caps, hoods, and hats with brims. All of the hats were dark and had strange ski-type masks that flipped over the front, covering their faces as if they were pretending to be cold but were actually hiding their identities. Ninja bootblacks. "Have you no sense of selective bilingualism, Devil-o?" Peter said. "You need to know when to play the dumb, mute gringo. You never know who's got a gun, and who's crazy enough to use it."

"I just wanted to know what he was saying."

"Because of you Santa almost got sexually assaulted," Peter said. "We're lucky that fat bastard didn't do him right on the table." Robert laughed out loud as Peter spoke. "First you try to kill Christmas by giving Santa the plague," Peter said, "and now this."

We left La Paz. The road was straight and dull. On the way to Cochabamba I daydreamed, first about sex, and then about flying without mechanical means, like Superman. I often wandered into sexual fantasies while on long, boring straights, but I noticed that I tended to do most of my saddle philosophizing when caught up in curves that demanded heavy concentration. Riding the bike every day gave me lots of time to think. Maybe too much.

We veered left at Caracollo and headed for Cochabamba. The road became a winding, twisting string laid up the hill, spilling over the top and then slowly falling down the other side to a wide valley stretching for miles. Red rocks and mud stacked up against sheer walls on either side, and the highway was a charcoal line down the middle. The blue sky lay like a sheet on the bed of earth. I had to remind myself to focus on the road and not be sucked in by the stunning landscape. We passed a totaled 18-wheeler on the roadside. The image of the huge crumpled wreck gave ample motivation to stay alert. Was the driver a victim of the pretty scenery, or did he just forget to feed the dog gods?

The town of Cochabamba is so very out of place, as though a city from some other country had been transplanted into the middle of Bolivia. The people are relaxed and seem to be well off economically, which is uncommon in most of Latin America, and in Bolivia in particular. There were many tourists, for no apparent reason, and there were large motorcycles like ours, which was very rare for almost any of the places we'd been.

The following morning we made plans to see a local site called the Palace between 5 and 6 P.M., the only time it was open to the public. We were to meet at the hotel at 4 P.M. I came back at the appointed time and saw that the guys were busy working on Peter's bike. That expanded to them maintaining both bikes, and then to washing them as well. I watched some TV and fell asleep on my bed. I came downstairs about quarter of six. "I guess we aren't going to the Palace," I said.

"It's six already," Robert said. "We could always see it tomorrow." His voice had a kind of humor in it.

"You want to stay another day?" I said.

"I don't know if it's worth another day here." I thought about what to do, and considered maintaining my bike as well. Fuck it, I thought, and walked out.

"Where are you headed?" Robert asked.

"Just going to stroll around." I don't think they had any idea that I was extremely annoyed with them. Once again plans were changing and I was being left in the dark. This lack of communication was getting really old. I spent the rest of the night around town, making a point to mingle with the locals and get away from the group for a while.

In the morning we saw a museum in town, which had a lot of impressive bashed-in skulls and stone and quartz maces on display, representative of the weapons used to do the bashing. The museum also had an amazing, near-complete skeleton of the Glyptodon reticulatus, or what looked to be a giant saber-toothed turtle.

Robert's back tire was finished. He'd been fretting about it for weeks, and on our trip here the rocks and pavement had shredded strips of rubber clean off. The tire now looked pretty unsafe to ride. Peter's tire was also well worn. In contrast, my tires still had plenty of tread; I rarely even had to put in air.

We managed to find a tiny shop, about as big as a vending machine, that could get Robert the unusual tire size he needed. The shopkeeper told us there was a Pirelli factory nearby in Brazil, and that he could have the tire in Cochabamba the next day. Even though it wasn't a dual-sport tire, Robert was happy and jumped at the chance. The other advantage of the Pirelli factory being so close was that the tire only cost Robert sixty dollars. And after all the pretrip worry about finding tires in Latin America, he found them in the most unlikely little town in the middle of Bolivia. We waited around the extra day for Robert's tire and then continued southwest to Oruro on very bad, unpaved roads.

14

The World's Saltiest Hotel

➤ ORURO, BOLIVIA, WAS JUST A STOPOVER; nothing really to see or do. As on most stopovers, I used the time to send e-mails and write notes. Peter and Robert also did their own thing, called their wives, and did laundry. Occasionally we'd busy ourselves with a game of chess at a bar or something, but most often stopovers were spent alone and introspectively.

The next real stop on the agenda was Potosi, home of the famous mine the Spanish empire exploited to amass much of their wealth. The way to Potosi was long and hard. Getting there was an eye-opener. As we toured the mountain roads we often passed crosses spiked in corners where vehicles had driven off cliffs. Mourners had come and marked the spot where the victims had fallen to their deaths. We rounded one corner and saw a truck that had recently fallen, its blue carcass still undisturbed in its resting place. We dropped out of the higher mountain elevations and worked our way along terrible dirt roads through the Bolivian altiplano.

We all took rougher roads at different speeds, and were often separated because of it. During one such instance, a careless driver in an

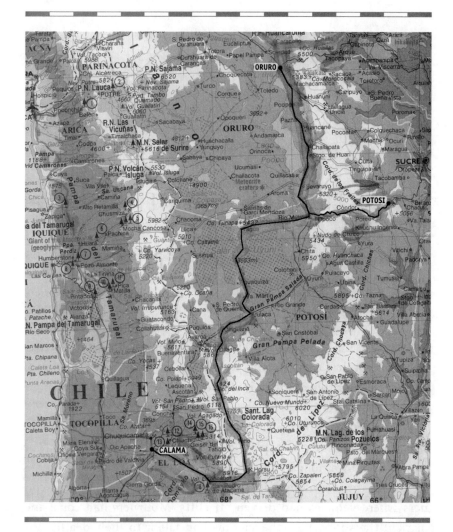

oncoming vehicle forced Peter off the road. As he struggled to maintain control, he ran down into a ditch. Peter somehow maintained the heavy bike's balance, and forced it to veer back up toward the road. He hit a bump on the way up and finally slammed to an upright halt on top of the berm. Peter wasn't thrown, but he was forcibly jarred forward when the bike stopped, and he slammed his testicles against the tank. After cursing and stomping around for a while, he calmed down and realized that the accident had caused an unusual oil leak on the Virgin Queen. A squashed oil line squirts only when the engine is under load, so at first, when the bike was stopped with the engine idling, he didn't notice it. If he hadn't stopped again later to inspect a bag lock that was also damaged in the crash, he might not have seen the oil that had splashed on the underside of the bike while he'd been riding. Looking for the source of this new development, he realized what was occurring and managed to temporarily patch it. If he hadn't, he could've burned out his motor and ended his trip right there.

I'd gained a considerable lead, so I waited for the others to catch up. Santa soon came along, but Peter was still missing. After about twenty-five minutes I suggested we go back and look for him. Although we were often separated and went along at our own paces in the rougher stuff, we generally never let each other get too far apart. By the time we found Peter he seemed frazzled from the ordeal, but was otherwise OK. Luckily he'd met some guys in a Land Rover who gave him some extra oil, and his bike problem was temporarily resolved.

We eventually arrived in Potosi, winding up the road past a river the color of a steel sink, which painted the river rocks an industrial gray with mercury, lead, zinc, and other nasty elements. Beautiful craggy rock walls, red as blood, stood at attention along the road as we passed. Behind the city loomed the magnificent fountain of precious metals, the Cerro Rico, which gave the town of Potosi a reason to exist.

Every town in South America has the same names for hotels and streets. There must be a thousand Hotel Libertadors and hundreds of San Martín streets below the equator alone. While Robert and I wandered one of them, Peter worked on his broken oil line and his again-broken bag mounting system. The right side of Peter's bag rack had by now been welded, reinforced, poorly painted, and rebroken a half-dozen times and looked absolutely repugnant. That bag mount had become an ugly wart on the Virgin Queen's backside.

Then we were free to explore the phenomenon of Potosi and its famous mountain, Cerro Rico. In 1545 the Spaniards officially began exploiting its riches. Even before then the mountain was being eviscerated by the native peoples, including the Inca. For as long as those first miners have been at it, the mountain has been producing vast quantities of silver, tin, lead, antimony, and zinc. Over the course of the mountain's generous life span, eight million workers are estimated to have died in the mines. Seven thousand people still work in them today. Such quantities of rock have been taken from the mountain that it's shrunk—the Cerro Rico of Potosi used to be 17,000 feet above sea level. It now measures in at just over 15,800 feet. The mountain coughed up so much wealth for the empire that even today in Spain, to describe something of inestimable value, one can simply say "it's a Potosi."

Veins in the mountain run anywhere from a kilometer to ten meters long, and all run north to south. There used to be one-and-a-half to two-meter-thick veins of pure silver. Today there is little pure silver, but every two years or so, one of the seven thousand workers finds an untapped vein with enough wealth to allow him to retire for good. All the men work with the hope of being that miner. Until that day arrives, each rents space in the mine from the cooperative and hauls carts of rock and ore to the surface, where they keep 80 percent of the profits after the valuable minerals are separated. The 20 percent the cooperative takes goes to the state. Two weeks of work can yield eight to ten tons of mixed rock per miner, valued at roughly three hundred bolivianos, of which one-third is spent in supplies like dynamite and blasting caps for making new shafts, and alcohol for making life bearable.

The outcome isn't totally bleak—if a miner is lucky enough to reach age fifty-five he can retire, after a lifetime of hunched-over toil in the mines, a hobbled, broken man. His reward will be thirty-five years of dynamite ringing in his ears, asbestos forming tubercles in his lungs, and a pittance of a social security check from the cooperative. But then again, most miners don't retire.

Conditions have changed little in the blackness. Spanish stone archways, centuries old, still support some mine shafts, and many sealed tunnels contain the bodies of workers that weren't worth being carried back out after their deaths. Engineers are unheard-of here. Apprentice learning dominates as knowledge is passed from father to son. Coca leaves are the diet of choice, and the sympathy of the devil is preferred when underground.

Miners pray to Jesus for protection when entering the mountain, but since Jesus only controls the heavens and land aboveground, they must pray to the devil for productivity below. They bring gifts for statues representing the evil angel, "the owner of the riches of the earth," whom they affectionately refer to as El Tio—"the Uncle." The miners make El Tio offerings of cigarettes, coca leaves, and the 95 percent pure alcohol firewater they drink, all in exchange for luck, the most precious mining commodity.

Each day miners set dynamite to deepen old shafts, dig west or east to find new veins and open up new air vents, and haul out tons and tons of mixed rock. The shafts in the mountain crisscross like holes in Swiss cheese. As you can imagine, such unnatural formations provide little structural support, and cave-ins are common. Like Chicken Little, these workers live in constant fear of reality coming crashing down about their heads.

These mines so dominated life in Potosi, we decided we absolutely had to explore one of them. Getting this done turned out to be quite a project. First there was finding a guide. Guides must be former miners with extensive experience underground. They must also be recognized and approved by the tourism industry in Potosi. We found a tour operator that seemed knowledgeable and legit and we negotiated a price. The rest of our group didn't show, so we had our guide, Efrain, all to ourselves. Efrain was short, caramel skinned, and black haired. He had laughing eyes and a red baseball cap with the Calvin Klein logo on it. He seemed to be making a decent living as a guide—at least a lot more than he made as a miner.

First stop on our tour was for needed supplies. At the market we picked up Argentine and Chilean dynamite (the Bolivian brand is reputedly of poor quality and unpredictable strength), slow-burning fuses, blasting caps, and ammonium nitrate to strengthen the explosions. We also got some chunks of calcium carbide—when mixed with water these small gray rocks give off a gas used to light the miner's headlamps. Then there was the much-needed firewater—supposedly six miners can drink a one-liter bottle of the 190-proof alcohol in a single day and still be productive. (This is a ridiculously potent amount— an average human would require weeks of blacked-out benders to polish off a bottle of the stuff). On top of all that we bought cigarettes, matches, coca leaves, and banana-flavored coca leaf activator.

Ethroxylon coca is the plant from which cocaine and other similar alkaloid compounds are made, but long before the refining process for these drugs was invented, the plant was taken orally to dull pain, lift exhaustion, alleviate the effects of altitude sickness, and make an otherwise dreary life a little more tolerable. When E. coca leaves are chewed with a calcium carbonate-based activator, small amounts of the alkaloid are released.

Although it's technically illegal for nonindigenous peoples to partake of the tradition, Efrain showed us the drill: put about twenty leaves into your cheek (carefully using your teeth to strip the elliptical leaf off the stiff stem, the stems aren't pleasant to chew), bite off dime-sized piece of activator (either regular or banana-flavored), then chomp and suck on the whole mess as a cow does its cud. After your illicit wad is all nice and soggy, shove it into one side of your mouth, adding a couple more leaves every few minutes, and insert more activator as needed.

The experience is like chewing on slightly bitter, dry grass at first, the flavor pungent and earthy. The pure activator tastes like bad medicine. The banana-flavored activator was much more palatable to my gringo palate. The result? Nothing. At first, anyway. After a half hour I felt a bit of mouth numbness. Over time, I did notice some of the purported effects, namely appetite loss, a feeling of calm, and a high level of energy, or perhaps I should say a lack of tiredness. I'm unable to judge how much of my results could be attributed to the placebo effect; Efrain could've been selling us tea leaves for all we knew.

Outside the mine we chewed our coca and watched as Efrain prepared some dynamite. We were loaned red windbreakers, hardhats, and big rubber boots. While Efrain detailed the finer points of TNT using my Multi-Tool as a poker, we posed in a masculine fashion in our mining gear. You may laugh, but this behavior was clearly expected of us—it's macho to wear a hard hat, chew coca, and discuss blowing things to hell.

Efrain unwrapped the paper from around one of the dynamite sticks and shoved the knife into the pasty green mix. He removed a pea-sized dollop of the explosive for us to admire. Efrain then lit a match and held it to the green blob on the tip of my knife. We all reflexively took a step back. "The dynamite will not explode from just heat," he said as the green paste turned black and ignited, burning tranquilly. "It takes heat and pressure—a lot of heat and pressure." He snuffed out the flaming mix and wiped the knife on his pants. He cut off the tip of a long fuse and shoved the fresh end into the blasting cap, crimping the cap around the fuse with his teeth. He then stuck the cap and fuse into the center of the green tube of dynamite, carefully wrapping up the stick again.

Efrain put the prepared charge in his mouth, cigar style, and lit the fuse—to demonstrate how safe the materials were. *Muy macho.* Robert and I took turns holding the lit stick of dynamite in our mouths, and Peter (the ex-safety inspector) demonstrated the proper way to hold the smoking, three-foot-long fuse. "If only my former coworkers could see me doing this," Peter said, "I'd lose all credibility." What can I say, we're just dangerous guys.

After watching the explosion of the dynamite from a safe distance we took the mine tour, making sure to bring along the extra explosives, blasting caps, fuses, coca leaves, sodium nitrate, and calcium carbide as gifts for the workers we met in our travels. The air was quite cold in the mines, but we were relatively well bundled. Most of the men were gaunt and worked in cotton T-shirts and pants. Robert pointed out the asbestos fibers dangling from many of the walls. These malnourished men and boys worked in horrendously unsafe conditions, mostly for the profit of others. I had a bag of crackers in my pocket that I gave to one miner who couldn't have been more than twelve years old. Our first impression when told to bring gifts was that these people were looking for handouts from tourists, just because they could. After learning what they went through every day, we deeply regretted that we hadn't brought more.

Just inside the main entrance we paused at the statues of Jesus and the Virgin Mary. "This is where the miners pray for protection," Efrain said. Llama blood, used in a kind of prayer ceremony, stained the walls. The religion practiced here was a combination of traditional native beliefs and colonial-enforced Christianity. Instead of converting entirely to the new faith brought by the Spanish, the natives had simply worked in the latest people—Jesus, Mary, and Joseph—with La Pacha Mama, Mother Earth, and the rest of their previous religion's cast of characters.

Smells of black powder and dust guided us down a narrow stairway. Deeper in the tunnels we found El Tio, the devil. His half-meter-tall likeness was painted red and seated in a rocky alcove. Colored papers decorated his little altar and coca leaves were piled at his feet. Burnt cigarettes dangled from his mouth; Efrain briskly flung these away and replaced them with some fresh ones, which he then lit.

Efrain sat down next to the statue and splashed a few capfuls of fire-water on the devil's black miner's boots.

We gathered around and shared conspiratorial sips of the blister-ing firewater, which went down like draughts of steam. El Tio smoked quietly next to us, grinning wickedly. Efrain told us that although most miners worked in groups of three, a few preferred to work alone. The reason, as Benjamin Franklin eloquently put it, is that "Three may keep a secret, if two of them are dead." Although there's a great sense of community between the miners, there's also an underlying savage competitiveness. Many accidents happen. Old mines are frequently cut off by blowing up the supporting arches. This is done for many rea-sons, most of them safety related. People have been found "acciden-tally" left behind in these suffocating shafts, their hands worn raw from scrabbling at the collapsed exit, murdered for the secrets the mountain holds. "For that motive more than any," Efrain said, "the working groups are kept small and usually joined by blood."

We walked deeper in toward areas that were being excavated. Efrain squatted on the packed dirt in a crossing of mine shafts, and we gathered around him. A musty breeze blew through the shafts, raising the hairs on my hands. "In 1993 a miner named Alberto Alave found a virgin silver vein like those of colonial times." While Efrain spoke, he scratched parallel lines into the ground and marked their ends N and S. "Almost as soon as he found it, other miners near him began cutting in from left and right." Efrain drew perpendicular lines, running east to west, crossing the N–S lines like a checkerboard. He told us how a group of rival miners had tapped the vein in front of Alave and cut him off. Traveling to the point where his vein suddenly stopped, Alave found only the tunnel where his rivals had entered. Beyond that was the hole they'd left as they stole his silver, as empty as his dreams and future.

A miner came charging down the shaft behind a runaway barrow loaded with rocks. We pressed ourselves against the wall for safety and waited for him to pass. "It's perfectly legal to cut across shafts," Efrain continued, "and Alave knew it. Fortunately for him he'd been making sixty thousand to seventy thousand dollars per week. That was more than enough to buy first-class pneumatic drills and other machinery."

Using the tools, Alave then dug a tunnel in the north–south direction, parallel with his vein, and rapidly passed the usurpers with the high-tech machines. By cutting east–west deeper in the mountain, he again found the pure silver, effectively doing to his rivals what they had done to him. He was not passed a second time. After kicking the vein, the clever miner retired and founded an overland bus tour company. His friends and respectful enemies now call him Alave the Wealthy.

We met several groups of miners, mostly friends of Efrain's, and Peter, Santa, and I doled out coca leaves, dynamite, cigarettes, firewater, and other goodies. It was like a dysfunctional family Christmas. But we weren't just handing out presents willy-nilly; we relied heavily on Robert's judgment of which miners had been naughty, and which had been nice.

We concluded our mine tour and headed back to the hotel to plan our next move. After much debate we decided to go check out the Salar de Uyuni, a salt lake to the southwest of Potosi. The decision had come down to either the Salar de Uyuni or San Vincente, the site believed to be where Butch Cassidy and the Sundance Kid met the end of their glorified criminal careers. Supposedly they'd made it this far south only to be killed by four patrolling soldiers.

The two American outlaws weren't the only famous people forced into permanent retirement here. In the mid-fifties, Argentine revolutionary Ernesto "Che" Guevara came to Bolivia after successfully helping Castro overthrow Cuba. He hoped to help spread the idealism of his socialist beliefs in a country that seemed ripe for change. He didn't make it back out alive, or even in one piece. Castro, incredulous that Guevara could've been caught and executed, received a gruesome parcel in the mail courtesy of the Bolivian government—the severed hands of his former comrade arrived as proof of his death. "Che's mistake," Peter once said, "was that he tried to hide out in a country full of short, dark Indians. He was a six-foot white guy with a beard. He stood out like a cold sore." Whether or not Che's appearance made a big difference is unknown. The moral of the story is, foreigners beware. Don't come to Bolivia unless you know what the hell you're doing. We would've done well to heed that advice as we started off on our trip to the Salar de Uyuni, because it's one mean, inhospitable place for the ill-prepared.

The Salar is an intriguing natural wonder, formed eons past when the continent currently known as South America was forced up from the ocean, carrying, among others, this vast lake of saltwater on its belly. Much of the water has evaporated over time, leaving the enormous expanse of white flatness. The salt's solidity varies through the year, depending on the amount of rain and other factors. With over 4,800 square miles of salt, the Salar de Uyuni is credited as the largest salt lake in the world. At 12,000 feet, it's also one of the highest.

The road to the former railroad town of Uyuni was better than that to Potosi, despite the fact that we had to ford several small rivers. For the first time during the trip Robert fell. He was coming out of one of the crossings and dumped his BMW in the muddy bank. This really wouldn't be a big deal, since in these conditions even very good riders fall often, but Robert's case was special, since Robert almost never fell. On his first trip to Ushuaia, he rode in an organized tour group with the famous moto-traveler, Helge Peterson, as the guide. Almost everyone, including Helge, took spills on that trip. Everyone except Robert. I wasn't happy that he fell, but at least now we knew he was human.

In Uyuni we made reservations to stay at the Salar's Salt Hotel, whatever that was supposed to mean (I envisioned a place decorated with six-foot-tall salt shakers cut out of cardboard). As we made our way along, Robert and Peter were both stopped by the washboards on the road. The rows and rows of bumps had broken Peter's bag mount again; he just hung his head in frustration. Robert's windshield vibrated loose, but he easily fixed it with a few turns of a screwdriver. The road entered the flats, mingling white salt and brown dirt like cinnamon and sugar on toast. There were dozens of three-foot piles of salt, and men scraping off the top layers of the Salar to make them. I followed the barely visible white tracks across the salt to the black speck, far off in the distance, that was the hotel.

Blinding white, as white as you can imagine, was the view, with mountains in the distance, a blue dome on top, and the sun pinned high above. The salt was crusty to ride on, perfectly flat, and looked like snow—but unlike snow, it gave excellent traction. Occasionally small ridges formed like long cracks in dried cake frosting, making polygons and other shapes on the ground. Bumps had also appeared, probably from small vents for subsurface water, creating millions of tiny anthill-shaped mounds. At this time of year the lake was mostly solid, and almost all of it could be safely driven on without sinking in.

The hotel, as its name implied, and as implausible as it sounds, was constructed entirely from blocks of salt. The roof was made from dried grasses and the windows were glass and wood, but other than that, it was pure salt. Even the furniture was made from big chunks of the white stuff. Our beds were salt platforms with mattresses and llama furs thrown over them. Our dinner table was a fat slab of salt big enough to satisfy a thousand horses for a thousand years. There were no showers, and the electricity was limited. The toilets were basic— to flush you grabbed a few buckets of water from the forty-gallon drum and poured.

After the initial whimsy of being in a hotel made of salt passed, we were struck by an immutable truth known to salt-flat travelers everywhere. There's really not a lot to do in a hotel in the middle of a salt flat. We ended up betting on liar's dice and getting drunk. Beginner's luck carried the day for me, as Peter and Robert were quite frustrated to see, and I soon won four out of six rounds. Peter won the other two. "Bunch of cheating bastards," was Robert's mantra whenever Peter or I won a hand.

The Salar the following day was a piercing white that could've easily burned out the unprotected eye. We rode in the general direction we were told to go, following the few tracks that indicated the way to the Isla de Los Pescadores, another landmark we wanted to visit. The "island of the fishermen" was just a huge rock jutting out of the white salt. Enormous cacti, some as tall as thirty feet, covered the island. The inhabitants were few: some people, a couple of pet llamas, and a smattering of wild viscacha. Viscacha are small rodents, cousins to the chinchilla, that somehow ended up here eons ago and now couldn't hope to make it across the miles of salt to move elsewhere.

After a short trip north to another island on the Salar, we doubled back towards the Isla de Los Pescadores and our next destination, San Juan. We passed the island and kept south. We were getting a little low on gas; we'd last filled up in Uyuni, and unwisely, we brought no spare gas cans. We also had only a few liters of water. We'd gotten some general directions back in Uyuni from a tour organizer, but our maps were incomplete and didn't show any landmarks on the Salar de Uyuni or the road through the seven lakes that we planned to take. We realized if anything went wrong we were going to be in serious trouble.

We'd heard stories about people who've had problems and been stuck on the Salar, such as the Japanese guy and his motorcycle that stopped running in the middle of the flats. The moist salt chewed up his electronics, and he had to abandon the bike and walk to the far-off black dot that was the salt hotel. He hired a truck the next day to drive him back to his bike, but it took him two days of roaming around to find it.

Our bikes weren't suffering electrical problems. Our problems started when we made it to the shore, or rather, just short of the shore. The salt went from hard to swampy near the edge of the Salar, and the last two-hundred-yard stretch to reach the firm earth was a salty muck that threatened to swallow our bikes without a trace. We needed to find one of the semipaved roads that we could follow safely toward solid land.

So there we were, stuck on the edge of an unstable salt lake with no obvious way to reach the road south. Information from a local was imprecise, as was the hand-drawn map given to us by the tour guide that booked our hotel stay. Even Robert's GPS was useless because it had no distinguishing landmarks programmed into it, and the cities it used as references were too far away. We simply couldn't find the road! We were trapped. There was the land, what we needed most, and we couldn't touch it. I felt like a salty Tantalus.

"Damn it, Andrés!" The stress was getting to Peter—he never called me by my real name. "We don't have enough gas to go riding around from one side to the other looking for the road."

"What do you want to do?" I said. "We can't sit around wasting all our daylight either." There were several tense moments as we sat under the blazing sun, debating our options. Peter wanted to go west and I wanted to go east. Robert didn't know what to do and just kept checking his GPS, perhaps hoping he'd somehow misread it, and would now find the answer to all our problems. Finally I convinced the guys that we needed to head southeast, where I was sure we'd cross the road. Fortunately (they would've killed me otherwise), I was correct, and we soon saw a tourist truck. "Sure," the tour driver said, "the road's right over that way." The road was just piled earth, built up like a bridge to cross the mush. So we weren't going to end up dead and salted like six-foot pieces of jerky after all.

Our plan was to follow a route through the famous multicolored lakes near the Bolivian border, and then to cross the border and head to San Pedro de Atacama, Chile. The roads through the lakes were the worst I've ever seen. Many companies like to claim their 4x4 vehicles are tough, and many of them have been tested here, but only one type of vehicle is used on these roads consistently: the older model Toyota Landcruiser. That was the only passenger vehicle that could cost-effectively handle the constant pounding of the washboards, rocks, and slippery sand. But even the Landcruisers were rare. When they passed, they were loaded with tourists that gawked at me as if I were the most insane person on the planet.

We were hopelessly underprepared for the rigors of the Salar and the trip south to Laguna Colorada and Laguna Verde. Our bikes should have been in top shape, our supplies maxed out, and our team morale and unity at a high level. Instead we went in with bikes that were beaten from four months of travel, limited fuel and water, and a group frustration that bordered on contempt. Now was the time that we needed each other more than ever, and our sense of community was at an all-time low. If one of our bikes broke down, we were in trouble. At night the temperature dropped below freezing, the winds blew bitterly, and I was the only one with a tent. The howling wind tore at everything, like the insistent tugging of a child on your shirtsleeve, and tormented us with abrasive blowing sand. I don't think a normal nylon tent a few microns thick would've survived a night in those conditions. If any of us had broken a bone and was unable to ride, we might've been stuck out there for days without food or water.

There were no gas stations, and we needed gas. The tourist Landcruisers packed all their own gas strapped to their roofs, but since they didn't carry much extra fuel we couldn't count on them for help. In San Juan, a pathetic, dusty village in the middle of this hellish desert, I fortunately found a farmer who sold gas from a rusting drum. Costing us about $2.25 per gallon, the gas was a bargain, considering there was nothing else around. I also discovered a man washing vehicles with a makeshift pressure washer, so we put our minds at ease by having the corrosive Uyuni salt cleaned off our rides. Separate rooms with baths cost us $5 each. I was ecstatic to get a hot shower. Dinner in the restaurant was followed by drinks and liar's dice by the hearth. As the evening cooled to bitter temperatures, we enjoyed a hot fire pungently fueled by yaceta, a small shrub that looks like petrified wood, but burns wonderfully.

That was the first day of our nightmare journey through the famous colored lakes. The roads, at first just varying degrees of annoying sand, gravel, and stones, graduated to endless miles of full-fledged, mind-numbing washboards. The choice was to either vibrate along violently on the endless bumps, or to venture off into the sand, which is smoother but much harder to negotiate. Sometimes we got the worst of both worlds, and the washboards would be covered with windswept sand. The sand often had large boulders casually lying about, waiting for you to screw up and make their day. My front wheel found several deep washouts, and every time it did I was thrown from the bike. After getting my bones and bolts rattled loose on the washboards for a while, I'd give up and try my luck in the sand. After falling a few times in the sand, I'd decide that endless pounding on the bumps was better than falling, so it was back to the washboards. The ride went like that all day: washboards, sand, big rock, pain, repeat. But I couldn't waste any time worrying about it. I knew I had to keep moving to make it to the next stop by nightfall.

My bike was running very poorly. The engine kept halting and didn't want to accelerate—the motor seemed starved for oxygen. I assumed it was the high altitude and bad gas, but it was neither. At one point on this miserable part of the journey, I hit a small bump, and I felt the back of the bike sink out from under me, which was a bad sign if I ever felt one. I stopped and inspected the bike.

A brief technical description (grossly oversimplified) before I continue: The KLR 650 is designed with a large frame, like a cage, that supports and protects the engine, transmission, and other internal bike guts. Both wheels are attached to this frame, the front by two telescoping tubes, and the rear by a set of bars shaped like a tuning fork, known as the swing arm. The subframe is a smaller cage that bolts onto the back of the frame and supports the weight of the rider and all the luggage. The KLR's subframe is mounted by four small bolts that are sufficient under normal conditions, but are pitifully inadequate to support the extreme loads caused by the weight of a rider and year's worth of luggage traversing the world's worst roads.

My cursory inspection of the bike revealed that the lower subframe mounting bolt on the left side had come loose and fallen out. No problem. I removed the identical bolt on the opposite side to compare it with the spare bolts I carried. I decided to replace both bolts, since the one I still had was badly worn. Two new matching spares in place, bike functional, mission accomplished. If only I had checked the upper mounting bolts.

Riding carefully to prevent damage, I saw Laguna Colorada come around a hill just before nightfall. The roads were so bad that I found myself counting the tenths of a mile on my odometer. The large red lagoon is named Colorada because of its red color, but it's actually more of a salmon pink. Strangely enough, it's home to dozens of flamingoes, and despite the freezing temperatures the birds wade around in the water, using their beaks to scoop up the algae that give the lake its hue. But I was too tired and cold to sightsee; I just wanted to eat and collapse onto a bed. The hotels at Laguna Colorada were terrible and overpriced, but we paid up without complaint. We were just glad to have a reprieve from the road.

We had a pretty terse night; we probably spoke about thirty words all evening. Earlier in the day we'd separated under uncertain cir-cumstances, and I was still furious at my companions. Peter had been psyched to take a small side journey to see some sulfur fumaroles that were spewing yellow gases from the side of the Ollague volcano. Although the detour sounded interesting, I didn't want to attempt the treacherous climb on a bike that wasn't operating properly, and I was forced to continue toward Laguna Colorada alone. Riding alone is not a problem—I was mad that I couldn't get either of them to listen to me. Peter was too far ahead and wasn't stopping, and although Robert heard me when I said my bike was having problems, he just contin-ued anyway. He blew me off without a word. So I turned back to the main road and continued alone, and I dealt with my minor breakdown alone. What's the point of suffering the constraints of numbers with-out being able to benefit from the safety in them?

I put the issue aside to face the immediate concern at hand: gas, again. Peter and I confronted the harsh night, wandering between hotels to beg tour drivers to sell us a few precious liters of gas. We got about two gallons each for seven dollars. Once back inside, I noticed that our hands had burned red from the frigid, sandy winds in just the few minutes it took to stock our bikes. That was when I knew that if we ever had to spend a night out in that weather we'd surely die.

We discussed, unsatisfactorily, the miscommunications of the day over a llama steak and spaghetti dinner. We slept fitfully, bundled under the covers with hot water bottles and oven-heated rocks. The next day, as we started out for Laguna Verde, every bike had complaints. My battery was dead—the fluid levels had gotten too low from lack of maintenance, and the freezing cold made the remaining liquid a useless, gluey mess. Robert discovered that his subframe had a fracture from the previous day's ride, but the bike was still roadworthy. Peter started his bike to find it was running on just one cylinder for the first ten minutes or so.

I had the battery charged, changed the spark plug, and told the guys to start without me while I put the bike back together. Although Robert had reservations about splitting up because of our various mechanical problems, it seemed a good idea to have him get a head start on his "second-gear adventure," as he called it. He needed to ride slowly with his cracked subframe, so I figured I'd catch up in no time. Peter said he was going to skirt around the lake to see some flamingoes and would wait for me further up.

They were twenty minutes gone when I started out. My bike ran worse than ever. After three miles I finally admitted I had to go back to Laguna Colorada to solve this problem. Sometimes the only way to learn is the hard way, and I've now learned that absolutely nothing can replace consistent, careful maintenance. In the end my bike was indeed starved for oxygen. The reason: the air filter was covered with a layer of hardened dirt like a thick leather hide. I'm amazed that any air got through at all. Because of the lack of air, my spark plug had fouled as well. I replaced the plug and cleaned the filter with gas siphoned from my tank. After reapplying air-filter oil and replacing the filter, the

motor roared anew and ran like a gazelle. I hurried to catch up to Peter and Robert.

Peter tired of waiting for me and had gone ahead. He soon met up with Robert, who wasn't really slowed down by the cracked subframe after all, so they gained a considerable lead on me. A few hours down the washboards they found a German camera crew doing a documentary on this desolate part of Bolivia. The Germans stopped them, wanting to interview the two strange bikers. Peter then obligingly demonstrated the proper technique for dumping a BMW in the sand while they filmed him; he was pretty embarrassed.

During the interview, Robert and Peter overheard the crew communicating via radio with another part of their team, a second film crew, in a 4x4 somewhere behind them. Their interviewers asked them about the "other rider," and they assumed that the Germans were referring to me. They were not. Putting things together, Robert and Peter also assumed, according to what they later told me, that the reason I hadn't caught up with them at that point was because I was wasting time with the other camera crew. I wasn't.

Actually, I was sliding over snow and ice, bounding off rocks and washboards, and falling in more fine sand, sometimes as deep as one and a half feet. Each new hill revealed a surprise of terrain. Sometimes there was gravel, sometimes sand, sometimes hard packed dirt covered with sheets of ice. Sometimes there was any combination of the above. There were a few fields of sharply pointed rocks like flint arrowheads, which looked as though they'd shred my suit if I fell.

After a while I made it to the reportedly green Laguna Verde, also home to a few out-of-place flamingos. The lagoon was actually more of a creamy jade color, like key lime pie. The guard posted there said that my companions had left for the Bolivian border over an hour before. "How long were they here waiting?" I said.

"Oh, I don't know," the guard told me, "not long."

Not long? What the hell was going on? Why weren't they waiting for me like they were supposed to? I decided it was best to keep moving. As I started out I thought, What a couple of assholes. What if I had a serious problem? What if I broke my leg and was stranded ten miles from a town? This is the most desolate place we've ridden, by far, and if something went wrong out here I'd be completely fucked.

That very second—the exact moment these thoughts crossed my mind—I heard a muffled crack, and I felt the entire rear end of the bike give out and sink from under my backside. For a split second I stood on my pegs, knees bent, butt poised ludicrously in the air while the bike's tail end slumped toward the back tire. I killed the engine and stopped.

The bike was in no condition to ride. The upper subframe mounting bolts, the ones that I'd neglected to check the day before, were snapped off. Normally that wouldn't have been a problem—just shove in some new bolts and keep riding. The difference here was that the broken pieces were stuck inside the holes. The heads, normally used to unscrew bolts such as these, were long gone. With no way to remove the broken bolts, there was no way to replace them.

I remembered I'd once seen my friend Mark Van Horn, the guy who shared the first few hundred miles of this trip with me from New York to Daytona, remove a sheared bolt with a Dremel tool and a screwdriver. First he etched a narrow notch in the top of the bolt piece still stuck in the hole, making it look like the head of a screw that had sunk in. The he used a common flathead screwdriver to work it out. Unfortunately I had no Dremel tool. Worse still, the bolts had been put in with a liquid thread lock in the factory, which makes even a perfect bolt tough to remove. I could tell that mechanically improvising my way past this problem was unlikely.

Things looked bad. The carburetor was completely separated from the air box and the muffler had pulled apart from the exhaust pipe. The weight of the entire rear end was supported by only two screws and some electrical wires. This couldn't be solved alone. I looked at the sand all around me. I looked up at the sun, ever creeping toward the western horizon. I lowered my eyes and looked at my boots, dusty and falling apart. I was right about one thing: I was completely fucked.

As I struggled to walk my bike back to the town I'd just left, Laguna Verde, the packing advice of my friend and motorcycling mentor, Carl Williamson, came back to me, as if mocking my predicament: "Only travel with as much stuff on your bike as you are willing to push fully loaded in all your riding gear." Closer inspection of the "town" revealed that it was really just three houses and six locals. They didn't have a phone or electricity. They didn't have any vehicles or the gas to operate them. Hell, they didn't even have a llama to drag me to civilization. My situation seemed hopeless.

I was suddenly overcome with tremendous anger at Peter and Robert. Where the hell were they? Why didn't they wait? I couldn't believe it. The one time I really needed them and they ditched me. They fucking ditched me! After all the sacrifices and shit we put up with to stay together, when help was really needed, it was nowhere to be found. In Laguna Verde, I learned from a cop changing shifts that my "companions" had left a message for me at the Bolivian border: they said they'd meet me that night in San Pedro de Atacama, Chile.

My last hope—that Peter and Robert would wonder what had happened to me and come back—was dead. I knew they wouldn't be coming back, because they'd left me a message they were sure I'd get. I looked closer at the bike, thinking to remove the tank and somehow wire the subframe up temporarily, but one of the tank bolts had failed and I couldn't remove it to get access to the frame. These damn bolts were really fucking up my trip!

For a while I just steamed. I wanted to kick the crap out of my bike. I wanted to kick the crap out of the two pricks that left me there. I began talking to everyone I could find, trying to get access to anything: a phone or radio to call for help, a hacksaw or manual drill to do something with the bike, a pistol or a slingshot to shoot myself. Some tourists in ridiculous bright red track pants and matching earmuffs looked at me, stared even. I guess I must have looked equally ridiculous stomping around a bent motorcycle in a space suit.

Perhaps I'm a child of fortune. I managed to get a ride out of that mess that very same day. A group of construction workers were repairing nearby roads in Chile, just across the border. The guard I'd spoken to said these men happened to be coming that day to get a diesel truck motor that had been left in one of the town's three buildings. Their plan was to illegally import the motor into Chile. I negotiated with the driver and scored a tow to San Pedro de Atacama, Chile, for forty dollars.

I had to admit I was getting out of Bolivia while I could. Scurrying away like a puppy hiding my tail. If it hadn't been for those lawbreaking engine smugglers, I could've been stuck there for a week waiting for a ride. No, this was not my finest hour. But sometimes you have to know when to cut your losses and accept defeat. I was beaten by this country as soundly as my three famous predecessors, Butch, Sundance, and Che. But unlike them, at least I was getting out of there alive.

15

The Place Where Bikes Go to Heal

➤ THE BIG DIESEL TOYOTA bounded down the road to Chile. The truck had a wooden bed with caked dirt and black grease intermittently splashed about. I was in the back, seated next to my bike on a saddlebag and gripping a tie-down strap for balance. Alex, one of the road workers who had come along for the ride, sat near me on an inverted yellow five-gallon bucket, the bottom of which had been burned and bubbled, as if by acid. He wore a wool cap, filthy coveralls, and work gloves. Scruffy and gregarious, Alex was instantly likable. We squinted from the dust and talked as we bumped along. His wife and kids lived in Santiago, and he worked near San Pedro de Atacama and sent them money.

He held out some of his uneaten lunch to me: bread, apples, and a chocolate bar. Although I was quite hungry after a day without food, I thanked him for his kindness but declined. This man worked hard for his family; I could get a meal in town in a little while. Thankfully the dirt ended and we started onto the International Highway, a paved road. "Yesterday a truck was driving on this road and the brakes failed," Alex said. "The truck sped out of control and crashed on its side. Both men that were in it died—one of them, the driver, was a friend of mine. He just baptized two of his kids last week."

We were on dirt again and bouncing our way into town, where we dropped off the motor. My benefactors then took me back to the customs and immigration checkpoint. Things got a little iffy when the portly customs guy wanted to know what they were doing picking me up from Bolivia. They said they found me on the Chilean side of the border, not in Bolivia. Learning my lesson from Peter, I used selective bilingualism to stay out of it. The road workers finally dropped me off at a youth hostel, and I chained the bike and went to meet up with Robert at the appointed place at 7 P.M.

The plaza was getting dark and Robert's white beard stood out like a homing beacon. "I thought we lost you," he said, smiling.

"You almost did," I replied. "I had a major failure and was stuck in Laguna Verde. Why didn't you guys wait for me?"

"You told me to go ahead."

"Sure, I said start out and I'd catch up. You didn't wait for me to catch up."

Robert led me to where Peter was e-mailing while we talked. I explained what had happened, the lucky turn at meeting the motor smugglers. He could see I was pretty upset. He told me the story about the German camera crew and their conversation about a third rider. "We were sure they were discussing you, so we figured you were fine," he said. Not having seen any Germans, all that made absolutely no sense to me. "So we waited a while, and when you didn't show we continued without waiting. I thought it was a bad idea for you and Peter to split up, but . . . "

"You know," I said, "I keep trying to see it from your point of view and look at it as an honest mistake. But what I keep coming back to is that it couldn't have happened to either of you. If you didn't show I would have waited or gone back. Like the time Peter was run off the road. Like just a few days ago when your windshield came loose and you stopped." I wasn't mad anymore, just really disappointed. "Every

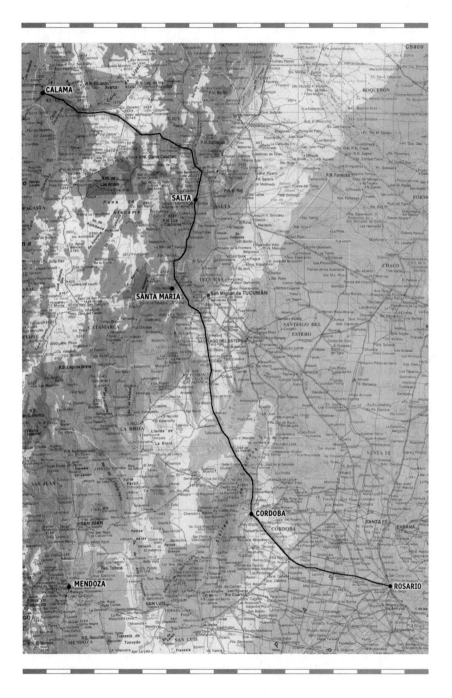

time there's been a problem I went back for you guys. What if I'd broken my leg and was stuck in the freezing desert right now? Where were you guys? All this time I just kept thinking about what I'd have done in your place. If you didn't show I'd have gone back, and if that were impossible, I'd have waited, sleeping in my tent on the road, if necessary. I'd be damned if I left a country without you."

"I don't know what's happened." He looked tired. As always, his words were carefully measured. "We held together fine for four months, and now everything is falling apart."

"I don't mind traveling alone," I said, "but that's not what I signed up for. I thought I'd joined a team, but when I needed you guys, you were gone."

"It's amazing how those Germans screwed us up," Robert said. "We thought you were just swapping information about your book and their documentary." So that's what it was about. Devil-o was goofing off with the Germans, trying to promote himself on TV and making us wait, so it's OK to ditch him. I could imagine them waiting, steaming at the border, finally saying, "Fuck it, let's go." I knew they must've been really mad to justify riding off without me.

Peter was busy at an Internet café so we began walking toward their hostel. "You can bring the bike over," Robert said. "We got a triple."

"I don't know—I don't really feel like dragging my gear. I think I'll just crash where I am tonight."

"I'll help you bring your stuff if you want," Robert said.

"That's OK. I'm going to the mechanic here in town early. You can meet me there if you want."

I went to the hostel, changed money at an exchange kiosk, and got dinner. I took a much-needed shower and climbed into bed. I was completely drained. A Japanese guy using one of the four bunks in my room came in later, loudly organized his things on his bed, and then climbed under the covers on the top bunk to sleep, still wearing his clothes and boots. He also left all the lights on and the door open.

In the morning I chained the bike behind a truck and towed it to the mechanic. Unfortunately, the mechanic was out of town. I climbed on the bike again and the truck driver pulled me outside of the village, where the only other mechanic in town lived. He had a large gated property loaded with junked vehicles and a massive toothy dog that didn't like me, or any strangers for that matter.

I found the petite mechanic inside working on a big diesel with the hood up. He wore a flannel cap with earflaps that hung down past his jaw and big wraparound sunglasses. All of this made his head look tiny. Positively shrunken. When I stated my reasons for coming, he rejected me gruffly. "I'm busy with this truck," he said. "And I'm sick in the eye." Whatever that meant. He didn't care to explain.

I rolled the bike down the street to the only other place I saw, just a shack with tools in it, near the customs house I'd passed the day before. There was a man outside, waiting around to change truck tires and perform light repairs. He helped me saw off the stripped tank bolt, and then he wanted to pound it out with a nail, but I stopped him. Using the hacksaw, I cut a slit in the top of headless bolt shaft and worked it out with a screwdriver. "That's a good one," he said. "I'll have to remember that." He was powerless to help me remove the embedded subframe mounting bolts. "There's no electricity in town until 5 P.M.," he said, "and the best mechanic in town is in Calama. Only the other guy can do it."

So I rolled the bike back to the shop of the "other guy." The small mechanic was bent over up to his waist in diesel motor, and his assistant looked at me like I was asking for trouble when I walked back in. "I don't mean to bother you," I said to the mechanic, "but you are my only option." He didn't reply. After a few silent minutes I said; "It will only take a minute of your time. Or perhaps if you could just let me use a few of your tools."

His tiny head sprung out from under the red truck hood. "Can't you see I only have two hands?" he boomed. "Can't you wait just a second?" Wow, this guy was irritable.

"Sorry, didn't mean to bother you." I slunk outside and waited. About twenty minutes later he poked his head outside the gate.

"What's the problem?" he said. I showed him the entrenched bolt pieces. "Bring it inside." I set the bike up inside and started to remove the seat and tank. He turned over a generator and then powered up an air compressor. I asked what he planned to do. "I'm going to drill those bolts out and tap new threads." Sure. Why not. Why didn't he just countersink the bolt and watch it unscrew itself? He probably didn't have the right tools. The plan he had could work, but it was tricky to drill straight into a bolt, especially if he was "sick in the eye." I was getting a little nervous watching this.

"You know, if these threads don't work the bike will be useless," I said.

"What does he want from me?" The little mechanic shouted as he raised his hands pleadingly to the heavens. He looked back at me haughtily. "I am not a magician, just a mechanic. I will try." I sensed I was in for a long day; the only mechanic in town was a psycho with a penchant for melodrama. I was beside myself with anxiousness. I resolved to sit quiet and let him work. For better or worse, this was out of my hands.

Just then Robert and Peter showed. Despite the fact I was still unhappy with them, it was nice not to feel completely alone with my problem. "How's it going, Devil-o?" Peter said.

"Not good. I don't know if this guy can do it. Plus I think I pissed him off."

Peter looked at the man working on the bike and walked up to him, asking him how he planned to fix it. The man threw an exasperated arm across his forehead. "Look here! I'm sick, only one eye works, and I'm just a mechanic, not a miracle worker. If you can do it better, you do it." He held the drill out to Peter.

"Holy shit!" Peter said to me in English, laughing incredulously. "Is this the attitude you've had to deal with?" I could sense his reaction wasn't going to help matters.

"He's not feeling well, and he has a lot of other work," I said in Spanish. I was trying not to make it appear that we were discussing the Napoleonic wrencher behind his back. I gave Peter a "don't mess this up for me" look.

"I don't have time for this," the mechanic said flatly. "May I do my job or not?"

"Look, I'm just asking an innocent question," Peter said to the man. "There's no need to react that way." The mechanic threw his drill to the dirt and walked away. Peter looked at me in disbelief. "What the hell is wrong with that guy?" he said. Great. The cavalry had arrived and it turns out I was better off alone. I just shook my head in defeat and walked up to the mechanic.

"Here, I'll pay you for your time." I held out some bills to him. "Thanks a lot for your help."

He regarded my cash with disdain, as though I'd just retrieved it fresh from a sewer. "No, of course I won't accept payment. I never take money unless I make a solution," he said. "But your friend doesn't seem to want me to do it. You should just leave."

"OK," I said. "Sorry to have bothered you." I started picking up bike parts. Peter walked over and talked to the guy.

"We can truck it to a larger city and get it fixed," Robert suggested, looking at the bike. Peter walked back over to us.

"Well," Peter began, "he's willing to do it, and I said that we'd leave and let him work in peace. We've demonstrated we are sufficiently submissive enough, so he'll lower himself to do the work." Peter looked at me for effect. "He's just another one of those petty tyrants you always complain about, Andrés." Maybe so, but he was the only petty tyrant in town.

They left, and I stayed out of the way while the mechanic worked. He was having a hard time, his drill bits kept breaking and he had to sharpen them with a grinder. After a while he relaxed. I found out his name was Adrian. "What happened to your eye?" I asked him after things had calmed down.

"I was welding and a piece of metal went into it." He pulled down his glasses to show me. A tiny shred of gray was barely visible under the white swelling and redness. The tissue was puffy and inflamed, the red veins stood out boldly. I tried to be casual, but reflexively I recoiled at the sight. I couldn't believe he wasn't screaming in pain.

"Christ!" I said. "Go to the doctor. Screw the bike. I'll come back another time."

"It's fine," he smiled. Without taking his good eye off what he was doing he stuck his thumb over his shoulder. "I have to finish that truck over there next. I was supposed to be at the hospital now, but that truck's owner needs it badly. I'm doing him a favor." After that I just shut up and watched Adrian work. I also took back all the unkind things I'd thought about him.

He tapped out the holes with standard threads, but all my spare bolts were metric. He only had one rusty bolt that fit, so we put it in and it was enough. I thanked Adrian, paid him, and rode back to my hostel. Knowing that Peter had some standard bolts, I went looking for him at their place.

I found Peter at the youth hostel where he and Robert were staying. He introduced me to Walter and Sandra, a German couple that was camping in the spacious backyard of the hostel. They'd both ridden older BMWs like Peter's from Alaska. Sandra's bike had the same problem with breakage of the saddlebag mount as Peter's. The break kept appearing in the exact same spot. Uyuni had gotten the better of them as well. Walter's bike took a beating but was now repaired. However, they couldn't continue their journey because they needed a new rear shock for Sandra's bike, which was trashed in Bolivia. The shock was being sent by mail from California, and the couple had been waiting three weeks, sleeping in a tent to save money. "San Pedro de Atacama," Peter said, "seems like the place where bikes come to heal."

Peter found some 10.9-grade bolts, gifts from his former job as a safety inspector, that fit my newly tapped threads. Unfortunately the bolts entered crookedly, because the holes were crooked. This was acceptable; Adrian the one-eyed, shrunken-headed mechanic had done the best he could and, under the circumstances he worked in, I was amazed his results turned out as well as they did. But sooner or later this situation would come back to haunt me if I didn't get the bike properly repaired.

As I reassembled the bike back at my place, Peter talked. He apologized for leaving me in Bolivia. "It's just that we were getting too used to riding apart," he said. "We were so sure because it seemed those Germans must've been referring to you. Why else would they talk about a 'third rider'? We were sure you were fine." Things smoothed over as we discussed it. Then he laughed, adding: "It's probably better that I was with Santa anyway. He fell again and was stuck underneath the Condor. If I hadn't helped he'd still be there."

They invited me to dinner that night. I didn't really feel like a part of the group right then, and they seemed to be at a loss for words. We loosened up with a few drinks and I asked Robert about his fall.

"There are no secrets here?" He looked at Peter accusingly, laughing. "It was a high berm of gravel," Robert explained, "and I got caught in Peter's track and the bike fell on my leg, pinning my foot."

"I thought a guy like you would've just gnawed your leg off," I said.

"Well, I had my knife out, eh?" Robert smiled. "I was ready to cut, but at the last second Peter ran up and helped me out."

"Yeah," Peter said. "I really wanted to take a photo to document the moment, but I thought, if he's really hurt, he'll be pissed. Now I really wish I had that photo."

Robert stared at Peter incredulously. "What a guy! Thanks a lot." He laughed. "Since it means so much to you, I'd be willing to do a reenactment."

"OK," Peter said. "But this time let's do it with the bike pinning your head."

Over the next few days the tensions slackened. They both felt bad about leaving me, and I'm sure that if they had known the trouble I was in, they would've waited. Obviously. But the fact was they did leave, and that was the one thing that was so hard to forgive.

Ultimately I decided to continue riding with them. We only had a couple of weeks left together before we split up, so I thought I'd try to finish the trip on a good note, instead of forever feeling that I'd been let down in the end. For four months they'd been good riding partners, so I shouldn't write them off for just one mistake. I decided to stick to the plan. In August I was going to stay in Argentina with my family, and they were to continue through the Brazilian Mato Grosso to Venezuela, and then home. I figured I might as well make peace until they left.

The next morning Robert and I made a day trip to Calama, a mining town near San Pedro de Atacama, where we could get our bikes repaired. Calama is home to the world's largest man-made hole in the ground, a two-and-a-half-mile-wide mine that produces more than forty tons of processed copper every minute, which, frankly, is a lot of copper. Because of all this mining, Calama is loaded with welders, machinists, mechanics, and just about anything one might need to keep a vehicle operating. And since these specialists are all located in Chile, the labor is still fairly cheap. In short, it was the perfect place for us to go. And on top of that, the ride was like a Möbius strip: curvaceously simple, yet intellectually stimulating.

Up close, Calama is an oasis of trees. The town was sufficiently modern and seemed to be doing well for itself. Robert and I picked the first place we saw that had a TIG welder. The welder was named Oscar, and we contracted him to do the work for us. We had a lucky turn picking his shop, because he was actually very good.

Robert's cracked subframe was relatively easy to weld, except for the fact that the welding had to be done near some of the bike's plastic and electrical components. We watched Oscar work, and all three of us wore welding face masks with darkened glass to protect our eyes from the bright fire of the torch. Everything was fine until I noticed yellow flames and smoke coming from Robert's bike. A plastic panel had caught fire. I didn't say anything at first because I assumed that both Oscar and Robert had noticed the fire and were fine with it, accepting a little bit of burning as part of the welding process. Why proclaim my ignorance by overreacting to a little smoke? was the idea. Finally I couldn't take it anymore, and when I noticed all the electrical wires near the plastic, I asked Robert if he knew his bike was on fire.

"What!" He ripped off his mask and looked around for something to put the flames out.

Oscar stopped working and looked up, annoyed at all the commotion while he was trying to work. Then he noticed the fire. "Quick! Water!" He screamed for his brain-dead apprentices, who sat in a corner chatting. They rushed around, fumbling with pans full of water in the sink. After that everyone was more mindful of where Oscar pointed his torch.

My bike was next, but the repair was a little more involved. Robert, Oscar, and I decided the best solution was to disassemble the bike, cut out the original upper subframe mounting bracket on the frame (with the misaligned bolt threads), and then replace it with a new one machined from scratch. After that we'd reassemble the bike and be on our way.

Robert and I took apart the Kawasaki's rear end and prepped it for the removal of the bracket. The tank, airbox, seat, panels, and screws were carefully organized on the floor for later reassembly. Disconnected wires stuck out everywhere. The bike was now just a frame, forks, drivetrain, swing arm, and tires, looking like something the A-team might've slapped together. I had half a mind to put on the tank and take the bike for a spin like that. "I pity da fool dat messes with my ride."

Oscar assigned one of his dingbats to the task of cutting out the bracket. I told the guy to take good care of my mechanical girlfriend. Next thing I knew, I saw the apprentice had started to cut without protecting anything, and that he had filled my carburetor with tiny shards of metal. I could've screamed. I stopped him, removed the carburetor, and then stuffed clean rags into any and all exposed holes. Now on top of all the other things to do, the carburetor needed to be cleaned to prevent the metal shards from entering and shredding the guts of my engine. Luckily I was spared that task—Robert did it for me while I was buying parts in town.

Oscar's father Hector drove me to the machinist's to place the order for the new bracket. The machinist was a fascinating man in his sixties with Einstein hair and glasses—his name was also Oscar. His shop lay hidden behind his house in an expanded garage. His work area was clean, organized, and filled with ancient machines: grinders, presses, sanders, vises. A poster of a woman on a motorcycle was the only decoration on the wall. We gave him the written measurements for the part we needed and left.

Robert's bike came out fine. The weld was reinforced, and after it was painted, the frame looked pretty good. Hector turned out to be a real peach, driving me around for other parts and discussing world politics. In a couple of hours Oscar the machinist had finished the bracket, a real work of art. He charged me sixteen dollars for it, including the needed bolts.

Back at Oscar the welder's, my bike was ready for surgery. We put the new bracket into the hole left by the original, measured twice, and then Oscar ironed it all together. Fortunately nothing ignited on my bike. We noticed that the rear shock mount had also suffered trauma— a fissure was climbing along the seam. With five seconds of flying sparks, Oscar nipped that future headache in the bud. Lastly, the subframe needed work where the gas tank mounting bolts had stripped. When that was completed, I put it all back together while the gathered crowd offered help: lights, tools, extra hands, extra eyes. Finally, after an incredibly long day, the bike was reassembled. All told it cost me about seventy dollars, a fraction of what I might've paid in the United States.

Back in San Pedro, Robert called it a day and Peter and I decided to go out. Peter had been out the night before, and had gotten himself lit up like a pumpkin at Halloween. That's why he didn't come with us to Calama. We saw some people he'd met the night before and proceeded to party in the grand style we'd grown accustomed to. Near 12:30 A.M. we hit another bar, the only one with lights. "After 1 A.M. the power goes out," Peter said. "So everyone comes here to generator heaven."

Peter got up for a beer and some young women began talking to me. They were all cute and friendly so I was pretty happy. We danced all night, and Peter and I spent eighty dollars on drinks for ourselves and all our new buddies, an absolute fortune in alcohol in most parts of South America. (Keep in mind that I had put six men to work all day on my bike for roughly the same price.) Unfortunately, just as the night was ending, all the men that the girls were dating suddenly appeared, and made all the girls disappear. Bummer.

"Come on, Devil-o," Peter said with his arm around my shoulder. "Time to take the walk of the losers. Well, loser—singular—I'm not a loser because I wasn't trying. I'm married." He laughed at me happily.

We shuffled to our hotel, stumbling and kicking up dust. I'd since moved into the triple with them. "You know the Germans camping out in back of the hotel, waiting for their new shock from California?" Peter said, chuckling.

"Yeah, sure."

"Get this: They got a package today, after three weeks of waiting." Peter could hardly speak for giggling. "You know what's inside? Take a guess. C'mon, guess." He looked at me and opened his eyes wide, for effect. "One thousand miniature lightbulbs," he said, before I could reply. He screamed with high-pitched laughter. His piercing glee echoed down the street and across the rooftops. I was afraid he was going to wake up the neighborhood. "A thousand fucking lightbulbs! Their shock was sent to a dealer in Santiago, and they got his bulbs. They tore up and down the backyard, swearing in German. They were so funny!" I was caught up laughing too, and as we came upon the hostel, Peter was still giggling and sighing. "A thousand lightbulbs."

Suddenly Peter's face got very serious, and he put his arm around me in a consoling manner. "Well, since you couldn't do the little hotties, Devil Boy, I have another plan. Let's do Santa Claus instead." He ran up to the window. "Oh, Robert!" Peter shouted. "Wake up, Santa Claus, we're coming to do you!" He laughed his maniacal laugh.

I knew the hostel patrons were going to lynch us, but I was laughing despite myself. "Shut up, you drunk bastard!" I hissed. I opened the door and Peter stumbled in past me, hitting an end table and crashing all the magazines and decorations to the stone floor. A broken seashell crunched under my feet.

"Robert!" Peter called out loudly. "Robert, I hope you have Vaseline...." I left him inside and escaped back out into the night. I didn't want to be associated with whatever bad results he brought upon himself. I went for a walk around town to get some air and think.

In the morning I was completely domestic. Socks and shirts needed washing, a pair of shorts needed to be darned, and for safety's sake I tightened every bolt I could reach on the KLR. Never again would a lack of maintenance cause me a problem like the one I had in Bolivia, I decided.

We'd been in San Pedro de Atacama long enough. The decision was made to head to Argentina. It would be a long trip: a total of 350 miles, half dirt, half pavement, and a border crossing as well.

As we left Chile on the international highway I was trucked in on, I saw Alex and the other road-workers-turned-smugglers that had given me a lift. They waved me onward, smiling and shouting as I passed. Alex took off his coat and whipped it around as I zoomed by, as if he were waving the checkered flag.

We took the Paso de Jama and entered Argentina. The view was like an old Western: eroded red hills, cacti, mesas, dried scrub, clear sky like a painted ceiling. I killed the engine and coasted down great dirt switchbacks into gorgeous canyons, listening to the wind, my whirling chain, and the crackling of rocks under my tires. The valley walls were dramatically split by the castings of the fading sun. The realization touched down that I'd made it to Argentina, the land of my displaced European ancestors.

Near Jujuy the front end of my bike became squirrelly and I pulled off the road. Having come all this way, I'd gotten my first flat tire. Thankfully it was a slow leak and not a blowout. I had a repair kit with a trick handheld tire inflator that used miniature CO_2 canisters. So very James Bond. I slapped one of canisters in the inflator and it coughed enough pressure into the tire to get me to the hotel. We took forever deciding where to stay, because all the places were of the same quality we were used to, but triple the price. Welcome to Argentina. I fixed the tire outside the hotel and at Peter's suggestion double-checked the inside. Sure enough, there I found a long tack driven through the thick part of the tread, and it was still long enough to have repunctured the repaired tube. "Cute little guy, isn't he?" Robert said, holding it up to the light.

The next morning Peter and I both woke up late, and Robert started off in a bad mood that lasted all day. The route we took turned out to be a great ride, beautiful, in fact. We passed Cafayatte, home to several famous wineries. Columns of tall trees lined the road. Casks big enough to hold a couple of cows each stood outside the drive to an estate. Rows and rows of vines, grayed and in tangles, lay dormant on fields of wires, waiting to be hung heavy with fat grapes.

We moved on to a ruins at Quilmes, a site of former Indian resistance against the Spanish. They were, well, ruined. They were also boring. However, just before we left we met Luis Alberto Calonga, a councilman for the commission of public works and services from the district of Quilmes in Buenos Aires. When asked, Luis explained that the popular Argentine beer, Quilmes, derived its name from the place in Buenos Aires where it was made, which in turn owed its name to the Indian peoples that moved there and populated it. Luis then introduced us to Francisco, the chief of the Quilmes Indians. We all posed for photos as Francisco explained how the tribe was petitioning the government to return lands taken from the Indians in the 1800s. A crowd had gathered around us. No matter where we went, the people always seemed bored enough that we could capture their interest for a little while. In Argentina the trend was even more pronounced. Men and women of all ages approached us, as motorcycling enthusiasts and curiosity seekers, asking us about our trip and bikes.

My bike was in top form. I'd stiffened the suspension in San Pedro de Atacama, and the ride and handling were significantly improved. I made a mental note to dial the shock a little stiffer still as we took the good dirt roads and paved streets to Santa Maria. We stayed at a hostel run by an older couple for the night. We also met a newsman who was excited to interview us, but he couldn't get the crew to come out in time. He drove us around town and dropped us off at a restaurant, promising to catch us in the morning before we left. We had a few drinks outside and we were joking with each other as we sat watching cars run circles around the plaza.

That night we discussed plans for the next day. Peter needed to go to Mendoza to pick up the spare rear tire he'd forwarded there. I planned to go to Córdoba for an interview with Radio Córdoba, which an Argentine correspondent in Miami had asked me to do at the beginning of the trip. There was no way to do both, so Peter and I decided to split up. Robert didn't say anything, but he seemed to have reservations about the radio interview and opted to go with Peter.

In the morning we were up and off to breakfast. On the walk back to the hostel I asked Robert if I could make a copy of his map for the trip. We walked into a copy center and he looked at me blankly. "So, can I borrow your map?" I said.

"I thought you were the guy that didn't need maps," he said. He was kidding with me in his stony-faced way, and I don't know why, but suddenly I was very annoyed. Just let me copy the damn map and don't bust my balls, I thought.

"Fine," I said, and walked out.

"I thought you were going to copy the map." Peter followed me out. Robert trailed behind, an amused look on his face.

"Guess not," I replied.

"Don't be a dork. Just copy the map," Peter said. I was walking pretty briskly back to the room. I turned around.

"I'm being the dork? You guys are the ones with the queer matching handkerchiefs around your necks." I don't know what came over me.

"Why are you acting like such a child?" Robert said. Look who's talking, I thought, you're the one that won't let me copy a stupid map.

"No, it's fine," I said. "The truth is, it's a straight shot to Córdoba, so I don't need the map."

"What about getting to Buenos Aires?" Peter said.

"I can't copy the whole thing anyway, so I'll just buy one later. It's better not to waste time now, I have farther to ride today than you guys." If we were getting along any better in the last couple of days, that pretty much killed it. It was glaringly apparent that our group problems were as much my fault as anyone's. All my anger from the past weeks had come out at once, and Robert was right, I was acting childish. I got my stuff, said "See you later," and left.

The ride was entertaining at first, but then became long and straight though the monotonous flatlands for three hundred miles or so. The steady vibrations and the droning of the tires almost put me to sleep. Passing towns occasionally provided enough interest to stir me, and then I fell back into a lull.

In Córdoba I found a room and called the radio station. They never called back. The following morning I got to know the city a little. It's beautiful and old, the second largest in Argentina. There were stunning plazas and tons of shops for big motorcycles like mine. I changed the KLR's filter and oil. Huge recycling cans were scattered about in blue, red, and yellow. They were over seven feet tall and shaped like an inverted thimble with a hook at the top, as if they were designed to be lifted by a crane. There were lots of buses, cars, and motorcycles that drove around way too fast. That night there was still no call from Radio Córdoba, so in the morning I headed for Rosario on my way to Buenos Aires.

The wind beat me around like a hackneyed overweight mafioso, cruelly, methodically, and with slight pauses to catch its breath. The currents kept me at a ten-degree angle and occasionally a truck would roar past and batter me with a wall of oncoming air. I stopped to lube my chain and the wind from passing trucks nearly knocked me over. Airborne hazards were everywhere. A big bird flew into my path and I had to duck behind my windscreen for safety. It was foggy and cold and I kept my electric vest cranked all the way up.

In Rosario I decided not to press my luck against the angry elements. Rosario was a busy, boisterous town, but I was exhausted and didn't really care to sightsee. In the morning I got right back on the road and finished the last leg to the capital. I was excited to get to Buenos Aires and see my family. I was also excited because in a few days, Elena, the lovely young woman I'd left in Guatemala, would be coming to town to meet me.

16

Bad News in Buenos Aires

➤ I'D ARRIVED. The culmination of nine months of planning and five months of riding had been achieved. I'd covered almost eighteen thousand miles to get to Buenos Aires, only to find that my uncle wouldn't even get off his chair to come to the door and greet me. A far cry from the warm celebrations I'd envisioned as a child. Then again, being that my uncle in Buenos Aires is a slothful man, I really wasn't too surprised. My cousin and aunt, however, were very happy to see me and welcomed me heartily.

With the help of a friend I managed to sublet an apartment in Palermo, a hip neighborhood in the center of the city. My goal was to spend the next three months there, practicing my Spanish, writing, and spending time with family. After that I planned to head further south and visit other relatives for another three months. After all that was over, I'd continue to Ushuaia for the millennium party, and then ride back home along the east coast, through Brazil, the Guyanas, Suriname, and Venezuela.

Peter and Robert showed up a few days behind me, and were kindly put up in the house of my aunt and lazy uncle. Elena arrived a short while after that with a friend of hers, a delightful redheaded Irishwoman named Maggie. Together, Robert, Peter, the two women, and I made plans to take a day trip on the bikes to see the Iguazu falls.

The telephone rang at 8 A.M. and woke me up in my new apartment. Robert was calling. I thought he wanted to finalize plans for the day's trip to the falls. Instead, he told me that Peter had gotten an e-mail from his wife saying she wanted a divorce. Peter had called the trip off.

As you can imagine, this came as a shock to all of us. We felt terrible. Peter's wife had made the announcement via e-mail and then became incommunicado. She flatly refused to answer her phone or respond to Peter's e-mails. We knew they were having problems, but apparently the long separation was the final whack that felled the tree.

I couldn't believe what was happening. Robert decided not to continue north through Brazil by himself. He seemed to feel that the risks of traveling alone were too great, so he was leaving for the United States with Peter. They'd already started making plans to ship their bikes back to Miami. In a moment, our trip together had ended for all of us.

What could be said? It was over. A strange four and one-half months had passed with my two unlikely riding partners. That's a long time to get to know all the good and bad of two people. We had a lot of fun. We had a lot of problems. We had shared the trip of a lifetime. In a few short days they had packed up their bikes, shipped them home, and followed right behind them on an airplane. The journey together had ended abruptly, and that was all.

※

OVER THE NEXT THREE MONTHS I spent a lot of time with my family in various parts of Argentina. Building relationships with the extended family I rarely saw growing up was more gratifying than I could've imagined. Now my future kids have a good chance of know-

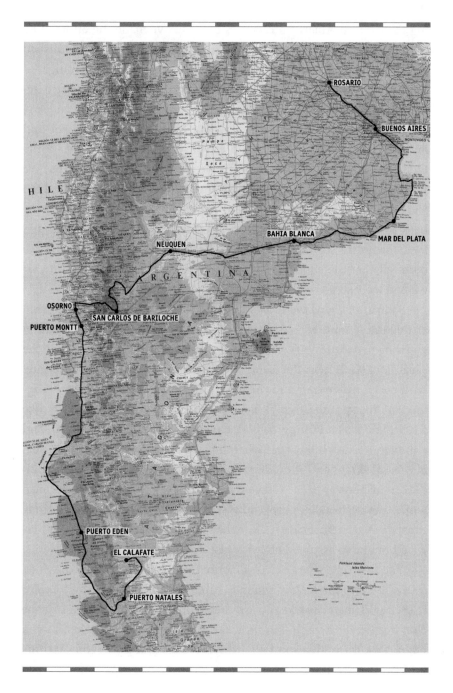

ing their South American relatives because I've made the effort to be a part of their lives. In the simple act of spending time, I accomplished an objective that was at the heart of this trip from the beginning.

During my stay in Buenos Aires I saw tango shows, the frigate-turned-museum *Sarmiento*, the Colón Theater, more museums, and several dance clubs. I studied some Brazilian Jiu Jitsu, ate some sushi, and overspent my budget. Buenos Aires is a very expensive city. While Elena stayed with me for a month, we made several short trips. We went to Bariloche by plane and to Mar del Plata, Bahía Blanca, and the Sierra de la Ventana by bike. The time was lovely and brief. She went back to her work in Guatemala, and I stayed in Argentina. Although I was happy to see her and we had a great time together, I think we both felt that the short time we spent together was enough, and that we had learned all we could from each other.

Soon after Elena went back to Guatemala, I met another woman. I settled into a kind of routine of work and exercise, and started dating a girl named Antonella. At the time she worked as a waitress at the Hard Rock Café near Recoleta. She was of Italian descent and petite, with curly brown hair and the most precious little face you can imagine. You just wanted to pick her up and stick her in your pocket like a doll. She was studying to be a dancer of both jazz and tango, and although I didn't know that when I met her, the tone of her physique, her muscled legs and shoulders, and her graceful walk were clear indications of her vocation. I have a policy not to make passes at women while they're working, especially waitresses and bartenders, but fortunately Antonella made it clear that she was interested in me, otherwise I might've assumed she was just doing her job.

The first time I saw her was before Elena had even arrived, which contributed to my lack of pursuit. After all, I'd been looking forward to seeing Elena for weeks. I wasn't really interested in meeting anyone else, but I couldn't help but notice this girl and wonder at her, as you might look through a shop window and marvel at a gorgeous antique piano you couldn't possibly fit in your living room, let alone afford. I was dining at the Hard Rock Café with Robert and Peter. Antonella was extremely friendly and floated around our table, enchanting all of us. Robert even gave her a Canadian flag pin to put with all the rock'n'roll memorabilia she had tacked to her uniform.

She spoke English well, and when we told her we were from the United States, she mentioned that she'd fallen in love with an American the year before. "But," she added, almost as an afterthought while she met my eye, "he's not my boyfriend." She asked us to come back and visit her at work anytime.

The second time I saw her, I was eating at the Hard Rock with two of my female cousins and their boyfriends while Antonella waited on us. At one point a swing tune came on, and I offered to show my cousin a few simple steps of the popular American dance. She agreed, and as we stood up and started, Antonella approached to check on our table. "You know how to dance swing?" she beamed at me. "I love swing, but nobody here knows how to do it."

I stopped my cousin in midtwirl and asked Antonella if she'd like me to show her. She glanced over her shoulder at the bar, to check if the boss was around, and then smiled at me as if to say "Hell, yes!" I practically threw my cousin back into her chair. Taking Antonella by her hand and her tiny waist, we began to dance. Though she'd never danced swing, in two passes she acquired the basic rock step like a champ. Like something from a Broadway show, busboys appeared and slid the empty tables away to give us more room. We spun and twirled while most of the Argentines, far too cool for their own good, pretended not to notice. This was all very silly and romantic. It was also very, very nice.

I'd pick her up from work on my motorcycle, and she'd stay with me most nights at my apartment. For two months I'd write and exercise while she was at work or at class, and we spent every free moment together. The strangest thing about this relationship was the simplicity. To be with her or to make her smile took no energy or effort. When there was nothing to say, we were silent. It's great when you can find someone to be silent with.

Nothing lasts forever, and neither did my time in Buenos Aires. I went to Bahía Blanca, where I stayed with more family before continuing south. Antonella and I kept dating, although it was hard not seeing her. I'd grown so attached that I impetuously invited her to take the trip to Ushuaia with me. How I felt about her was sure—I wanted her with me. How I felt about her coming along on the trip itself was confusing. I was afraid that I'd have no adventures, that I'd shut myself up in hotel rooms with her and not meet any more people. (This was not an unreasonable concern. We sometimes went days locked up in my apartment, never feeling the need to step outside and interact with the rest of the world.) Aside from the fear of ending up like a duprass from Vonnegut's *Cat's Cradle*, perhaps the biggest reason I hesitated to take her was that I needed a chance to ruminate about the spiritual side of my life. I sometimes need to be alone, just to think. Part of the motivation of this trip was that it would give me time to mull over things, to find the right questions and to see where I've been. I still needed to do this, because, between Peter's constant joking and Robert's, well . . . being Robert, there was a side of me I felt I'd somewhat neglected. I expected to be having a kind of motorcycling epiphany, learning about myself and life along the way. I don't know why I assumed that having Antonella along would get in the way of that.

Antonella seemed excited to come with me. She'd planned to spend her vacation with friends in Thailand and Singapore, but changed all that for me. When I expressed my reservations about her coming along and—to put it bluntly—uninvited her, she was understandably not impressed. I thought I was making the right choice at the time, and went about my business preparing myself and the bike for the remainder of my trip.

I left Bahía Blanca on a Sunday in December, alone. This was the beginning of the final leg to Ushuaia. In my usual style I started out late, around 11 A.M. I rode through the hot day to Neuquen, passing a dozen mint antique cars heading to a car show. Rows of trees resembling giant asparagus passed. That night I camped at a place called, appropriately enough, "Camping 2000." There were showers, clean facilities, even a pool. I found paying just three dollars to spend the night there refreshing, because the rest of Argentina is painfully overpriced.

Getting a chance to finally use the camping gear I had been dragging around was not the only nice change. Now I only had myself to answer to. Camping out, I awoke and left when I wanted to. I stopped for lunch near Piedra del Aguila and was served a slab of meat as thick as a phone book with a side salad as an afterthought. About a half hour later I was extremely tired while my gut fought to digest all that protein, so I pulled far off the side of the road, popped the kickstand on the bike, folded my arms across my chest, and leaned back on my top case for a half-hour nap while perched on the saddle. The day was cool, so I slept with all my gear on and my visor cracked open a half an inch for air. If anyone noticed me, they probably thought that I was just looking up at the sky or basking in the sun. The best part was that nobody could complain about me wasting time, slowing them down, or otherwise doing something wrong. I woke up and took a sip of cool water, looked around, and smacked the sleep from my mouth. What a great trip.

Back to the boring altiplano, which was broken up with occasional scrub, sand, buttes, muddy hills, mesas, and scree. One-hundred-sixty-five miles outside of Neuquen the familiar white points of the Andes appeared above the sparse brushlands. They shocked me anew. There are only a few countries in South America not blessed with the beauty of the Andes chain running through them, and they are worse off for it.

I detoured north from my track to Bariloche, taking Route 40 in order to check out Junin de los Andes and San Martín de los Andes. I perused both towns. Junin had great motorcycling roads, and San Martín had gorgeous tin-roofed houses, many of them owned by movie stars. I continued south on the Camino de los Siete Lagos. The road bisected the typical Andean setting of stunning mountains and lake scenery, dotted with a variety of pine and deciduous forests.

Smoke rose over a hillside in the distance. Uniformed men stopped traffic up ahead, giving all the drivers the same travel advisory. There was a forest fire in progress near the first lake, Lago Machónico. There wasn't any danger as long as we kept to the road. Huge swabs of light gray smoke puffed up over the side of the mountain as I skirted along. If the fires moved too close to the highway, the guard told me, I'd be sent back by men working further up ahead. As I rode, the smoke occasionally parted and I saw a yellow wall of flame creeping sideways up the hillside. A fire helicopter passed near me, dipping its bucket into the lake and then flying over the fire to drop its load.

Later I came upon an accident. A small rental car sat in the middle of the road, its windshield shattered. The sides and roof were dented and the front wheels pointed in opposite directions. Someone had obviously rolled it, but now the car was right side up again. The accident seemed recent, but nobody was around. I pulled up close to the window to see if anyone was hurt inside. Empty. No blood anywhere, no footprints in the dirt, nothing. No sooner had I pulled up than an ambulance and tow truck arrived behind me. I looked at the ambulance driver questioningly, but he just waved me on. I started to leave and the ambulance followed me; apparently they weren't going to wait around to see if anyone showed up. I watched the news later that night to see if the accident would be mentioned but there was nothing. This appeared to be just another roadside mystery.

I arrived in Bariloche by 7 P.M., completely wrecked. I needed some time to readjust to the 350-miles-a-day routine. After five days in Bariloche relaxing with family, I headed for Chile.

On the Chilean side of the border I met Christel, a German woman traveling through all of Chile and parts of Argentina on her BMW R80. We chatted a little while and decided to ride together to Osorno, just a short distance west. After that we'd split; she'd take the route north and I'd move south. The road was great; it was interesting to see the changes in the scenery across the borders. The Argentine side had been mostly hardwood trees and tall forests. The Chilean side had those trees as well, but it also had more tropical-looking shrubs, under-growth, ferns, and vines thrown in.

Chile was instantly odd when compared to the rest of Latin America because the drivers I saw were excellent. They were courteous, calm, and patient. I was used to being ignored or muscled off the road, of having to fight the entire highway from every on-ramp. But here the drivers slowed and politely waved me into traffic ahead of them. I didn't know what to make of this strange behavior.

We reached Osorno and stopped for lunch. Christel had been headed south on Route 40 in Argentina with two other German bik-ers. She'd gotten tired of the constant wind and turned back north again. Her plan was to ride around Chile until her friends made it back from Ushuaia, Argentina, and then meet up with them again. Appar-ently she'd been just about everywhere on that bike of hers: Africa, North America, Central America, India, Tibet, all over Europe. We took some photos after lunch, wished each other well, and parted.

In Puerto Montt there was not much to do. I found a hotel and didn't even try to deal; my heart wasn't in it. This was a good-sized town, lots of shops, but nothing that I was looking for. I couldn't find a cinema and was bored walking around. I went to the local museum, used an Internet café, and watched a few stray dogs fight over a bitch in heat. I walked from one end of the shore to the other, always with the overshadowing mountains above me.

For dinner I found a place that specialized in *curanto*, a curious local dish recommended by my family in Bariloche. The waiter first brought some bread, a small fried empanada, and some broth in a bowl. Then he placed an immense empty blue oven dish on my table and walked away. The tray looked like something a busboy might've used to clear the dishes from a dining hall, but it turned out to be for the scraps and bones from my main course. Then I saw why.

The waiter came back with an enormous bowl stacked with what appeared to be everything they had in the kitchen. The mound of food was as tall as a bottle of wine. There was chicken, beef, a hot dog, a sausage, two boiled potatoes, fried dumplings, boiled dumplings, a truly bizarre seafood called *picoro* that I can only describe as having a head like a crab claw shoved inside of a little barnacle-like cave, and two dozen clams and mussels, all open and gaping stupidly at me. "Is this what I ordered?" I asked the waiter. He smiled and nodded. Surely I was going to hell for wasting this much food because I didn't think there was any way I could eat it all.

The following day I prepared for the next stage of my travel, which was to take a ferry from Puerto Montt to Puerto Natales, in the south of Chile. My ticket and bike passage cost me four hundred dollars for the four-day trip. I figured it would've taken me at least a week to do the ride on Route 40, one of the most notoriously bad roads in Argentina, and a windswept torture test for man and machine. Including the cost of food, lodging, and gas to ride through Argentina, I figured I was saving a small amount of money, time, and wear on the bike by taking the ferry through Chilean waters.

We weren't boarding until 10 P.M., so I had some time to kill. I bought a bottle of rum at a grocery store and some cherries from a vendor in the street market. I rode to various ATMs trying to withdraw cash. All the machines told me I had insufficient funds, which I knew to be incorrect. Finally one of them took my debit card and kept it. Bummer. I sent an urgent e-mail to my family in the United States, asking to be forwarded the spare card I left at home.

After dark I went to the docks to wait. Outside the boat I met two English bicyclists who planned to pedal around South America in the coming year. And people call me crazy.

Our boat, the *Puerto Edén*, was enormous. If you stretched out all the trucks it could carry in a row they'd measure a kilometer in length. In addition, it could hold sixty cars and more than 150 passengers. The *Puerto Edén* was a Finnish vessel, made in 1971. The normal life of a ferry of this kind is fifteen years, but according to the engineer she was in good shape and was still usable. I found it a little worrisome that this vessel's age was now twice its estimated life span. The boat had two main diesel engines that generated 3,000 horsepower each and used about 2,600 gallons of fuel per day. Although the boat was capable of thirty days of travel between stops, our trip took less than the normal four days because our captain was certified for night navigation in the channels. The trip was indeed fast. We arrived in Puerto Natales ahead of schedule with no problems, aside from the fact that the sheep stacked up in the tractor-trailers began eating the wool off each other's backs after a few days without food.

The morning we arrived, I rode to the Torres del Paine national park. Along the way ranchers on horseback waved and a pack of thin-legged guanacos flanked me, spooked by the roar of my bike and running at top speed. The stupid animals seemed unable to realize the scary noises were coming from me, so instead of running away, they huddled around me in a pack and escorted me toward the park entrance along the dirt road. They call me Dances with Guanacos.

The Torres del Paine park is impressive; the rocky towers are gothic, imposing, and cruelly serrated. The cold, sterile power of nature resides up there—old trees are dried and bent like broken scarecrows, the frigid winds are constant, and the looming mountains spike upward from the ground like giant jags of broken glass tearing the sky.

That evening I stayed in the refugio, a wooden building with showers, toilets, and a kitchenette downstairs, and mattresses for travelers stacked up on the second floor. There was a French couple I'd seen earlier sleeping there, and also a couple of single men in the corners, but since I arrived later than expected, around 12:20 A.M., and left by 8:30 A.M., I didn't interact with any of them. However, it was

comforting to know that I wasn't the only weirdo roaming the world alone on Christmas Eve.

From the Torres del Paine park I rode to El Calafate. Most highways in this part of South America are made of rocks called *ripio*, which is an appropriate-sounding name since the sharp gravel used to grade the roads is excellent for shredding tires. I got a flat and patched the tube at a service station in El Calafate.

I rode on to the Perito Moreno Glacier. The road was dusty and washboard laden, and when I reached the steeper rough roads near the glacier I discovered the design limitations of my saddlebags. The locking mechanism gave out on my right-side bag, causing it to fall from the bike. Later it dawned on me that, like my motorcycle, the bag's lock needed regular maintenance—it needed lubrication and the screws had to be tightened. Two of the four screws had worked themselves out, and the lock collapsed under the pressure. The bag still opened and closed fine, but I lost a few parts and the lock no longer served to hold the bag to the frame. Another lesson learned the hard way. I strapped the bag into place with a tie-down and pressed on.

By the time I pulled into the camping area, the sun had already started to fall behind the horizon. The fading light reflected glaringly off the glacier and the lake. The massive ice field crept tirelessly forward, as it had been doing for more than one hundred years. That evening I camped near the shore of the water and listened to the far-off crackling of the glacier. I heard passing laughter and voices speaking. Sounded like Americans. I turned from my camp stove of boiling cheese ravioli and saw a group passing, two men and a woman, around my age or younger. "Hello?" I called out. No response. They continued walking, not looking my way. Perhaps they hadn't heard me. "Hello, are you guys Americans?" The guy in the lead threw up his hands in exasperation, like I was his crack-addict brother that had just asked him for another twenty dollar loan. He continued walking without further acknowledging my presence. Guy Number Two followed him without looking my way. The girl looked in my direction as she passed. I was confused by their behavior and said, "I don't mean to bother you."

"No, you aren't bothering us," she said cheerily, still walking, "we're from Chicago." Was that their excuse? Well Merry Christmas, I hope Santa brings you a bad case of diarrhea.

They next day I visited the glacier, setting myself up on the wooden walkway to watch and listen. Robert once described the Moreno glacier as "humbling" to witness. I couldn't agree more. I felt dwarfed next to such a powerful, active force of nature. The glacier is massive—it's shaped like a giant arrowhead with a varying width of roughly two and a half to four miles and a surface area of over 170 square miles. The craggy frozen peaks reach heights of up to 170 feet. The Moreno glacier moves as much as seven feet per day in its center, but the real action happens underwater.

As the glacier pushes its way down from the mountain into Lago Argentino, its tip is forced up against the peninsula of land, damming the lake's Sur and Rico arms. This creates uneven water levels on the two sides of the ice, and the water, in turn, tears at the glacier's underbelly as it conforms to gravity. The result is a cataclysmic explosion of ice and water as the weakened glacier's massive ice bridge crashes spectacularly into the lake. This much-anticipated event happens only once every five years or so, but for reasons not quite understood, the glacier hasn't crashed in recent years.

I sat watching the massive ice worm crawling down the mountain and listened to the mythical cracking sounds coming from deep within. I was far enough away on the observatory deck that by the time the sound reached my ears, the calving pieces of ice, some as big as a six-story building, were already tumbling into the water with devastating crashes. Tour boats and floating icebergs bobbed in the giant swells raised by the falling pieces of ice like toys in a bathtub. There's a fine of up to five hundred dollars for straying off the walkways. A sign read: "Danger—NO TRESPASSING—When ice falls, pieces are thrown violently dozens of meters away. This action caused the death of 32 people between 1968 and 1988." What's not stated on that sign is why it took twenty years and thirty-two deaths to figure out they ought to post a warning.

After I rode back to the town of El Calafate, I got a shock. I didn't know how I'd done it, but suddenly I realized I had a big problem—so big that my trip was in jeopardy. In fact, it was almost over. I checked my e-mail and found I was out of money!

17

The End of the Road

➤ SINCE MOST OF THE BANK MACHINES in South America didn't display the totals in my bank account when I withdrew cash, I usually didn't know how much money I had left. Although I had what some might loosely call a budget, I was never really organized with it. So I was shocked when my family in the United States, who had been taking care of most of my business at home, sent word that my account held about eight hundred dollars. Damn. What a surprise. What a drag. I didn't know what to think or do. What happened to my cash? Who the hell spent all my money? I went outside the cyber café where I'd gotten the news, sat down on the hard curb, and squinted at my bike for a while. The sun blazed proudly above. I stood back up, tightened the chain, and then lubricated it; it had been getting really loose lately. I sat down and looked at the bike some more.

After thinking for a while, it seemed entirely likely that I had indeed spent all my money. Argentina, by far the most expensive place I stayed, was also where I'd been living for about five months. Barring the low beef prices, everything in Buenos Aires cost as much, if not more, than similar items cost in New York City. Movies were expensive and I'd seen a lot of them. Dining out was pricey too, and I did plenty of that with my girlfriend, Antonella. I partied a lot with my cousins and that added up as well. Damn. I'd blown all my cash for the rest of the trip.

I pulled a half a sandwich I'd saved from lunch out of my pocket and split it with a dog that had wandered up to me. She happily scarfed it up and wagged her tail. The dog was a pathetic thing, friendly, skinny, and inoffensive. She looked at me and I looked at her. Here we were, a couple of losers, without the foresight to carefully plan our futures and conserve enough resources to accomplish our goals. Well, OK, the dog had no goals. I was the only loser. Damn dog. Give me back my food. I'm going to need it.

Even if I couldn't ride back home, I knew I probably had enough money to make it to Ushuaia. Crap. At least I could do that. Crap, crap, crap. Maybe I'd have to sell my bike and buy a scooter. Maybe I'd have to get a job. I might have to become a shepherd in Ushuaia in order to get out of town. I dejectedly got onto my bike and dejectedly rode out of town, toward Rio Gallegos. The whole way there I was kicking myself, which is hard to do while seated on a motorcycle. What could be said? I'd had a great time in Buenos Aires.

Time to face reality. I had to deal with this. Fine. I can handle it. What were my options? I could sell the bike, fly back home, and use the leftover money to pay off any remaining trip debt on credit cards. Or I could ship the bike back, and have big credit card bills and no way to pay them back until I start making some cash. I thought about this as I rode from El Calafate.

Coming over a hill, I saw the headlight of an approaching vehicle. This was unusual because most people in South America drove around without headlights, day or night. As I suspected, the headlight was from another motorcycle roaming the earth, like mine.

I pulled over and a couple riding two-up on a red BMW 100GS parked beside me. They had matching black and purple suits and red helmets. "Howdy," the man said. He had a full graying beard and

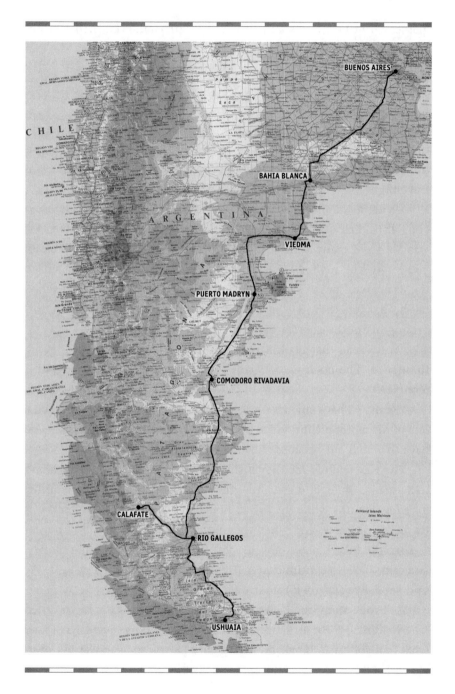

glasses. "I'm Eric Haws and this is my wife Gail." Gail had straight shoulder-length hair and a kind face. "Are you coming from the glacier?" Eric asked as we posed together for photos. "How was it?" Gail seemed content to let Eric do most of the talking. There was something unusual about this pair but I couldn't put my finger on it.

"Yes," I said. "It's astounding." We talked more and I found out they'd traveled over much of the world two-up, and planned to continue to do so. They asked me about my trip, myself, and where I was traveling.

"What a coincidence, we've written a few things about motorcycling also," Eric said. "And I made a Web site." I commented that Eric was a man of many skills. "Everyone has strengths and weaknesses, you know," he replied. "For example, my strength is that I'm smart. Gail is my weakness." He beamed at me and Gail just smiled and shook her head. "You know, we have a friend who wrote a book about motorcycling in South America. His name's Greg Frazier."

"Yes, I read that book actually. It's not bad." I said. I was trying to be nice. The book wasn't bad—when compared to a book that is terrible.

"Really? That's surprising, knowing Greg," Eric said. "I've seen a few of his motorcycling videos. That's another thing about Gail—you have to watch out because she talks behind people's backs."

The Hawses told me they'd shipped their bike from New Zealand to Santiago, Chile, and somehow they managed to leave it in-country for a few months while they went home. What they did, in effect, was travel to one place, and when they ran out of cash they didn't bother to ship the bike home, they just left it, went home for more money, and came back to continue later. "It's cheaper that way," they said. We said good-bye and took to our own directions.

As I rode along the beautifully paved road I passed a town called La Esperanza. I got an inspiring revelation, a hope even. I realized what that conversation meant—suddenly I knew the trip was not over. No way. All I needed was the customs people to give me a year, or even just eight months, on the bike's importation permit. Then I could leave the motorcycle in Buenos Aires, go home and make some cash, and come back and finish my trip through Brazil later. I was starting to get excited again. This is probably how that dog felt. There I was, all alone in the hot sun, when along comes a stranger with a tasty scrap—just what I needed.

A gorgeous sunset chased me into Rio Gallegos. The flat horizon extended in 360 degrees, and the violet and orange flames seemed to circle me in all directions. The colors bounced off the clouds, lighting the sky like an inferno. I had to stop on the side of the road just to watch.

I left my things at a hotel and rode into town. I spoke to my girlfriend Antonella on the phone; it was great to hear her voice, though she sounded very far away. I called around to my family in the United States but nobody was there. Back at the hotel I lingered in the shower, which was nice after so many days without.

The next morning I found a note left on my motorcycle from the night before. Gail and Eric Haws had left the message, asking me to stop by their hotel. When I showed up at their place they were just getting up. In the sort of off-handed way that someone might tell you they like to play tennis, Gail and Eric mentioned to me that they're in the *Guinness Book of World Records* as the first motorcyclists to cross Russia, the world's largest country, from east to west purely by riding a motorcycle. No ferries, trains, or other vehicles were involved—an impressive feat when you consider that Russia covers a maximum lateral distance of 4,774 miles. That's like driving from New York to Los Angeles—without all the nice highways, bridges, and places to eat and sleep—and then turning around and driving back again. The pair did the trip by riding together on a single motorcycle, as they always did. They were besieged with setbacks. Mosquitoes devoured them every time they stopped, and at the beginning of their journey they had all their dried foods, spices, and cooking supplies stolen. "We left it all hanging from a tree, which is normal when camping in bear country,"

Gail said. "What we didn't realize is that the people were even hungrier than the bears, and they saw our food dangling there like a present."

"After that we lived off toast, noodles, and tea sweetened with jam," Eric added. "We both lost 15 percent of our body weight."

Gail asked me where I was headed. I mentioned Ushuaia, and suddenly it was decided that we'd all head there together. I felt like I'd been adopted. The last leg of my trip would be finished with none other than this curious, world-record-setting couple from Oregon. And so began my journey with the Hawses. "Don't worry, we're great to travel with," Eric smiled. "But occasionally Gail can talk too much."

Ushuaia is reputedly the southernmost city in the world. If you want to find the honest-to-goodness end of the road, at least the southern end, that's the place to go. You can't ride much farther than that. The city sits on the "Great Island of the Land of Fire," commonly known as Tierra del Fuego, which rests at the bottom of South America like a thimble knocked from a finger. Ushuaia has about three thousand steady inhabitants and was about to get twenty thousand guests for the new millennium bash.

We rode through countless customs checkpoints on our way to Ushuaia. We ferried across the short channel, a free trip for motorcycles and pedestrians, and continued south on the unpaved roads. High-velocity winds blasted us along the ripio. In San Sebastian, just before the roads became paved again, we stopped for soup and coffee.

I looked up from our snack to find we had a visitor. Like a burst shot from the sun, a packet of raw strawberry-blond energy, the exuberant man strode boldly inside, hiked up his riding pants, and sat down in front of us. We instantly pegged him by his motorcycle gear—he was another freak like us, riding to the end of the world. His name was Nat Crewe, and he'd come all the way from Alaska to raise money for the Muscular Dystrophy Association in the name of his father: gourmand, Renaissance man, and muscular dystrophy sufferer, the late Quentin Crewe. Nat was originally from England, but he'd lived in Argentina for five years and spoke near-perfect Spanish. He wore a crew cut and stubby five-day beard, and his black suit and yellow moto boots were coated in road dust.

"I almost didn't make it here," Nat said. "I was held up in Quito waiting for the bike." What a coincidence, I thought. He made it sound as though he'd just been there. In fact, he had. He'd run a bit behind schedule and had to bolt down from Ecuador in a matter of weeks to make it to Ushuaia in time for the millennium party. Like the rest of us, Nat heard about the collection of motorcyclists that were going to be there and wanted to be a part of it.

When we'd all finished we stepped outside and saw Nat's bike. He rode an Africa Twin with a monstrous, custom-built, twelve-gallon tank. Nat was of average height, but his bike was stacked up so high with gear on the tank and tail that, in order to mount it, he had to make a bold, running leap with his right foot forward, throwing himself onto the sheepskin-covered seat as if performing a flying front kick from a bad Kung-fu movie. We all found this tremendously entertaining. I could sense that Gail wanted to adopt him right away.

We roared out of there. The excitement was building, ready to boil over. We were now just a couple hundred miles from our goal. There were so many expectations: dozens of riders from around the world, meeting up in Ushuaia for what was sure to be motorcycling's equivalent of Woodstock—every biker having endured countless hardships and great expense to cart themselves and their two-wheeled beasts of choice to the end of the world. And we were going to be able to say, "Ushuaia Millennium Party? Yep, I was there." There would be masses of people, Pavarotti would sing, the festivities would last all night.

In the north, people planned parties at home with candles and canned goods for the Y2K disaster that never came. Companies braced their bank accounts and many would-be revelers stayed in their towns, afraid to fly because the airplanes were going to spontaneously explode when the clock struck 2000. We weren't worried. Down here the threat of technological failure was limited to bad gas blocking up our carburetors.

At the next immigration checkpoint the Hawses went through first. Nat and I followed. Nat displayed a bit of charm, flirting with the woman behind the counter. He was thin and confident, with enough boisterous energy bubbling out of him for two men. The customs woman wanted us to take the office address so we could send them a postcard from home. "Yeah," Nat said, smiling broadly at the young woman, "put your home phone number in there, too."

I was chatting with the man working next to her, and she interrupted to have him write his personal information down for us. She was still blushing from Nat's comment. The man noticed his co-worker's state and suddenly leaned over the counter, shaking Nat's hand. "Congratulations pal, in one year of working with this woman I've never seen anybody get to her. But one sentence from you she can't even remember my name."

A friend had given me a contact in Rio Grande, our last major stop before Ushuaia, who helped us find a place to stay—actually a yacht club. The club's caretaker, Benjamin, was in his late twenties and was tall and thin like a post. His brown hair had begun to recede off his forehead. Benjamin was about as nice as they come. He offered us food and wine from his personal larder and loaned us mattresses and fresh towels. He even let us park our bikes inside the club for security and protection from the elements.

We pulled the bikes into the warehouse-style building and Nat noticed oil dripping from the Hawses machine. "That's quite a spill you have there, Eric," Nat said. "I suppose you just drive around dripping away like some roving Exxon disaster?"

"It's actually not that bad," Eric said, "it only collects in places where I stop."

"You may have the Greenpeace beard," Nat said, shaking his head reproachfully, "but you certainly don't have the Greenpeace attitude."

We headed out in the morning, and as Benjamin predicted, there was a lot of wind. About eleven miles from town we took the F road toward Lago Yehuin. My ankle was sore from a fall the day before. I'd turned to check a passing sign and caught my foot under my saddle-bag, taking the weight of the bike onto the joint. Luckily it didn't break, but it now complained intermittently. I'd also gotten sick again. I'd picked up some bug, which by now had tired of the free intestinal tour and was dying to get back out into the world. I was forced to use a rustic facility I found off the side of the road, an old outhouse on an abandoned plot of farmland. The ancient latrine should've been destroyed—the rotted wooden beams crumbled to dust when you touched them and the whole thing was as drafty as a screen door. I had to arrange myself just so to prevent the decayed structure from collapsing around me from my weight. Luckily I always carried my own roll of toilet paper in my top case, a habit I picked up from Peter.

My stomach improved after lunch. Nat and I were impatient to reach our goal and kept pushing ahead. The Hawses had found some German bikers that were taking their time and decided to keep pace with them as we tallied the final miles to Ushuaia. I rounded the dirt road that circumvents Lago Fagnano, and the sun burned orange-yellow obelisks through the haze on the lake—they looked like columns of gold pointing toward our destination, now just a few miles away. I couldn't believe it. Ten months after I started, I was about to make it.

Unlike most of the Argentine Patagonia we crossed to get there, Ushuaia actually has mountains and trees. The entire southern end of the island is an unlikely oasis on the big toe of South America. As we got closer the road became paved, and the first building we sighted was an empty police checkpoint. We rode past a traffic circle and bright pastel prefab houses. Nat and I began shouting as we rode down the main drag. We'd taken completely different tracks here, but suddenly it was as if we'd come the whole way together. This was what it was all about. Ushuaia, baby. Don't talk to us about road trips. We know road trips. We pulled over and dismounted, beating each other on the back and jumping around. We strutted and screamed. We climbed back on the bikes and rode a victory lap around town.

I went to look for a cyber café and groceries, and I got separated from the others. Near midnight I arrived at the campsite where all the international bikers were to meet. After a long and winding dirt trail through the Tierra del Fuego National Park, I turned a dark corner and saw the campfires burning. I heard hooting and shouting, greetings for the appearance of my lone headlight. The motorcycling masses came out to welcome me in leather and ballistic nylon jackets, with unshorn faces and filthy boots. They offered cups of hot German wine and warm handshakes. Steam escaped their smiling teeth. People I'd never seen before hugged me hello.

Tents were everywhere. Bikes were everywhere. This was a road warrior convention. Fifty bikers from Denmark, Germany, the United States, the United Kingdom, Scotland, France, Australia, and Japan among other places had gathered together in Laguna Verde campground at the end of the Pan-American Highway. Even Walter and Sandra were there, the two Germans who'd been waiting in San Pedro de Atacama for three weeks to get a box of lightbulbs.

There was an incredible feeling of camaraderie and togetherness. We were the dedicated few, the privileged crazies. We were a group the likes of which had never been formed before. This comraderie was exactly what I didn't know I was hoping to find. I was a member of a strange and magnificent species of migratory bird that, for some reason, had come to the end of the world only to discover myself surrounded by all my waiting siblings. Welcome to Ushuaia, they said. Have some hot wine, they said.

As far as the actual millennium party was concerned, I got all that I could ask for, except Pavarotti. The portly tenor was a no-show. What we did see was a stunning performance by Julio Boca and Eleonora Cassano of a ballet-tango called Tango 2000, culminating in a perfectly timed final pass just as the clock struck midnight and the fireworks began. I was with the Hawses, Nat, and a lanky Scottish rider who'd come down to the party on a Triumph. The twenty-minute fireworks display that followed had our motorcycle group screaming. There was just one thing missing. Antonella, my girlfriend, should've been with me. The only thing that could've made this the perfect end of my trip would've been to have her there.

As glittering orange willows wept in the sky and violet and magenta sunbursts exploded, I was finally hit by the enormity of my journey. I had actually made it. I somehow survived, and therefore, succeeded. Twenty-two thousand miles, ten months, countless falls, illnesses, frustrations, and one head-on collision later, I was finally in Ushuaia, the end of the world. Another rider who'd come along the Pan-American from Alaska described the feeling as "an overwhelming sense that there is not a thing on earth I cannot accomplish." Although I can't concur completely, that's a damn good description of the feeling.

The next couple of days the camping motorcycle pack hung out in the wilderness. One afternoon I met a guy, whom I will call Sam, a short man in his late twenties, who rode a big GS just like Robert's, only he didn't take care of his bike as well as Robert did. (Nobody can maintain a bike like Robert.) Sam was a former stockbroker from New York who had made a wad of cash and finally asked, "What's it all for?" He then began traveling the world on his BMW. He recently had found a good purpose for his trip by raising money to help an orphanage he got to know in a third world country. Sam was an intelligent person, spoke four languages, and had a lot to talk about, mostly himself.

When in the company of people like Sam and Nat, those that lived their trips raising money in the name of others, or even Gail and Eric, who put their quirky minds to setting world records, I couldn't help but feel that my trip was a bit silly and selfish. Narcissistic even. Motorcycle masturbation, if you will. In reality, people do trips like this all the time. Mine wasn't special; I had just ridden my bike south. It wasn't as if I landed on the moon or anything. I hadn't discovered anyplace where people didn't already live.

After all the hot wine was finished and the town had begun to settle back down to its normal, freezing self, we bid the other bikers good-bye. Accompanied still by Gail, Eric, and Nat, I made a fast ride back up to Rio Grande. Benjamin, the skinny Yacht Club manager, was there for us again, with room for our bikes. My time on the Bolivian hell roads taught me well; I made it back early and did some maintenance. I cleaned the air filter, tightened the chain, and unstuck the rear brake light switch.

I couldn't sleep for stress. That night I fretted over money blown in Buenos Aires. I was bummed that I couldn't go to Brazil. Around 2 A.M. I headed downstairs to read. I picked my way through a field of sleeping twenty-year-old Israeli ex-soldiers and their camping gear to find Benjamin at the kitchen table, reading the paper with a cigarette in his hand. Having an understanding nature and the typical Argentine awareness of how to deal with such situations, he prepared a classic maté. The very strong tealike drink has more caffeine that a triple espresso, but since I wasn't sleeping anyway I figured what the hell. He asked me what was troubling me, and I told him my story.

"Everyone makes mistakes with money," Benjamin said. "I used to work in a photo lab, a good job, but I wanted a vacation. I told my boss I needed three weeks, but he only offered me two. So I went anyway, without worry, even though my boss said that when I came back I'd probably be out of work. He was right. I came back from my trip with ten dollars in my pocket and he'd hired someone else." Benjamin smiled and laughed, taking a long drag from his cigarette. He seemed an imperturbable kind of fellow. "So I sold my house and lived off of the money for two years. I did absolutely nothing. When I was finally broke I came here to Rio Gallegos and went to work. Now I'm building a house." He paused, putting the cigarette in his mouth to free both hands, and he drew a rough sketch on the newspaper of how his future home would look. "First I bought the land, then I had a hole dug, and now it's just a pit with a tarp over it. I'm building it one piece at a time. I hope to rent it and travel off the money later." Benjamin's tale of woe did the trick. Nothing like a little perspective. I went to sleep around 4 A.M. with a clear conscience.

The next day my new group split. We rode as far as we could together, and then stopped and said our good-byes. Nat and I were

going to ride together to Buenos Aires, and the Hawses were heading
off to see some national parks. Gail hugged Nat and me warmly. Her
little moto-ducklings were all grown up and leaving the nest. We'd
spent less than a week together, but it felt like much more than that
(especially when Eric was talking). Nat and I made Eric uncomfortable
by giving him hugs as well. "You're making him get in touch with his
feminine side," Gail said.

"Yeah. It's sweet," I said. "Turn around, Eric, we want to touch
your feminine side too."

The buffeting winds were fierce on the route north; they pushed
hard, forcing us to push back. Sometimes a gust knocked me onto
looser gravel, or if the wind suddenly died and I remained leaning into
it, I'd veer off at weird angles, my balance threatened. Nat said that at
one point he almost bought it in a curve. I was tightening my chain
once or twice per day now. That was a bad sign; it was bound to go
anytime. We paused for lunch near Sombrero. Four cute Israeli ex-mil-
itary girls came in and sat near us. We started to talk, and a short one
with great teeth asked us about Ushuaia. "Yeah, we were there," Nat
smiled at her warmly. "Did you see me?"

We burned our way up Argentina's Route 3 toward Buenos Aires.
I wanted to get back to the United States and make arrangements for
the trip through Brazil as soon as possible, and Nat was in a hurry to
get to Mar del Plata, so we flew across the dry landscape. Arid brown
earth lay in every direction, flat and unending. We hunched on our
bikes uncomfortably, leaning deep over the tank to hide behind our
windscreens. Numbness quickly set in on the long, flat roads. For ten
miles I'd ride on one side of my butt until it started to fall asleep, and
then I'd shift my body weight and switch to the other.

The Patagonia could be summed up as the most expansive stretch
of nearly naked, harshly winded, sheep-and-guanaco-dotted, flat, dry,
interminable, boring nothingness in all of South America. Of course
there's a lot more than just that, but that's pretty much all you notice
when you whip through it at 90 MPH in a huddled position. One good
thing about the Patagonia, however—it's got the best sunsets ever

seen. The rays fanned out, encircling the dome of the sky, and brilliant colors lined every angle of the horizon, creating the illusion that there was more than just one sun setting. I hardly knew where to point my camera.

That night we camped in Piedra Buena, near a river's edge. We talked across the fire about the bikers in Ushuaia. "I don't know," Nat said. "I found Sam to be a little too Wall Street. A bit of a braggart." Nat described Sam boasting about his glory days, some former sexploits with a stripper. "Oh, how good for you," Nat had said mockingly, right to his face.

"Yeah," I said. "But you handled him OK. In fact, he seemed to like you."

"No, I don't think he did too much." Nat said. "There was a moment as we chatted and we both realized there's no way we'd ever ride together."

"He seemed really noble when he talked about his charity ride for the orphanage," I said, "but what got me was how he described his New Year's celebrations. Something about his conquest of 'some pig' he'd met. I just kind of pretended I didn't hear him."

"I feel sorry for the pig." Nat laughed. We finished our dinner and slept under the open sky, listening to the flapping of the motorcycle covers in the breeze.

Black-neck swans drifted in the river, poking their heads in and out of the reflected morning sun. Blackflies nipped our flesh as Nat patiently watched me remove a link from my overstressed chain. The chain was so far gone that the only way to tighten it now was to begin shortening it. At Robert's insistence I'd agreed to bring along a chain breaker. Even though he was gone, Robert was helping me out in spirit. My sprockets were also pretty worn. The teeth had become needlelike fangs and were ready to start snapping off.

Back on the highway we surfed against the constant wind, riding at a twenty-degree angle into the breeze to fight it. We saw a group of Italians from Macedonian Motorcycle Tours at a gas station. We pulled in to say hello, but they just curtly greeted us and roared off on their Moto Guzzis. We walked into the dining area and the greasy-haired older man behind the counter asked us to sit right down. He seemed friendly but strange.

"Where are you from?" he asked. We told him the United States and the United Kingdom. He took a step back and reached under his apron, as if to withdraw a hidden knife, gaucho-style. "Oh, friends of Pinochet, eh?" he said. He did this act in a dopey, joking manner, but I sensed that if we did, in fact, speak favorably in any way about the ex-Chilean dictator, he would've instantly hated us. For all I cared Pinochet could rot in a cesspool for eternity. But since neither Nat or I wanted to rehash political events that happened when we were in kindergarten, much less convince this village idiot of our lack of camaraderie with Pinochet, we ate our sandwiches outside.

Another stunning sunset greeted us that night while we camped: the blue sky formed massive welts of cool roses and lavenders, just above the horizon, and they heated and expanded higher, roasting and swelling until they burst forth and stained the clouds with flaming orange and bleeding magenta. The Patagonian skyline is so expansive that it pains the eye to perceive its borders. It hurt to look too far into the distance.

That night we stared up from our cozy sleeping bags and counted satellites. We slept most nights under the open sky, enjoying the astronomical shows that can only be seen in the southern hemisphere, in a place as desolate as the Patagonia. With no nearby cities to add distracting light, the visibility of the heavens is unsurpassed. Satellites and shooting stars floated by. Several falling stars blazed through, yellow-tailed and fleeting. The last one was long and straight like an ignited rope, its huge red tail scourging the sky and burning its image in our eyes. Unbelievable.

We smoked a trail up the Patagonia, averaging 85 MPH on the flat pavement. The ambient temperature rapidly increased as we scaled the coastline. Whenever we stopped, my tires felt like heated sponges. In a couple of short days we'd passed Puerto Madryn, and the midday weather became exceedingly hot.

On the third day of our trip north we stopped for gas near Santiago del Oeste. The gas station attendant, a black-haired kid about seventeen years old, approached me at the pump. He asked me where I was from. I told him New York and he said, "What happened to your friend?" I looked around. Nat was walking toward the restroom. He seemed fine.

"What do you mean?" I said.

"There's an article about you in the paper," the kid continued. "About your friend that died." Oh, I thought, he must be talking about Nat and his dad, who had died of muscular dystrophy. Nat was doing his trip for charity in his father's name, and had spoken with some reporters about it in Ushuaia. I concluded the article must've been about them. Nat came back from the bathroom.

"Hey, Nat," I said. "There's an article about you and your dad in the paper."

"Oh. Good," he smiled.

"It was his father that died," I said to the kid while pointing at Nat.

The kid eyed us strangely. "Oh. Well, the paper is inside," he said.

"Excellent, thanks!" Nat replied to the boy, smiling and waving as he ran inside to read the article. I came in soon after and sat down. The front cover was a photo of a crashed motorcyclist. His bike was laid over and he had onlookers peering over his immobile body. There was another shot of the biker being put into an ambulance on a stretcher. This article clearly wasn't about Nat and his dad. I now realized what that kid meant. He was telling us that someone from the Ushuaia group of bikers had been killed in a crash.

I didn't even read two sentences when I recognized the bike. It was Sam's poorly maintained GS. The dead man the gas attendant referred to was Sam. I went into a kind of shock. The poor bastard had gotten himself killed. I was suddenly overcome by the emotion of it.

We were just with that guy and suddenly he was dead. Sure he was boastful, a bit of a jerk maybe, but he wasn't a bad person. He dedicated his trip to charity. He couldn't be dead. What the fuck was happening here?

Scanning the article further, I quickly realized he hadn't died. He'd fallen and been knocked unconscious. But he was alright. Sam had been awake enough to respond as they loaded him on the ambulance and the first words out of his mouth were, "Where is my bike—is it OK?" They took him to the hospital and he turned out to be just fine. That kid outside had assumed the biker in the photo was dead and passed the misinformation along to us. I told all this to Nat with relief in my voice.

"You thought he was dead? What a shock—no, I read he was OK." Nat eyed me with concern as he casually sipped a can of orange juice. "Wow, what a horrible feeling you must've just gotten. . . . I saw you start to well up there."

"Yeah. Damn. I really thought he bought it." I laughed off some of the tension. "What an idiot. That bike is way too big for him. No wonder he crashed." We both chuckled. Nat found this particularly funny.

"The first words out of his mouth were 'How's my bike?'" Nat made a goofy voice as he said the last part, imitating Sam's New York accent. He dripped juice down his chin as we laughed at his impersonation. "What a dickweed," Nat roared. I know it's not nice to laugh at the misfortune of others, but we were really rolling now. I mentioned how the kid at the pump must've seen us. He thought that was Nat's father lying dead in the photo, and when I told Nat about the article he'd replied "Oh. Good. Excellent." and smiled like it was a happy thing. The attendant must've thought we were whacked. The situation didn't really merit it, but we practically cried on the floor from laughter.

The ambient temperature got hotter still on the road north. Near Viedma my engine was overheated and steaming from lack of oil. Nat loaned me some and we made it into a town and stopped for more. My chain now jangled loosely on the sprockets like dentures on old gums. We didn't have much further to go, but I didn't know if the chain would make it.

We crashed for the night at the house of my aunt and uncle in Bahía Blanca, where they prepared a typically excellent Argentine barbeque for us. Many writers that visit this southern country like to comment on the sensuous Argentine tango, the stunning architecture of buildings in Buenos Aires such as the Colón Theater, or the mysterious beauty of the Patagonia. Let me tell you about the least noted wonder of Argentina. It's the *asado*. The classic Argentine barbeque incorporates virtually every part of the cow, which is raised in the sweeping green pampas, with more freedom to roam and better nutrition than almost anywhere else on earth. The meat, when properly prepared, is as succulent as a ripe plum and tender as a loaf of fresh bread. The flavor is astounding. Not surprisingly, with such great beef available, there are very few vegetarians in Argentina.

A good asado incorporates several classic components: the specialty cuts of Argentine beef that most tourists will try, including the ribs; the regular chorizo and the *morcilla*, or blood sausage (provincial and family recipes for both are guarded secrets, but most all are delicious); and then there are the specialty items that shouldn't be missed, including the kidneys, throat glands, and tripe, which are best with a stiff lemon squeeze and lots of salt. And don't forget the *chimichurri*— the wonderful, pungent, garlic-flavored condiment that resembles a thick salad dressing. Whatever you do, leave your ketchup at home, lest the *asador* (the barbecue artist) skin you alive after watching you defile his food with it.

The following day Nat and I took our separate paths. We said good-bye and waved as he rode west to Mar del Plata and I continued north to Buenos Aires. Just like that, I was alone again. My chain survived and I made it back to the capital without a problem. But I discovered a very lonely and depressing moment when I got back.

Everything was different. My subleased apartment had returned to its rightful owner. My Argentine girlfriend, apparently fed up waiting for me, had left on a trip of her own to Asia and Australia. I was out of money and I couldn't ride back through Brazil. I had no cash, no pad, no girl, and the odds of making enough money to ride back home in the depressed Argentine economy were not good. It was time to face the suffocating truth. I had to go home.

Of course I was dying to see my parents, my siblings, and my friends back home. But leaving Argentina on a plane was just too depressing a thought to consider. Why did I have the feeling that it shouldn't have ended this way? I guess Peter and Robert must've had the same feeling when they suddenly had to drop everything and admit their trip was over. Maybe it's not what I wanted, but that's what happened. My days of motorcycling mountain roads with guanacos,

dodging careening Latin buses, and battling eagle-sized mosquitoes were over. For now.

I sat in the back seat of the cab, heading toward Ezeiza airport through the Buenos Aires congestion. The world seemed to move in slow motion around me. The bike was taken care of—Pablo Maggiani of Kawasaki Argentina offered to store it in a warehouse for me, where it would be started and ridden weekly to keep it in shape. This was a big relief, because to keep a motorcycle inert is to kill it. As much as I disliked the thought of leaving my KLR in another country, that seemed the only way. I knew I'd come back and finish the trip sooner or later.

As we drove, the taxi driver talked to me about Argentina's new president. He rattled on, and I listened absent-mindedly as I looked out the window. The sun was strong, but the clouds gave the sky a hazy gray tone. Cars were everywhere, stopping and starting, surging and lurching forward, each driver moving toward a private destination. Outside on the highway, a few motorcyclists wove between the cars, braking, leaning into turns, and accelerating past the other vehicles. I watched them go, weaving and playing between the cars, making faster headway in the endless traffic.

APPENDIX I

Detailed Trip Lists

➤

Andrés's List

Motorcycle and Accessories

1999 KLR 650A
Givi 36L saddlebags (2)
Givi 45L top case
Progressive fork springs
Progressive rear shock
Corbin custom saddle
Russell steel-braided brake lines
Clearview windscreen
Avon AM24 Gripster tires
Aerostich cloth tank panniers
Heated grips
Acerbis hand guards

Motorcycle cover
Tie-downs (2)
Kryptonite lock and cable

Maps and Books
Maps: Central America,
    Southern North America,
    Northern and Southern
    South America
Lonely Planet Guides—
    Uruguay, Paraguay,
    Argentina, Chile
Kawasaki KLR 650 repair manual
    with addendum

Clothing
Underwear, T-shirts, socks
Long-sleeve shirt (2)
Short-sleeve shirt (2)
Jeans (1 pair)
Casual pants (2 pairs)
Swimsuit (1)
Sneakers (1 pair)
Belt (1)

Riding Gear
Aerostich Darien jacket
Aerostich Darien pants
Widder electric vest
Asolo hiking boots
Summer gloves (2 pairs)
Tourmaster winter gloves
    (1 pair)

Shoei helmet with spare tinted
    shield
Camelback Pakteen water
    system
Aerostich neck warmer
NOS Quiet Rider helmet system

**Documentation and
Finances**
Driver's license
Passport
Debit card
Credit cards (3)
Cash
Address book
Dummy wallet (including
    expired license, credit cards,
    and a few dollars in cash)
International driver's license
Inoculation record
Motorcycle registration, title
Letters of introduction and
    contact information from
    Kawasaki USA
Medivac insurance,
    international medical
    insurance
Copies of all documents

Miscellaneous
North Face sleeping bag
Eureka tent
Camp stove, cooking utensils

Canon Rebel G camera with
strap
Camera carrying case
Film rolls (24)
Portable (7″) tripod
Journals (3)
CTX laptop computer with
power converter
Earplugs
Lens cleaner
Crazy Creek folding camp
chair
Toiletry kit
Sunglasses

Tools

Kawasaki tool kit
Kershaw Knives Multi-Tool
Adjustable wrenches
Ratchet kit
Chain breaker
Hex wrenches
Multihead screwdriver
Small mallet
Tire levers
12V air compressor
Progressive tire repair gun with
CO₂ cartridges
12-gauge electrical wire
Reversible Velcro
Assorted nylon ties
Electrical and duct tape
K&N filter oil

K&N filter cleaner
Flashlight with head strap
Tire pressure gauge

Spare Parts

Spare spokes, front and rear
Spare bulbs
WD40 lubricant
Small can grease
Spray can chain grease
Spare inner tubes, front and rear
Miscellaneous nuts and bolts
Clutch lever
Brake lever
Front brake pads
Rear brake pads
Spark plugs
Oil filters (2)
Fuel filter (1)
Spare fuses
Spare keys

Medical

Medical kit
Malaria pills
Water purification tablets
Mosquito repellent
Eurax topical antiparasite cream
Sunscreen
Multivitamins
Ibuprofen
Intravenous and intramuscular
syringes (6)

>

Peter's List

Motorcycle and Accessories
1995 BMW
BMW saddlebags (2)
Custom aluminum top case
Tires
Motorcycle cover
Tie-downs (2)
Fender bag
Bungee cords, net
Cable lock and disc lock with
    alarm
Map case

Maps and Books
AAA maps
Travel guides—Brazil,
    Venezuela
Repair manual

Clothing
Underwear, T-shirts,
    socks
Long-sleeve shirts (2)
Casual pants (2 pairs)
Walking shorts (1 pair)
Swimsuit (1)
Sneakers (1 pair)
Belt (1)
Hat (1)

Riding Gear
Hein Gericke Kilimanjaro jacket
    with water bladder system
Hein Gericke pants
Widder electric vest
Tall riding boots
Fingerless riding gloves (1 pair)
Summer gloves (1 pair)
Winter gloves (1 pair)
Shoei helmet with spare visor
Neck warmer
Rain gear

Documentation and Finances
Driver's license
Passport
Debit card
Credit cards (2)
Cash
International driver's license
Tax returns, 401K rollover
Inoculation record
Motorcycle registration and
    title
Medivac insurance,
    international medical
    insurance
Copies of all documents
List of BMW dealers
List of cyber cafés
Spare passport photos (6)
Traveler's checks

Miscellaneous

Sleeping sack
Waterproof packing bags (2)
Miniature camera
Film
Portable (7″) tripod
Earplugs
Lens cleaner
Toiletry kit
Sunglasses
Highlighter
Watch
Binoculars
Compass
Batteries
Super Glue
Flask

Tools

BMW tool kit
Leatherman tool
Victorinox Swiss Army knife
Adjustable wrenches
Ratchet kit with various sockets
Small vise grip
Hex wrenches
Multihead screwdriver
Siphon hose
Tire levers
Tire repair gun with CO_2
    cartridges
Assorted nylon ties
Electrical and duct tape

K&N filter oil
K&N filter cleaner
Flashlight with head strap
Tire pressure gauge
Matches
Light stick

Spare Parts

Spare spokes, front and rear
Rear tire
Spare bulbs
12-gauge electrical wire
10 feet of 14-gauge wire
Crimp-on ends for wire
Carburetor diaphragm
Diode board
Valve cover gasket
Spare clutch
Accelerator (2)
Muffler seals
Fork seals
Center stand cap
Tubeless tire patches and rubber
    cement
Tubeless plug drivers
Miscellaneous nuts and bolts
Clutch lever
Brake lever
Brake pads and shoes
Rear brake pads
Spark plugs
Oil filters (2)
Fuel filter (1)

Spare fuses
Spare keys

Medical
Medical kit
Malaria pills
Water purification tablets
Mosquito repellent
Sunscreen
Crack cream
Multivitamins
Ibuprofen
Immodium
Phazyme
Celexa
Allegra D
Rolaids
Alka-Seltzer
Antibiotics

➤
Robert's List

Motorcycle and Accessories
1995 BMW R1100GS
Givi saddlebags 36L and 45L
Top case (generic plastic toolbox—lockable)
Michelin T66X tires
Garmin GPS III+
Thermometer

BMW heated grips
BMW hand guards
Givi windscreen
Map case
Reinforced Givi metal luggage rack
EZ Touring motorcycle cover
Bungee cords
Tie-downs (2)

Maps and Books
Maps: Mexico, Guatemala, Honduras, Nicaragua, El Salvador, Costa Rica, Panama, Ecuador, Peru, Chile, Argentina
Lonely Planet Guides—Ecuador, Peru, Bolivia

Clothing
Underwear, T-shirts, socks
Long-sleeve shirts (2)
Short-sleeve shirts (2)
Casual pants (2 pairs)
Walking shorts (1 pair)
Casual/dress shoes (1 pair)
Belt (1)
Eyeglasses (2 pairs)
Toiletry kit

Riding Gear
Hein Gericke Kilimanjaro jacket
Hein Gericke leather pants

Caroline lineman boots (18″ tops)
Summer gloves (2 pairs)
Winter gloves (1 pair)
Rain gloves (1 pair)
Rain pants
Electric vest
Nolan helmet

Documentation and Finances
Daily record books (2)
Debit card
Credit card
Cash
Phone numbers (North American dealers)
Phone numbers (North American friends)
Canada Direct phone card
List of critical information (for traveling partners)
Copy of driver's license (fake)
International driver's license
Inoculation record
Motorcycle registration and title
Copy of all documentation (passport, driver's license, and birth certificate)

Miscellaneous
Sleeping bag
Olympus OM-4T SLR camera with strap

35-105mm zoom lens
21mm and 28mm wide-angle lenses
2x extender
Spare camera battery
Camera carrying case
Film rolls (72)
Lens brush
Canon binoculars
Toiletry kit

Tools
BMW tool kit
Needle-nose pliers (miniature)
Bent-nose pliers (miniature)
Needle-nose vise grips (miniature)
Regular vise grips (miniature)
Ratchet kit with various sockets and extenders
Ratcheting screwdriver
12v air compressor
Stop 'n Go tire repair gun with CO_2 cartridges
12-gauge electrical wire
Rubber bands
Velcro
Heavy-duty rubber bands (inner tube pieces)
Large Phillips screwdriver
Large flat screwdriver
Twin Max
Assorted nylon ties

Electrical, duct, and double-
  sided tape
Punch for brake pad removal
K&N filter oil
K&N filter cleaner
Oil filter wrench

Spare Parts
Valve stem
Spare spokes, front and rear
Front wheel bearings
Front wheel bearing seals
Fork seals
Spare bulbs
Three-in-one oil
Tincture of grease
Spare alternator belt
Miscellaneous nuts and bolts
Clutch lever
Brake pads, front and rear
Spark plugs

Oil filters (2)
Fuel filter (1)
Fuel injector cleaner
Rags (2)
Spare fuses
Spare keys

9. Medical
Medical kit (band-aids, scissors,
  gauze, iodine, and peroxide)
Malaria pills
Antiseptic
Nose Cote
Polysporin
Hydrocortisone cream
Alka-Seltzer
Sunscreen
Imodium
Dulcolax
Multivitamins
Ibuprofen

APPENDIX II

Evaluation of Equipment

➤ 1999 KAWASAKI KLR 650: The KLR is a rugged and cost-effective answer to long-distance dual-sport riding. Like all bikes, it requires patient and consistent maintenance—if maintained, it's nearly indestructible. The pros of the KLR are too many to list, but include the stock tank, low-end torque, reliability, simplicity of design, fuel economy, etc. Major failings, in my view, are the underpowered brakes and the weak front suspension.

PROGRESSIVE SUSPENSION ROESELER 420 SERIES SINGLE SHOCK: The shock performed flawlessly and was simple to adjust for various conditions. The Progressive spring design was a significant comfort improvement over stock.

PROGRESSIVE SUSPENSION ROESELER SERIES FORK SPRING KIT: Although a major improvement over the stock Kawasaki front springs, these were not enough to overcome the KLR's front-end failings off-road. I suspect this has more to do with Kawasaki's inadequately sized fork tubes than with Progressive's aftermarket solution.

GIVI E45, E36 HARD SADDLEBAGS AND MOUNTING HARDWARE: These Givi bags survived dozens of spills, and I was always happy with them. The saddlebag mounting system available from Givi at the time left something to be desired. Without reinforcement, the original mounting system is suspect under normal conditions, and doomed to fail under even minimally stressful conditions. I've been informed that Givi has corrected this problem, but I've yet to try the new mounting system for myself.

WIDDER ENTERPRISES VENTURA II LECTRIC VEST AND LECTRIC CHAPS W/ASSOCIATED HARDWARE: The Ventura II was an indispensable part of my riding uniform, and one I used every day in colder weather. It often meant the difference between meeting a day's mileage quota, or quitting early.

CLEARVIEW SHIELDS +11IN. KLR 650 WINDSHIELD: The shield made significant reductions in both wind buffeting and road noise. Furthermore, this shield survived a head-collision that crushed the bike's front headlight and fairing and doubled back the forks. A very tough, very satisfying add-on.

AEROSTICH, INC. DARIEN SUIT: Custom-tailored to fit my long limbs, this riding suit was comfortable, reliable, and made motorcycling in wind, snow, and rain a minor inconvenience, as opposed to a ride-ending hassle.

AEROSTICH LARGE TANK PANNIERS: These soft-sided tank panniers provided additional storage and helped front-load weight for balance. They worked well for the most part, but required minor re-stitching of two strap attachment points about midway through the trip.

CORBIN SADDLES KLR 650 DUAL SADDLE: This seat's foam is a major improvement over stock, and helped prevent me from experiencing the blisters that Peter suffered during the long days in Mexico. Unfortunately, the design has a deep depression in the middle that I found disagreeable. The intention was to lower the rider's center of gravity in rougher terrain, and to help a shorter rider touch the ground when mounted on the tall KLR. With my taller frame I simply found myself uncomfortably sliding crotch-first into the tank during even moderate braking.

RUSSELL PERFORMANCE STEEL-BRAIDED BRAKE LINES AND SPEED-BLEEDERS: When a product performs well, its benefits become expected as a matter of course. These tough cables provided superior brake feel and response, and were so effective and trouble free that I soon forgot I even had them. The system was so trouble free that I never had to use the speedbleeders.

KERSHAW KNIVES MULTI-TOOL: An excellent product that I would recommend to anyone. Its unique vise-grip design and one-handed opening blade make the Multi-Tool an easy first choice for a motorcyclist. The vise-grips can act as a temporary replacement for a broken brake or clutch lever, and the thumb-release blade is an unobtrusive, easily deployed crime deterrent that can be drawn with one hand even while mounted on the bike.

AVON TYRES AM24 GRIPSTERS: I was amazed at the longevity of these tires. I put 10,000 miles on the rear Gripster before replacing it, and I typically averaged about 65 MPH on the highways. I met a man with Gripsters on his BMW that got 15,000 miles out of his rear. As the name implies, the AM24 also gave good traction both on and off-road. Peter and Robert suffered multiple flats on the trip. I had just two with the Avon front tire, one of which was caused by a 1/2 inch tack driven through. The Gripsters are worth every penny if you don't like worrying about your tires.

Epilogue

➤ ROBERT resides in Canada and the United States with his wife Sandy. He continues to work as a petroleum engineer on a consulting basis, and has done several short trips since ending this Latin American adventure. We have not kept in close contact.

PETER, after finalizing his divorce in the United States, returned to Colombia, where he lived for two years. In Colombia, he met and married a beautiful young doctor. In his words, the stay was an opportunity to see what his adult life might've been like in Colombia. Having grown accustomed to the (relative) safety of life in the United States, he has since returned and is currently living with his wife in Miami. Strangely, I was not invited to the wedding.

ELENA, the lovely Spanish/Irish girl I met in Guatemala, continued to work in Central America, but recently began a master's degree program in London. I visited with her briefly when she passed through New York City recently, and she is as charming and sweet as ever.

Immediately after finishing his trip, NAT CREWE went to work on a cattle ranch in Montana. We still entertain the idea of organizing a motorcycle trip from Norway to South Africa.

ANTONELLA, the Argentine girl I dated at the end of the trip, has continued to pursue a career in dance and regularly dances in small productions in Buenos Aires. She hopes to someday move to New York or London to work as a performing artist and dance teacher. Despite two trips to Argentina and my best efforts, we never got back together.

GAIL AND ERIC HAWS are still making their eccentric way around the world. When they are not traveling, they spend their time updating their 400-plus-page international motorcycling Web site.

SINCE I RETURNED TO THE UNITED STATES I have been working as a technical writer to pay the bills and writing creatively on the side. I have been training in Brazilian Jiu Jitsu for fun. I've been to Argentina twice since returning home and collected the motorcycle on my most recent trip. I've been unable to complete the journey through the remainder of Latin America so far, but I plan to eventually.

Index